# *ACROSS CHINA*

*Also by Peter Jenkins*

A WALK ACROSS AMERICA
THE WALK WEST *(with Barbara Jenkins)*
THE ROAD UNSEEN *(with Barbara Jenkins)*
THE TENNESSEE SAMPLER *(with friends)*

# ACROSS CHINA

*Peter Jenkins*

*A William Morrow/Sweet Springs Press Book*

Library of Congress Cataloging-in-Publication Data

Jenkins, Peter, 1951—
  Across China.

  "A William Morrow/Sweet Springs Press book."
  1. China—Description and travel—1976–  .
2. Jenkins, Peter, 1951–  —Journeys—China.
I. Title.
DS712.J43    1986    915.1′045     86-21646
ISBN 0-688-04223-6

Printed in the United States of America


3  4  5  6  7  8  9  10

*This book is dedicated to Frederick Davis Jenkins, Jr.,
also known as Fred, Pete, Curly, Bam Bam, and most
important to me, as Dad*

# *Acknowledgments*_____

Thanks to many talented and gifted people who contributed much to this book.

Skip Yowell, you started the whole trip rolling. Lou Whittaker and Jim Wickwire, thanks for allowing me to be part of the team. Team members Phil Ershler, Dave Mahre, George Dunn, John Roskelley, Peter Whittaker, Greg Wilson, Carolyn Gunn, John Smolich, and Dr. Ed Hixson and Steve Marts, your cooperation with many long interviews is greatly appreciated. I also appreciate the families of the team for their assistance and support during this expedition.

Thanks to the support team: Russ Cole, Ingrid Widmann, Skip Yowell, Dan McConnell, Laszlo Pal, Susan Pal, Tom Annanie, Linda Nerven, and George Bright.

Research played a significant role in this book. Thanks to the following for their efforts. Most significantly to Rita Jorgensen for the reading, reports, and intricate research on Tibet, Mongolia, China, and Communism. Rita, your contribution has been most influential. Thanks to William Stenson, Ph.D., at M.S.U., and a special note of appreciation to the Michigan State Library, Nashville Public Library, Maury County Public Library, and the Spring Hill Public Library. To Dr. Bill Fuqua for his readings and advice on classical mountaineering and to Mel Mihall, Charles Hambrick, and colleagues at Vanderbilt University for advice on "when in China . . . ." To Lucy Scott Kuykendall for her advice on Chinese art. And John Pollack for advice on the best mountaineering books.

The maps in this book were done well and professionally by Dee Molenaar (Mount Everest, Tibet, and base camp) and by Markie Hunsiker and Jim McClelland, Jr. (China and the world). Thanks to Dennas and Ruthie Davis for graphic design. A special note of thanks to Jim Wickwire for suggesting Dee Molenaar, for researching routes on the mountain, for his expert advice, and especially for his concern for the accuracy of the China/Everest part of this book. Thanks, Jim.

Thanks to the generous organizations that assisted in sponsoring the climb: JanSport, William Morrow and Company, Wrangler, Shaklee, Allied Corporation, Dupont/Cordura, Dupont/Quallofil, C. Itoh and Co./Entrant, Knight International, New Balance, _Outside_ magazine, Edmund Chung, and Sweet Springs Press.

A special thanks to the makers and executive producers of the movie _Winds of Everest,_ Pal Productions: Producer/Director Laszlo Pal; cinematographer, Steve Marts; production manager, Susan Pal; sponsors who supported making the film, JanSport, Inc., Blue Bell, Inc., and Wrangler. Special thanks to Executive Producers Dan Spalding and Phillip K. Vanderhyden, Jr.

Again, thanks to William Morrow, my co-publishers. This is our third book together, and I hope our best. Thanks to Larry Hughes, Al Marchioni, Sherry Arden, Tom Consolino, the skilled folks in sales and production, Joan Amico, Jennifer Williams, Linda Pennell, Lela Rolontz, Michelle Farinet, Jean Griffin, art director Cheryl Asherman, and the rest of the group that make Morrow the best. Most important, a giant word of thanks and a bunch of love to Pat Golbitz, the superwoman of editing. This book would not be what it is without Pat.

Also, based on a new agreement with Morrow, this is my first book co-published under our companies' new imprint, Sweet Springs Press of Spring Hill, Tennessee. My staff, both present and past, have done a great job assisting me with this book: Terri Loveless Baker, your readings and commentary on drafts, careful attention to plot accuracy, computer work . . . you do it all! Mary Margaret Reed has done remarkable work on our computers and much more. Thanks so much, Terri and Mary Margaret. Thanks, too, to Wally Hebert for preliminary research and correspondence and to Judy Roberson for patient skills at transcript production and slide organization.

I would not have experienced one tenth of what I did in China without the help of Ran Ying Porter. Thank you, Ran Ying and Ed Porter, and your three young sons Michael, Patrick, and Ron Adwell. Thanks to Peggy and Ray Porter, and Corinne Wells.

Family and friends, as always, played an indispensable role. Heartfelt thanks to Lacy (our Alaskan husky), Lamar and Honey Alexander, Jim and Shirley Dobson, UFO (our Brahman bull), Robert George, Calvin Scott, Tim Scott, Mike and Gail Hyatt, Bob and Bobbie Wolgemuth, Jess and Mary Lou Morton, Billy Weeks, Ernie and Betty Pennell, Homer Kelley, Aubrey Harwell, Bob Sullivan, John and Patti Thompson, Gary and Jean Wysocki, Dot and Horace Murphy, Zephyr Fite, Bruce and Lawanna McIver, Wally and Brenda Hebert, Tracy Smith, Tom Smith, Phil Yancey, Mike Blanton and Dan Harrell, Betty Sain, Harold and Marjorie Yowell, the subscribers of "Our America" newsletter, CoCo (our Welsh Corgi), and a deeply felt thanks for all of you who have expressed concern, prayed prayers, and reached out on my behalf.

To my Mom and Dad and sisters, brothers, and in-laws: Winky, Scott, Fred, Betsy and Abbi; and Randy, Alex and Jesse; Bonnie; Coleen, Molly and Sarah, all my love, as always.

And to my loving family: Barbara, Rebekah, Jed, and Luke, your work, compassion, love, prayers, long-suffering, humor, and inspiration make the words "thank you" sound very inadequate.

I love you.

# Contents

*Where liberty dwells*
*there is my country.*

—BENJAMIN FRANKLIN

# *ACROSS CHINA*_____

# 1

## *A Low-Slung Mood*_____

I was hungry and bored and I was in such a dreary mood that I didn't feel like going anywhere. I was looking at some old slides, sitting in the funky green and white trailer that I used as an office, not even wanting to look out the window. The sky was a low-slung oppressive gray and it seemed that dismal winter skies and lifeless trees would always be here. It was the end of February. For the past two years I'd been working in this drafty trailer that sat behind Mr. Luther's grocery store.

Since our five-year walk across America had ended we'd moved to

Spring Hill, Tennessee (native pronunciation "Sprang Heel"). It's a town of less than a thousand and our 135-acre farm borders Spring Hill's eastern city limits. Here, just thirty-seven miles south of Nashville, there aren't many eating places for humans to choose from. There are many more cows and horses around here than people, and plenty more hay and clover fields than restaurants. For lunch I could go to the Poplar House Restaurant and eat a fine hamburger of fresh-ground prime local beef and leave stuffed and smelling like smoke, or I could go to the Cedar Inn and get meat and three veggies and cornbread for a few dollars.

The Poplar House was next to Spring Hill's only combination Laundromat and barber shop. The Cedar Inn was between the Red Raider Market (the only place in town to get dog food or diapers after 8:00 P.M.), and Anderson's Hardware. Lloyd Anderson hadn't been open too long, and that was the only place to get bolts and nails within ten miles.

No, I didn't want to be friendly today. And if you live in a small town where you know just about everyone, it's better not to go out in public when you're in a raggy mood. Maybe I should just walk across the gravel parking lot to Luther's and get a Diet Coke, a bag of cashews, and taco chips. Nah. Bubbly little Mrs. Luther would want to talk. She would talk to me while I was in line at the cash register, and then sometimes follow me out the door talking. I could learn more from Mrs. Luther about the folks around here than from the combined daily output of the *Daily Herald,* WKRM radio, and Channel 5-TV news.

I'd been sifting through hundreds of boxes of slides jazzing up my slide show. For the past few years I'd been invited to many colleges to "lecture" about my walk across America. I picked up the slides again, holding them up to the dull light coming through the window. I'd taken these on the high plains of New Mexico. The colors were the saturated golds and the electric purples of late summer, the western cowboy's sky. I could see, too, the black silhouettes of gnarled fence posts and windmills. The slides took me there.

Why couldn't I just get in my Ford pickup, head straight up I-65 to the Nashville airport and fly somewhere to warm sun and warm wind and warm, green ground? No, my wife, Barbara, was expecting me home for dinner. It was my turn to bathe the kids, Rebekah and Jed, and read them bedtime stories like *The Muffin Munchin' Dragon.* There were our wood stoves to stoke. Then there were other demanding ladies, my herd of about fifty cows, and our bulls,

UFO, PJ Snap, and the Barbon Kid, who needed their hay. Shocker, my Tennessee Walking Horse stallion, needed some "sweet" feed and Lacy, our Alaskan husky, needed some Alpo Liver Chunks, unless she'd caught some woodchuck who'd waked up early from his winter's sleep.

I held up another slide. It was a shot of me in gym shorts and a yellow sweat shirt. I was a lean-mean traveling machine. My legs were tan and muscular. The rest of me was lean and ready to live off the wilderness, with just a small load of possessions in my backpack. Where did I get all these responsibilities? The farm, the family, the tractor, the one-hundred-year-old farmhouse and the total restoration we'd been doing for the last six months. The taxes . . . The phone rang.

There was the hiss of a long-distance call.

"Peter, this's Skip."

Skip and I had been friends since I'd made contact with him while still on the walk, in New Orleans, less than halfway across America. I'd already worn out my first backpack and sleeping bag and tent. Having heard about JanSport equipment more than once, I decided to use some of their products. Skip, who with his cousin Murray had started JanSport less than ten years ago, let me buy a new pack, a dome tent, and a couple of sleeping bags at cost, and shipped them to New Orleans. During the walk we became friends.

"How's Murray doing?" I asked right off. Usually, I'd ask about Murray later in our conversation, but I was in the mood to hear something wild and crazy and Murray was one of the most originally uninhibited people I'd ever known. Once he had swung on a wagon-wheel chandelier hanging out over the floor of a crowded Houston disco, and escaped a swarm of bouncers and Houston police. He could be dared to do almost anything, like jump up on a bar, Wild West style, and walk the length of the bar kicking off the occasional bottle of Bud Light. Murray was very creative when it came to outrageous human behavior and designing backpacking gear.

"Murray's the same as ever. How's Barbara?"

"Have I told you she's pregnant again?" We'd only found out a few weeks before. It seemed like our third pregnancy was not quite as all-consuming as the first two.

"When's the baby due?" Skip responded more quickly than usual.

I counted on my fingers as I said, "The first week of October."

Skip didn't say anything. He stayed quiet for a few moments, just long enough for me to wonder if something I'd said bothered him.

We both began talking at once, then Skip interrupted me. "Did you hear what I said about China?"

"About China?"

"How would you like to go to China?" His voice was deadpan.

"Come on Skip, be serious."

"I am serious. Would you like to come with us and go climb Mount Everest? We'll be going through China and Tibet."

I couldn't even take it in. "Why, ah, I mean, what are you going to Mount Everest for?" I was stalling to let my mind and heart catch up with Skip's questions. I was shocked, and that was very rare.

"Lou Whittaker has organized an expedition called China/Everest '84. They want to be the first Americans to get to the top of Everest from the Tibet side. You know his twin brother, Jim, was the first American to climb to the top of Everest in 1963."

"When is everybody leaving?" I asked, stuttering slightly.

Skip now had his hand over the phone. I could hear him talking to someone. "Can you hold on a minute?"

COME ON, Skip. How could you possibly put me on hold, NOW!!

I was transported far away from small-town, settled-down, winter boredom. My memory raced around like a hungry computer searching for information. Anything that could help me picture these exotic places I never imagined going to, at least not lately.

I saw old color pictures from *National Geographic* magazine, of rock ridges as sharp as a knife, partially hidden by the clouds of Mount Everest. Mountain climbers appeared like little black dots against gigantic blinding-white glaciers.

Lessons on Chinese sculpture from art history classes in college popped up. I could visualize the perfectly proportioned lines of a running bronze horse, huge ceramic lions, and incredibly intricate stone carvings that took years to complete.

I could recollect dreamy Chinese paintings of the Great Wall. There in my mind was my art-history prof, in his wire-rim glasses, pointing out the skillful brushstrokes of a Song Dynasty artist. The painting was done on long, delicate paper with eroded mountains in the background and twisted, ancient trees filled with storks.

"Peter, you there?" Skip asked.

"Yes . . . I'm here!"

"Sorry about that, but we've got a deadline to meet on a catalog. Now, where was I?"

"You were about to tell when the expedition would be leaving."

"If all the funds can be raised, and all the details worked out with the Chinese, Lou wants the team to be leaving Seattle sometime in early August, and arriving in Beijing the next day. From there we'd head for Tibet, which is thousands of miles from Beijing."

"Where is Tibet?" I asked. Skip paused, trying to figure it out himself.

I could not picture that part of the world. I felt stupid. For that matter, I couldn't even decide what countries were next to China, other than Russia, and I wasn't sure which side Russia was on. And as far as Mount Everest was concerned, I'd always thought of it as being in Nepal, not Tibet.

"Tibet's in the far southwestern corner of China. At least, I think it's southwestern. Who knows? It may be southeastern." I still could not get a vision of where Tibet was, the way I could picture where Mexico was in relation to Texas and Arizona.

"I think Tibet borders with India, Nepal, and Bhutan. . . ." Every country he mentioned sounded more intriguing than the last one.

"So what do you think, Dr. Jenkins? Your calendar too filled up to go to China or what?"

"What calendar, Dr. Skip? . . . I'm going," I said.

"You're making a decision that fast?" Skip said, disbelieving.

"I guess so. Hey, this is a trip that comes down the trail once in a lifetime, and I don't want anyone else to take my place."

Skip had to rush off to a meeting. He would call back later.

"Thanks for calling, Skip," I said before I hung up. Somehow, that didn't sound like enough to express the overwhelming excitement I felt.

I jumped around the trailer like a stork doing a mating dance. I yelled and hollered as loud as I could. There was so much adrenaline pumping through my body that I felt like I could jump from the United States to China. It'd been years since I'd felt so full of the expectation of adventure.

# Tigers of the Snow _____

The back door had to be latched to keep it shut. We'd been living in a run-down, leaky house in "downtown" Spring Hill since the summer before, and would stay here until we finished restoring our century-old farmhouse, a mile down the road.

Faded, dusty pieces of water-stained wallpaper were peeling off the walls and chunks of plaster hung from the ceilings. One night about fifty pounds of plaster had fallen on my visiting cousin Billy as he slept. Billy's a stocky, strong young man and it didn't hurt too much. Thank God he was family.

Tonight I couldn't tell a trash pad from a mansion. I was flying without a plane, the thoughts of this incredible expedition powering me higher and higher. I wanted to run to Barbara and tell her about it. I just knew she'd understand.

She was not in the kitchen, or the bathroom. I could hear Rebekah, our four-year-old, happily talking to herself. I peered into the living room and saw no one.

"Barbara, where are you, honey?"

"I'm in here," came her reply. It sounded like a moan.

Barbara lay on the couch, a quilt over her, looking pale and sick. It wasn't morning sickness because it wasn't morning, but she said she'd been feeling weak all afternoon. She looked as though she didn't have the strength to walk across the room, much less hear about me going off to China, Tibet, and Mount Everest. She was two months pregnant with our third child.

"How was your day?" she asked weakly.

"Oh, it was all right."

Jed, our one-year-old, heard my voice and woke up from a late nap. I walked over and picked him up and sat down across from Barbara. I figured the worst thing I could possibly do was tell her about China/Everest now. Even though I'd told Skip that I'd go, I wouldn't go if Barbara felt strongly that I shouldn't. I'd keep my dream-come-true to myself until she got over this early-pregnancy sickness.

"Peter, I'd planned to go to Kroger's and get some diapers and things. Would you take Rebekah and Jed and go get them? The list's on the kitchen table."

Who could think about eating, now! And diapers!

"Sure, no problem. Let's go for a ride, kids," I called, rounding them up.

Rebekah, my precious little princess with the graceful movements and always-ready-for-adventure eyes, was by my side as quickly as I'd said I'd go to Everest. Jed was different. He could be very difficult about rapid change or unusual circumstances.

I was heading them down the hall and out the door when Rebekah protested, "Daddy, it's cold out in the yard. We need our coats on."

I turned back, got the coats, and stuffed the kids into them. I could hardly focus my eyes I was trying so hard to act normal and not let China/Everest show.

Almost out the door I heard Barbara's call. "Peter, I'm feeling too sick to cook. Would you please pick something up at Kentucky Fried Chicken?"

I was a mile down Highway 31, on our way to the city of Columbia, when I realized I'd forgotten to get Jed's car seat. If I kept on this way, my family might not survive till I took that trip.

As we passed the pet cemetery, where our farm neighbor Mary Lou Morton buried one of her precious Pekingese dogs, I had a vivid flashback to my early teens.

My Aunt Rhoda bought us six children a long-term subscription to the *National Geographic*. I knew about what time of the month it came, and I would always try to be the first one to get it, before my younger brothers and sisters got it and messed it up. That magazine and my *Boy's Life* were about the only things I cared about that came in the mail.

When I was ten and eleven, I would take the magazine out of its brown wrapper and scan the cover, looking for the stories I loved best, the ones about the impossible-sounding expeditions to the other end of the world.

Riding along with my kids, I remembered reading about the mountain peoples of the Himalayas, who were called "Tigers of the Snow" because of their seemingly supernatural endurance and bravery. These Sherpas could climb above glaciers, loaded with the white man's equipment, barefoot, with no extra oxygen, while Western climbers struggled to take ten steps.

I could see pictures of their prayer-flags and stone temples growing out of the mountaintops. The mountains were gods to them, some loving, some evil. I could recall their odd-looking yaks. The yaks carried loads of supplies through the narrowest rock-strewn mountain passes. The Tibetan people used the yak's dung for fuel, ate the meat of the yak, spun its hair and wove it into cloth, and used their hides for leather. I remembered pictures of the Himalayan people, their faces lined by the glare of their sun, dressed in bright-colored wool.

It surprised me that I had not thought of any of this for years and one phone call brought it all back as if I'd read those old *National Geographics* last night.

We made it to Kroger's, purchased our three bags of groceries, got our chicken nuggets, and headed home. I had no idea groceries were so expensive. Barbara was still lying on the couch when we came home. I knew I'd have to wait till she felt a lot better before I could tell her about China/Everest.

# *Attempt Number 2*

For the next couple of weeks I kept China and Mongolia and Tibet to myself. It was like winning a five-million-dollar lottery and not being able to tell anyone about it. Maybe, when our pastures began to shed their dead winter grasses and come alive with the greens of spring, Barbara would feel better. With the other two pregnancies she hadn't felt sick this long. I'd wait till the right moment, especially since going on this trip meant being away for the end of the pregnancy. If something happened to me in China, like falling off Mount Everest, being thrown into a roach-infested prison, or no telling what else, I could miss the birth of Jenkins baby number three. I knew that would be incredibly tough on Barbara. Would she ever forgive me?

The more I thought about IT the more I wanted to go, no matter what the price might be. However, the father and husband in me realized it was the wrong time, that leaving Barbara pregnant, alone with Rebekah and Jed for months, would be very difficult. I decided that I'd not go if she felt strongly about it. Well, she'd have to feel SUPER strongly.

Attempt Number 1

After the first week I decided to start talking about IT in some subtle way and see what Barbara's reaction would be. *Nightline* was on Channel 2.

"Barbara, did I tell you that Skip is going on an expedition to Mount Everest?" I tried to sound casual.

"Can you hold on a minute, honey, I'm trying to hear what Ted Koppel's saying."

After ten minutes or so she said, "Now what did you say about Skip?"

"I asked if I'd told you that Skip's been invited to go on an expedition through Tibet, to Mount Everest?"

"Is Skip married yet?" she responded. Barbara was always wanting our unmarried friends to tie the knot. Skip used to say that the knot would feel like it was tied around his neck. For the nine years I'd known Skip, he'd never been close to marriage. But lately he'd met some beautiful, curly-haired lady from San Francisco and he actually sounded serious.

"No, he's not, but he may have met someone lately. Her name's Susan."

"Well, good. I hope he comes back alive so he can finally get married. The time to travel is before you get married, and ESPECIALLY before you have kids!"

O . . .K . . . So much for that attempt. I discreetly camouflaged the book I'd been reading, *In the Throne Room of the Mountain Gods,* in the magazine rack. It was about an expedition to K-2, which was the world's second-highest mountain and over five miles high. Five miles high! That's higher than some rides I'd taken on American Airlines. K-2 was considered to be the most strikingly magnificent peak in the world, and two of the leaders of "my" climb, Lou Whittaker, team leader, and Jim Wickwire had been on that trip. I'd wait for a better opportunity to let Barbara in on China/Everest—if there would ever be a better time.

Attempt Number 2

About a week later I got a letter in the mail with a round blue logo on it that said something Chinese in the middle. On top it said China/Everest 1984. The bottom of the logo read "Chomolungma." It was some kind of press release, about four pages long. However, there was no personal note of explanation with it.
It read:

_CHINA/EVEREST_

_1984_

_CHOMOLUNGMA_

_IMMEDIATE RELEASE_

_EVEREST NORTH WALL II_

_Lou Whittaker, 54, famed mountaineer and co-owner of Rainier Mountaineering, Inc., has received permission from the Chinese government to return to Tibet in the fall of 1984 and again attempt to reach the summit of 29,028-foot Mount Everest via the unclimbed North Wall._

_In 1982, Whittaker attempted the same route with a large team of Americans but was unable to reach the summit after bad weather and the tragic death of Marty Hoey, who hoped to be the first American woman to climb the world's highest peak, pushed them back._

_For the China/Everest '84 Expedition, as it is being called, Whittaker has drawn from the strengths of the 1982 team and sought to improve further his chances for success by adding some of the strongest, most capable American climbers available._

_With Whittaker will be Jim Wickwire, 43, much-noted climber and one of the first Americans to top K2, the second highest mountain in the world. Wickwire was with Marty Hoey in 1982 when her tragic accident occurred._

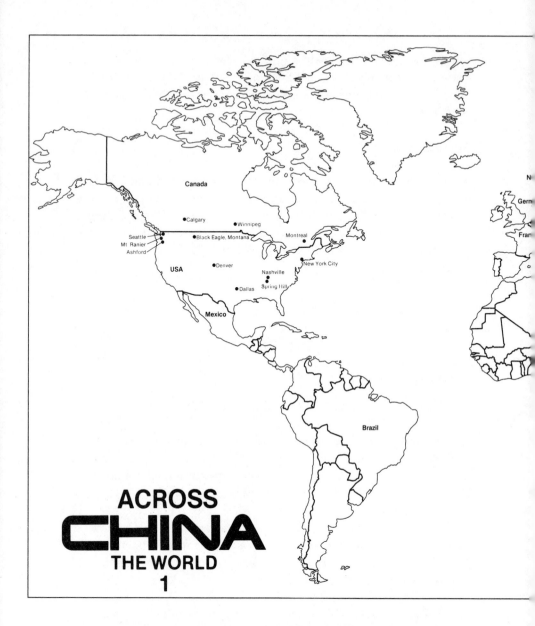

Canada

● Calgary

● Winnipeg

Seattle ●
Mt Ranier
Ashford

● Black Eagle, Montana

Montreal

USA

● Denver

Nashville
●
Spring Hill

New York City

● Dallas

Mexico

Brazil

N

Germ

Fran

## ACROSS
# CHINA
## THE WORLD
## 1

"Do you want to go to the other side of the world?" my friend Skip Yowell asked. His friends were headed to China to climb Mount Everest on the Tibetan border. Tibet, China, Everest. Of course I wanted to go. In Tibet I befriended a holy man and yak herders. After establishing base camp with the mountaineers, I left these incredible adventurers and met my skilled interpreter, Ran Ying Porter, in the city of Chengdu. We traveled together across China. From the restaurants of Sichuan Province, through famous Xian,

retracing the path of the ancient silk route through Lanzhou and Yinchuan, we experienced much. We had a rare opportunity to live with a Mongolian family on the grasslands of Inner Mongolia. On the China coast I was shown the stone carver's art by an Old Master; then in a rusty ferry, we sneaked to an off-limits coastal fishing village. Now when I see the shape of China on a map of the world, it is not a vague mystery but the motherland of many new friends.

*Also joining the team is John Roskelley, 35, considered by many to be the premier American Himalayan mountaineer. Roskelley has climbed three 8,000-meter peaks—K2, Makalu, and Dhaulagiri—and has pioneered difficult routes on several lesser Himalayan peaks. While high on Everest in 1983, Roskelley contracted pulmonary edema, a dangerous buildup of fluid in the lungs, and was forced to return to base camp before making a final attempt via the difficult west ridge.*

*Dave Mahre, 55, well-known in Northwest climbing circles and father of the world champion ski twins Phil and Steve, is also returning from Whittaker's 1982 climb, where, according to Whittaker, Dave proved to be a strong, cool-thinking asset to the team.*

*Phil Ershler, 33, is also coming back from the 1982 team. He served as climbing leader on the 1983 Seven Summits Everest Expedition, which succeeded on the often-climbed South Col route. During that expedition, Ershler was forced down after suffering frostbite while climbing above 26,000 feet without oxygen.*

*Rounding out the climbing team are professional guides George Dunn, 30, who proved himself to Whittaker on the 1982 Everest Expedition; Whittaker's son Peter, 25, Greg Wilson, 27, and John Smolich, 35, all veterans of Whittaker's guide service.*

*Dr. Ed Hixson, 42, a member of the 1982 Expedition as well as the 1983 Seven Summits Everest Expedition, will go with Whittaker in 1984 as team doctor. Hixson suffered a mild stroke while climbing above 26,000 feet on Everest in 1983. He is fully recovered.*

*With nine climbers and a doctor, the 1984 China/Everest Expedition will use yak support to move up the mountain faster into assault position. They will use a longer, less technical approach up the mountain to reach the high point of their 1982 route in the Great Couloir, a large ice-packed gully, at approximately 27,000 feet. From there they will attempt to complete the unclimbed North Wall route.*

*"In 1982, seventeen of us carried 2½ tons of equipment up the mountain with no support. I think it took too much out of us. With a smaller team this time, we'll move up quickly to over 21,000 feet where we will establish an advanced base camp. From there, we'll have a much better opportunity to reach the summit in early October," Whittaker wrote. "With the knowledge we*

_have from the 1982 Expedition, I think this team will have an excellent chance of succeeding. We all have climbed together and can work well to-gether and I feel very good about China/Everest '84. Each of us has the ability to go to the summit, even old-timers like Dave Mahre and me. As always, though, it will depend on the mountain."_

## CHINA/EVEREST '84 TEAM ROSTER

| NAME | AGE | OCCUPATION | HOMETOWN |
|------|-----|-----------|----------|
| Lou Whittaker | 54 | Co-owner Rainier Mountaineering, Inc. | Ashford, WA |
| Jim Wickwire | 43 | Attorney | Seattle, WA |
| John Roskelley | 35 | Mountaineer, lecturer, photographer | Spokane, WA |
| Dave Mahre | 55 | Ski Area Operator | White Pass, WA |
| Phil Ershler | 33 | Mountain Guide | Bellevue, WA |
| George Dunn | 30 | Mountain Guide | Seattle, WA |
| John Smolich | 35 | Mountain Guide | Sandy, OR |
| Greg Wilson | 27 | Mountain Guide | Edmonds, WA |
| Peter Whittaker | 25 | Mountain Guide | Ashford, WA |
| Dr. Ed Hixson | 42 | Medical Doctor | Lake Placid, NY |

## CHINA/EVEREST '84 TRAVEL ITINERARY

| | |
|---|---|
| _Departure from Seattle_ | _August 8, 1984_ |
| _Arrival in Beijing, China_ | _August 9, 1984_ |
| _Arrival in Lhasa, Tibet (12,000 ft.)_ | _August 13, 1984_ |
| _Arrival at Base Camp (17,000 ft.)_ | _August 20, 1984_ |
| _Establish Advanced Base Camp (21,500 ft.)_ | _August 28, 1984_ |
| _Establish Camp 1 (North Col 23,000 ft.)_ | _September 1–25, 1984_ |
| _Camp 2 (25,500 ft.)_ | |
| _Camp 3 (27,500 ft.)_ | |
| _Summit Attempt_ | _October 1, 1984_ |
| _Break Base Camp_ | _October 15, 1984_ |
| _Arrival in Lhasa, Tibet_ | _October 22, 1984_ |
| _Arrival in Beijing, China_ | _October 24, 1984_ |
| _Return to Seattle_ | _October 27, 1984_ |

I'd never read and reread anything so many times. There were things in it I didn't understand. Like what's the big deal about an 8,000-meter peak and what's pulmonary edema? Why did they need permission from China to climb a mountain? I didn't realize there was such a thing as a professional "mountain guide." What's a couloir? And I just couldn't imagine what it would feel like to live at a base camp that was over 17,000 feet, much less to live at over 20,000 feet above sea level at an advanced base camp. I remembered what 10,000 feet up in the Colorado Rockies would do to me before I got used to it. (Actually, I never did get used to running around at 10,000 feet.)

A stronger sense of reality in relation to this expedition came to me as I read the release. The team had its own logo, stationery, special permission from the Chinese government, not to mention some of the world's greatest mountain climbers. They were also bringing their own doctor. I doubted there were any hospitals anywhere near Everest.

It was also obvious from the Team Roster that my name was not there. Even though I'd walked across America and climbed "mountains" in the Smokies, Rockies, and Cascades, I was definitely not an elite mountain climber. These guys were like the hottest of the hottest Special Forces combat units. The climbers wanted me there to write about their expedition, but I would have gone to wash their dishes in cold water. The only foreigners allowed deep into Tibet, to be near Everest, were mountain climbers.

This release in its crisp white envelope with its tersely worded information would make an excellent piece of mail for Barbara to discover on our dresser. I only wished that there were no references to the climber who had died on the team's last attempt in '82. I wished they hadn't mentioned strokes, frostbite, and pulmonary edema. But then I'd always heard that one of the big draws of mountain climbing was confronting all the life-and-death situations that came up and living to talk about it.

I brought the envelope home from the trailer and placed it so that it would stand out on the cherry-wood dresser. Barbara didn't notice the news release for a couple of days. When she did finally read it, she didn't say anything till I asked her about it one evening.

"Barbara, what did you think about the info on that China/Everest expedition?" I asked. We were savoring the quiet we never had while our energy-kids had their eyes open.

"It sounds dangerous. I hope Skip's going to be careful."

"Me, too." Well, it was obvious to me by now that I would have to come right out and tell her that I had been invited to go, too.

"Barbara?"

"Yes," she said, carefully.

"I wanted to tell you that I've been invited to go on this expedition, too. BUT! They don't want me to climb to the top of Everest. They want me to write a book about it." I didn't take time to breathe or give her a chance to say anything yet.

"There's no doubt that this is a once in a lifetime open door and I want to go, VERY badly. . . . And"—I breathed a little—"I just _know_ that I'll make it back before the baby comes. I just know it."

She never flinched, as though she knew exactly what she was going to say. "Well, it says in that letter you put on our dresser that the team would not be returning until October twenty-seventh." She'd obviously read it very carefully.

"That's right, but I wouldn't have to stay with the team the whole time, just part of the time."

"Well. . . ," she said very slowly, "I know you well enough to know that if you couldn't go because of me, you'd never get over it. . . ." Long pause. "I think that you should go ahead and plan to go."

She continued, "If something bad happens between now and then, you'll just have to cancel. . . . Besides, I just feel right about this. I've known for a long time that you would have a chance to see other places in the world, and this would be a great place to start." What a remarkably wise and brilliant lady Barbara was! I really loved that lady.

# 4

# *Clawed in My Sleep*——

Later that night the dreams began. They were nothing like my normal dreams, most of which I couldn't remember. . . . They were "wake-up-sweating" dreams that happened in places I'd never been, with people I didn't know. What was so unusual was that I could remember them like I could remember the best books I'd ever read.

I remember the first dream almost completely. It began as *five Tibetan horses flashed through the narrow flats of a mountain valley. They were surprisingly small horses, yet obviously surefooted as there were stones of various sizes everywhere and they were galloping wide open. Running in* _front of them was a blur. The blur was low to the ground and long, covering ground in high leaps. I was on the back of the gray horse, and the men riding next to me were smaller than I, their skin dark red-brown from the sun. They shouted instructions to each other in a strange and poetic-sounding language, and somehow I understood._

_"Quickly, we must not let that leopard make it to the end of the valley," said the lead rider, whose soiled sheepskin coat blew open in the wind. We rode on the crudest wooden saddles, and my Tibetan friends never even bounced. The snow leopard was headed for an opening in the steep stone walls that closed in this end of the valley._

_The leader yelled to fan out, so that we could better direct the frantic leopard away from its only escape route._

_In a moment we would have it cornered. Then we would draw bow and arrows, tipped with poison, and aim to kill the snow cat. Its pelt would be used to make the Dalai Lama a sacred headdress. This leopard was said to have a pelt given to it by the gods, so perfect was the placement of the spots and so deep was the fur._

_The leopard had nowhere to go. It leaped high onto the stone, pawing and scratching desperately. Amazingly, it clawed up on the cliff even higher. Just as it seemed it would supernaturally claw its way up and onto a wide ledge, it slipped, and the magnificent body sprang back in midair, twisting and flipping. In a second it would land on one of us. It was coming for me. I lunged with my right arm to protect my face and hit something._

"Peter, what is wrong with you! Why did you hit me?" Barbara cried out. It was dark as a cave, and too humid for Tibet. I was at home in Tennessee and obviously I had not been chasing a snow leopard.

"Sorry, I was just dreaming."

"Well, be careful; that hurt," Barbara growled. She was instantly asleep again.

But I couldn't get back to sleep. Whatever was energizing my mind would not slack up. It was as if my mind were an engine that just kept on running and running. Lying on our hard mattress, I looked out the window and saw long shadows cast by the streetlights on our road.

I wondered if there were streetlights in China. Were there high-speed subways that blurred by their towns? Was it a country of ox-carts and bamboo bird cages, or did they have video games? Did the people own anything of their own, like televisions and washing machines, or did twenty people share the same weathered outhouse?

Would all parts of the country look alike? After all, I'd thought the USA would look like one huge shopping center connected by cities and suburbs—before I walked across it. Is all of China covered with rice paddies? Are the roofs on all their buildings curled up at the edges, and is there rock and roll on the radio?

I'd learned long ago that depending on preconceptions of a place turned out to be a trap. If you believed just what you heard or read, you'd be headed for lots of surprises. I rolled over on my back so I could think better. Would I be able to answer any of these questions just by being with the expedition to Everest? Based on the itinerary they had set up in their news release, it didn't seem that there would be time for anything but the expedition. That made sense for them since their goal was to get on top of the world's tallest mountain, but it didn't make sense for me.

If I was going all the way to China, I should take the time to see more of it than just Tibet and Everest. Besides, I might never get to go back, especially while the kids were young; who knows, China could shut its doors to the world again, anytime, for a year or a decade.

It was true that the villages and mountains of Tibet around Mount Everest were off limits to all foreigners except mountain climbers. And even then, very few permits to attempt Everest were given out each year to the hundreds of demanding teams from countries like Japan, Australia, the United States, Canada, France, Germany, and Italy, who wanted to be the first from their nations to make it to the top from the China side.

I knew I could never expect to get as close to China as I did to the USA while walking across it, but with all the experience I'd had meeting different kinds of people during my walk, I was confident I would learn much. "BUT," I asked myself, "are you forgetting that you're thinking about traveling around China, not Chinatown? They all speak Chinese, or worse than that, maybe they speak hundreds of different dialects!" Like any dream, China/Everest was becoming more complicated in real life. Hopefully, it would never become a nightmare. Rolling back on my right side I saw the red numbers on the radio alarm clock. It was after two A.M. That night I dreamed continually but I remembered only a portion of a dream about baby number three being born two months early. I decided I'd get in touch with Lou Whittaker soon, and ask him if he could help me work out the arrangements for my possible journey, alone, through the rest of China. As much as he'd dealt with that nation, he probably knew what to do.

I called Lou at the new underground stone home that he'd built for himself and Ingrid, his second wife, at the base of Mount Rainier. They'd met on Mount Rainier where Lou and his partner, Jerry Lynch, own and operate Rainier Mountaineering, Inc., a climbing school. Fact is, many of the climbers on the expedition team were guides at RMI, and had learned much of what they knew from him. He was as close as you could get to being a guru to many of the most talented mountain climbers in the United States.

Lou thought my idea about taking off on my own and exploring the rest of China was a fine one. He said that if he weren't going to be trying so hard for the summit of Everest, he'd like to come, too. He said it was somewhat frustrating to him that during an expedition there had to be almost fanatical dedication to the goal. There was little time for any exploring beyond finding the safest route up some vertical rock wall covered with ice.

"Peter, why don't you give Jim [Wickwire] a call," Lou said as he was hanging up. "He's a Seattle lawyer and mountain climber, and he can probably give you some good ideas about how to get permission to travel around China and get the appropriate government permissions, et cetera."

Hearing Jim's name reminded me that just a few weeks before, I'd seen a story about him on *60 Minutes.* He looked like a dark-haired preppy with the blue suit, striped tie, and the works . . . except when there was footage of him on a mountain. Then his whole countenance changed drastically. Then he'd have a bandanna around his sun-reddened, bearded face. His eyes darted with the energy generated from the risks he took.

Lou said that Jim corresponded with climbers in many countries and had all kinds of connections in the elite climbing circles of the world. The way he talked, it sounded like a very exclusive club, joined by some men and a few women for what they did miles up, where humans were measured by their ability to live and climb. Lou said most climbers he knew felt, "It's not how long you live, it's *how* you live."

Lou went on to say that Jim, being a lawyer, handled the team's work dealing with the Chinese and American governments, and that he had excellent contacts with the important mountain-climbing countries: Pakistan, Nepal, China, Bhutan. There were mountains of paperwork and details in organizing an expedition to China. There were travel permits, passports, telexes to be sent to Beijing, embassies to talk with, budget negotiations, and armfuls of official documents and correspondence to deal with.

I got the address of the American Embassy in China. Feeling confident that my reputation as a writer and appreciator of all kinds of people and their differences would translate into quick help from our embassy and China, I dashed off a letter to our ambassador.

Throwing the letter into the mailbox that afternoon from the window of my Ford pickup, I figured it was more of a formality than anything else. Surely a quick, decisive reply would follow. Just to cover myself, in case the Chinese intercepted my letter to the ambassador, I wrote our Tennessee senator, Howard Baker. He was majority leader of the United States Senate, so all he'd have to do was pick up his special phone, make a call, and click, it would be done.

I was so proud of myself for getting things started so early in the planning stages of the adventure that for a few weeks I relaxed, talked to anyone who knew anything about China, and read guidebooks. It was the end of March and I'd heard nothing yet. I'd be leaving in a bit more than four months.

I didn't expect to hear back from the ambassador or Senator Baker immediately, but when I heard nothing for two months, I began to get a "bit" nervous. I wrote the Office of Congressional Relations in Washington. I mailed a letter to the Chinese Mountaineering Association. Then I called Tennessee's Office of Economic and Community Development. After all, they had recruited Nissan, a Japanese automotive giant, to Tennessee. I was beginning to get desperate. Then I fired off a letter to the Chinese People's Association for Friendship with Foreign Countries. I got a few replies, some helpful-sounding attempts from the Americans, but no results, and nothing out of China.

It seemed everywhere I went people had heard I was going to China and Mount Everest. People would start up conversations in the check-out line at Kroger's, while I was pumping gas at the Shell station, while eating meals at local restaurants, anywhere. It wasn't just me—there was a fantastic curiosity and interest in China. People, including myself, acted and talked about it like it was located on another planet. I'd store nuggets of apparent wisdom, knowing that once I got there, *if* I got there, anything I might know could help. People, a few who had been there and others who had just read about it, would say things like . . .

- When in China always, ALWAYS smile. Never show anger.
- It's a good idea to bring maps of the United States.
  A. To show the Chinese where you live. They are VERY curious.
  B. To give as a token of appreciation for some favor, like a special dish at a restaurant, or directions to a restricted area.
- When talking with Chinese in groups, always be very smooth and polite. They are afraid that you could be a spy or that one of their comrades could be one. They will warm up much more alone. They never trust one another.
- If you're a guest for a meal, always eat some of everything and compliment your host, politely, but don't clean your plate unless you want a lot more food. Each emptied plate brings a bigger portion.
- Never discuss politics or religion.

# 5

## *Lead Bags*

The smoke was especially thick at the Poplar House Restaurant during this noon rush. The back corner table that had a sign over it saying "Reserved for Truckers" was full and noisy. The other back corner table was empty now, but early every morning many of the local farmers met here to talk of the latest rumors, truths, lies, and all their possible combinations. Usually I didn't eat alone, but today I sat in a row of empty tables, reading the menu. I waited for Mary or Vivian, my favorite waitresses, to take my order. Mary always had a perm and wore her uniform pants tight. She lived in a trailer park with her kids. Vivian lived a few miles past our farm with her good ol' country-boy husband, cheerleader daughter, and two little boys.

The best-sounding thing on today's lunch specials was BBQ'ed backbone, green beans, corn bread (I always wanted the well-done thin pieces) and squash casserole. I asked what kind of homemade cobbler they had today, hoping to hear cherry. I looked up, expecting Vivian, but saw instead a lady I didn't know standing next to me. I hoped she'd mistaken me for someone else. I was cranky and in no mood to talk to a stranger.

"You are Peter Jenkins, aren't you?" she said in a reserved manner. Her hair was dark brown and she was neatly dressed.

"Yes, I am," I answered flatly.

"Are you really going to China this summer?" She had a composed, unblinking stare.

"Yes, that's right." I was trying to discourage her by saying as little as I could, as coldly as I could. Ben Gary, a local auctioneer, was eating a heaping dish of cherry cobbler with vanilla ice cream melted over it. I wanted to get on with my lunch so I could get to the cherry cobbler part.

"Are you excited about going?" She was persistent.

"I sure am," I said, letting some emotion slip.

"I wanted to let you know that my daughter-in-law is Chinese." The first thing I thought was "So what?"

"My son's name is Ed Porter and his wife is Ran Ying Porter. Eddie met her while he was teaching English in China," the woman continued. "Did you know that Ran Ying's mother is one of the editors of _The China Daily_?" she asked.

"What's _The China Daily_?" I was suddenly intrigued.

"That's the largest English-language newspaper in China," she answered.

I felt guilty for being so standoffish moments before. "Won't you please sit down, Mrs. Porter. I'd love to hear more."

"Thank you, I will." She was a bold woman.

"Please tell me about your son and daughter-in-law," I urged, just as friendly as I could be.

She proceeded to tell me about her eldest son, Eddie, who had been caught up in the sixties and the peace and love movements, just as I had. She knew about me, she said, because she'd read _A Walk Across America_. However, she said her son's attitudes were a bit more unusual in the conservative, God-bless-America South than they would have been in New York or California. When Nixon went to China and it opened its doors to the West, Eddie applied for one of the very first English-teaching jobs. He ended up an instructor at a Chinese university somewhere between Beijing and Shanghai. While teaching there he met and married a fine young Chinese woman who was a student.

"Wouldn't you like to meet them?" she asked.

"Yes, I would," I answered, caught off guard by the sudden invitation, "but I'm not sure when I'll get the chance to, I'm so busy."

Lately the demands of life seemed to be running over me. There was too much going on. We had two small children and we lived in a house that was about to fall in. We were restoring our home and writing another book (*The Road Unseen*). Barbara was pregnant again. I had a farm to keep running and all our cows and their problems. Lacy, our Alaskan husky, had just had a huge litter of pups and they howled all night. I didn't know if I could get anyone to answer my letters and calls about help in traveling around a tightly controlled Communist China.

Mrs. Porter and I arranged that I would meet her son Ed and his wife, Ran Ying, the next Saturday, here for breakfast. I thanked her for her interest.

I was ten minutes late for our appointment. I'd been stuck in a "traffic jam" coming through town because a big John Deere tractor loaded down with a huge cart of fertilizer for someone's wheat crop was going about five mph.

There were the usual farmers and country people at the vinyl-covered booths and tables. Ed and Ran Ying (pronounced Ran Ying) were sitting by the window. I'd never seen an Oriental in Spring Hill before this. Come to think of it I'd never known anyone who was Chinese. We exchanged greetings. Ed appeared to be in his thirties, had brown hair, was medium tall and wore glasses. His face was alert, and it was obvious to me once we got to talking that he had a probing intellect and an adventurer's heart. Ran Ying had stylishly short, black hair and was quite thin. She had the innocent smile of a young girl and her skin was creamy yellow. I was surprised when she ordered a large breakfast of country ham, piles of hot, homemade biscuits, scrambled eggs, and hash browns. It was the biggest breakfast you could get at the Poplar House, which made its living dishing out servings big enough for farmers and truckers.

I sat across from them and immediately felt that Ed was doing everything he could to figure me out. I was so frustrated with the lack of assistance I'd gotten from both my own government and the Chinese, that I started right in. Why could I not even get the Chinese to reply to letters sent months ago? Did Ed think they would come through and provide me with an interpreter? I mentioned that although I was going with a mountain-climbing team to Tibet, I desperately wanted to travel to other places in China, like Inner Mongolia, Manchuria, Chengdu, the Chinese coast. By now I knew that I'd need special travel permits even to go there. I was afraid my intense frustration at the slowness of the Chinese was apparent to Ran Ying and Ed, and I hoped it wouldn't offend them.

Ed told me how he and Ran Ying met while he was teaching English and how they'd married even though there was a lot of negative reaction to them because of Ran Ying's marrying an "American capitalist, noncommunist Westerner." Marrying a foreigner was considered by many Chinese an act against the motherland. Ed told how they'd left China and worked at an East-West Center in Hawaii. He said they wanted to raise their children in the States because there was so much more opportunity. Ran Ying said little. She ate, smiled shyly, and did not make much eye contact. I couldn't get a fix on what she was thinking or what she was like.

"Why did you move back to Tennessee?" I asked. It seemed like a drastic switch from Hawaii, where there was a large Oriental population. About the only Chinese experience anyone can have in Tennessee is watching a show on the local PBS-TV station.

"We moved back to Tennessee because I was offered a job at Bethel College. That's in McKenzie, Tennessee, over towards Memphis. We live out in the boonies," Ed reported.

He began to explain how he'd felt going to China to teach, having been raised in a small, very southern town. "For the whole first year I was there I'd catch myself thinking that I was in the midst of a yearlong episode of _The Twilight Zone_. Everything was that different."

"Oh, come on, Ed," Ran Ying said, her tone of voice urgent. "It was good being in China, wasn't it?"

"Sure it was good; it was just very different," he replied.

The rest of our talk was like a bag filled with ancient jade carvings. Each piece of information would prove to be very valuable to me then and later. The great thing was that Ed was born and raised an

American and been in China for a couple of years and Ran Ying was born and raised in China and had been in the USA for a couple of years.

Ed had a writer's eye and would often share observations about life in China that were very perceptive. "Ran Ying has a close friend," he said, "who is a very serious member of the Communist party, yet he always wears a Christian cross around his neck!"

Ed and Ran Ying went on to share much of their knowledge of China and the Chinese with me:

"I would say that it's a must for you to go to Guilin, where the pillarlike mountains grow out of the rice paddies. This place of paddies and water buffalo and mountains and clouds is where the famous Chinese painters have worked," Ran Ying said. When she talked of China there was a powerful pride that emerged, like that of a Texan, more subtle but no less intense.

"Most Americans hear that there is no dancing and "Western" things, but there is much 'underground' dancing among the young people. The young people are getting much more rebellious," Ed said. I couldn't tell if it bothered Ran Ying for Ed to make such statements.

"Chinese love to smoke, but cigarettes are expensive. When you're there, Peter, buy packs of the best brands and always offer one," Ed said. This was excellent, practical info. I hoped I'd get the chance to use it.

"If you should decide to travel above the Yellow River," Ran Ying said, "the government has provided heat in the rooms." Who provides it below the Yellow River, I wondered? Maybe there wasn't any.

"I know you're a photographer, Peter. Whatever you do while you're there, don't take any pictures of anything that looks like it could be military, or off limits. Of course, so much of the country is off limits, it's doubtful you'll even get near one of these places." I couldn't wait to take some off limits photos.

Ran Ying quickly mentioned, "It would be nice to bring postcards of scenes of America, especially around Tennessee." She added, "Do not choose postcards that picture examples of America's great wealth, like big-city skylines or mansions. It would be better to have scenes of the countryside." She explained that the Chinese got their feelings hurt very easily and were so proud of China and what they had, and didn't know that they had so little compared with the rest of the world, especially America. The Chinese were told by the government and media, until very recently, that they were the world's greatest and most advanced nation and they had no way to find out differently.

"Never tip in China. No one does and it might be confused as a bribe or something." I was in a state of fascination over all I was learning. I was planning to give Mary a bigger tip than usual.

"The Chinese try to keep all foreigners in their own hotels, their "own" parts of town, shopping in their own stores called Friendship Stores, where the prices of everything are five to ten times what they are for the Chinese. You will have to use a different kind of money, just for foreign travelers, and have a special travel permit for all places you want to go except for the few open cities, like Beijing, that don't need one," Ed said. That was food for thought and the first time I'd heard about special money and stores and hotels and areas. I wondered what would happen to me, a curious foreigner, if I didn't stay in the places I was supposed to. Could they throw me in jail and lose the key?

"Always keep receipts for everything you buy in China, in English and Chinese, with how much you paid, date, where bought, when, and from where, in a special envelope. That way you will have a better chance of getting it out of the country, and you will not be sold anything illegally." I was planning to buy as much as I could afford.

"Bring pictures of Barbara and the kids and a few of some of the cows but not of your house and cars. Pictures of your house and cars might embarrass many Chinese and they might take it as a put-down, thought not intended." They said it was hard to imagine how primitive and poor China was. That was not the picture _I_ had of the place.

"Many Chinese are learning English now, it's the in thing, on TV, et cetera. But don't count on it," Ed said. "You must have a translator, just for you, if you are going to learn much of China."

"Buy lead bags for your film as their X-ray machines at the airports are much more powerful than ours and will erase all your film."

"Always remember that the concept of Revolution is a positive one in China. They speak of their Revolution in almost holy terms."

Ran Ying wound up her part of this exchange by informing me that the Great Wall was the only man-made object visible from the moon. She sounded proud.

The second to last thing Ed said was the most exciting thing he'd told me so far, if I could have confidence in it. "This is going to be hard to believe, after all we've said and all you've heard about China, but I wouldn't worry too much about the dead ends you've run into trying to get something out of the government. The way to do what you want in China is to just DO IT. Work out the details after you get there." Yeah, sure, Ed. I must not have been able to hide my reaction of disbelief because he reaffirmed his message.

"With the Chinese you must be very pleasant and VERY persistent. If you have a knowledgeable interpreter who will not take no for an answer, then you'll be amazed at where you will be able to go and what you will be able to do. The worst that can happen is that you get deported." I wanted to believe him, considering the lack of assistance I'd gotten so far, but I was also fearful, too. What if I got over there and everything was closed to me? I could only compare it to my walk across America. I'd let that adventure just happen. Was it possible in Communist China? Maybe I'd be finding out.

# 6

# "All My Rowdy Friends Have Settled Down"___

While I was emptying my last cup of coffee, Tanya, one of the younger waitresses, plunked two or three quarters in the jukebox and one of my favorite songs by Hank Williams Jr., came on. It was "All My Rowdy Friends Have Settled Down."

Ed spoke one more time. It was his most potent statement. "Peter, after talking all morning I would like to make a suggestion. Is that okay?" He seemed more nervous than he had been earlier. Maybe he'd had second thoughts and he was going to advise me not to go.

"Sure, Ed, shoot." I had a tension knot in my stomach.

"What would you think of having Ran Ying serve as your interpreter during your trip to China?"

"How is that possible?" I asked, taken by surprise.

"Well, she's been away from China for about four years now, and she is very, very homesick. I think it would do her a lot of good, plus she thinks she would like to get into this line of work, if we continue to live in the United States." Ran Ying sat quietly, showing no reaction to her husband's offer. Must be they'd already discussed this possibility and had come to check me out for themselves.

Thinking as fast as I could, I considered the glacier-slow movement of the Chinese government and how many days remained before I was to leave. I realized that Ran Ying spoke English quite well; she had a heavy accent, but I could understand her. If it was okay with Barbara, I told them, I'd be honored. I told them I'd think about the details of how to pull it all off, and call them in the next few days. My head was overloaded with information. It didn't seem possible that this could all have happened at the Poplar House.

That night I dreamed that I was taken into custody while traveling down some off-limits country lane in rural China, and charged with spying for the U.S. government. The shrill-voiced Chinese agents confiscated all my film and stomped my cameras. When I was put in a bamboo cage over a dirty canal with hundreds of leeches crawling up the sides toward me, I was scared awake. Ran Ying was nowhere to be seen in the dream.

It wasn't long before I called Ed and Ran Ying and said that I'd thought through their offer. I'd talked with Barbara and checked it out with the Everest team leaders. It didn't seem as if help would come from the official Chinese so I would take them up on their offer.

A couple of days later when Ran Ying called I was afraid she might have had second thoughts. After all, she had a husband and triplet sons, three years old, more than enough to keep her close to home, let alone going off with a comparative stranger to the ends of the earth.

Ran Ying explained that her parents and brother lived in the capital city of China. Her mother was an editor for *The China Daily* newspaper, and her father was a senior researcher with some government office. When I asked her what office her father worked with, she started talking about her brother instead, who was a doctor of traditional Chinese medicine.

"It may be a good idea for me to go to China a few weeks before we meet so that I can stop in Beijing and try to make some arrangements for travel permits while you're in Tibet. What do you think of that?" she asked, still not calling me by name. I was already getting the feeling that Ran Ying, although she seemed painfully shy at times, usually got what she wanted.

"That's fine. I'm just thrilled to have an interpreter." Before she hung up she told me that her parents had served in the early days of Mao's rule as interpreters to the Chinese Embassy in Denmark.

"Daddy, Jedy's sleeping. Let's go to the farm and see the puppies," Rebekah said. She was four and had that flashing light of high spirit in her eyes and her laugh. She moved with the easy grace of a dancer and she loved to run. Lacy's seven pups were in a dog house next to the barn and it was time to feed them all.

I couldn't have stood it if I'd made Lacy move into town with us, so I went out to our farm twice a day to feed her. She often caught her own food, mostly woodchucks and rabbits. Lacy was the most sensitive dog I'd ever known. With Cooper, my first dog, I could raise my voice and he wouldn't even hear me. If I raised my voice to Lacy, she'd never forget it, and would slink away from me for days, wondering if I was still upset with her. She could leap over five-foot-tall farm fences as graceful as a gazelle. She was sleek, her fur slick and shiny, but when she had pups she got awfully skinny, giving so much of herself to those forever-thirsty pups. She raised the fattest puppies.

We got out of my pickup, onto our gravel driveway. Rebekah stayed as close to me as a Siamese twin. This big open farm of ours must have seemed as big as a country to her. To me its 135 acres was as familiar and comfortable as a very close friend. Her insecurities about this "huge" piece of land reminded me of how big and scary the halls and drinking fountains seemed when I was in kindergarten. Someday, this farm would be nothing for her to be afraid of. It would be a place for her to come home to, to be secured by the sweet smells of the earth. She would come back to visit, from the confusing collisions of ideas during her college days, and walk over the soft curves of our pastures, sorting life out for herself. This land wouldn't change much, but she would certainly change her feelings toward it.

We rounded the corner, by the old smokehouse that was built with hand-hewn cedar beams, and saw the pups all lying in the sun, round and contented. Rebekah ran over to them, getting braver. She still wasn't totally relaxed around Lacy with her wolfish grin. I bought Lacy from an Indian in Alaska who raised sled dogs on a small sand island in the middle of the Nenana River. He'd said there was no doubt she was part wolf, and watching her lope along, either coming home or hunting, there *was* absolutely no doubt. She loved the children and would have killed to protect them. Often, she would watch over them while they played.

I walked behind a woodpile and in less than thirty seconds Rebekah noticed I was gone. She shrieked for me with a fearful, "Daddy, come back. Where are you!" It was very scary for her to think she was alone on this farm.

"I'm right here, sweety."

"Daddy, this one's name is Browny." She was holding one of the pups. Rebekah was too proud to admit she was afraid once she saw me.

"Daddy, how do they know who their daddy is?"

"They don't. Their daddy doesn't take care of them, just Lacy does."

"Oh . . . Daddy? I heard you talking on the phone. You said you were going somewhere on a big trip. Where are you going?" I thought she'd been engrossed in *Sesame Street* on TV.

"I'm going to China."

"Is that in our town?" She sounded excited for me.

"No, that's in another country, far across the ocean."

"What's an ocean?" she wanted to know.

"It's a lot of water," I said, realizing that it would be awfully hard for her to visualize where I was going.

"Is it bigger than our pond?" She looked out past the garden, toward a pond that I'd had dug for the cattle to drink from.

"Yes, it's much bigger than our pond."

"How long will you be gone to this place? Will you have to spend the night?" She'd recently spent her first night at one of her friends' and that had been one of the most exciting and anxious experiences in her life. She called us about five times that night to make sure we were still there.

"Not too long, honey." I wanted to call the trip off right then, thinking about how long I'd be away from my sweet family. I hoped someday she would understand that her daddy had to go places, sometimes. It was a part of his job and more important, necessary for his life.

In mid-July, a month before I was to leave for China, there was a barrage of official-sounding letters from staff assistants to senators, and commissioners of departments, but still no official assistance or, more important, permission to travel freely from the Chinese.

On July 19, Lou Whittaker received a telegram from China. It said:

*Mountaineering Association of the People's Republic of China*
9 Tiyuguan Rd.
Beijing, China

Mr. Whittaker of American Chomolungma expedition.
[Chomolungma is the Chinese word for Mount Everest.]
Extend our respects to you.
We received your letter dated July 10th. Here are replies.

1. We sent telex telling you to take the invitation telegram we sent you to China's embassy in America for visa.
2. Regarding the visa problem of Mr. Combu, we have sent telex to our embassy in India. Please notify Mr. Combu to go to our embassy in India immediately for visa. [Mr. Combu is a world-famous Sherpa mountain climber who has stood atop the summit of Everest twice, once with Lou's brother, Jim. He spoke Tibetan and was a part of this team.]
3. Regarding Mr. Peter Jenkins' plan to spend an additional period of time traveling in China, please notify Mr. Peter Jenkins to turn to Chinese International Travel Agency, immediately, for arrangement.
4. We agree in principle with your budget. But please leave some margin for your budget. We will make final accounts according to your actual expenditure in China. If the expenditure is less than your budget, we will return you the money. If it exceeds your budget, you will give us more money.

Finally, we hope you have a good preparation.

I'd already written them months ago and heard nothing. I couldn't believe that I still could get no help and wondered if this was their way of keeping me from seeing more of China. It was common knowledge that the Chinese did not like to come right out and say, "NO." At least the team had been issued our visa for travel into Tibet, one of the rarest travel visas in the world.

Finally, fifteen days before I would leave for China and Tibet, I got what I figured was the official reply from the Chinese government, just in time to do absolutely nothing about it except consider not seeing anything but Tibet. It said:

*The Chinese People's Association for Friendship*
*with Foreign Countries*
Beijing, China
CABLE ADDRESS: Youxie

Dear Mr. Jenkins:
Your letter of June 29, 1984, has been received with pleasure. We highly appreciate your interest in China and your friendship toward the Chinese people.

Regarding your visit to other parts of our country, I must tell you frankly and regrettably, that we have already been so overwhelmed with our previous commitments for this year that it is hard for us to receive any more guests, even harder to arrange your visit at such a short notice. I hope you will understand.

Anyway, we have contacted other departments concerned, they all expressed the same reason as our Association for not being able to comply with your request. In the meantime . . . we wish you great success in your forthcoming trip to Tibet.

With best wishes.

*Sincerely yours,*
Yu Shilian
Council Member

FINALLY, it happened. I was turned down, officially. Now my hoped-for, dreamed-about adventures in Inner Mongolia and around the rest of China seemed nothing more than that . . . a hope, a dream turned lifeless. My only chance now was to rely on Ran Ying and our ability to slide through the maze of official China.

# 7
## *During Detention*_____

"QUICK . . . Hurry . . . He's got it down . . . He's going to kill it. . . ." The voice on the other end of the phone line was breathy and high-pitched.

I should have recognized that voice, but I was somewhere else. Namely the Orient.

"Daddy, listen to me!" she shrieked.

"What's wrong, Rebekah?" I tried to sound calm.

"Shocker's out of his pasture and he's got a cow on the ground and he's biting it." Rebekah was calling me from the farm where she and Barbara were checking on the restoration the carpenters were doing.

"I'll be right there!" My car sped up our gravel driveway spewing a long trail of white dust. I swerved past our young orchard and leaped over the fence into the field that Shocker had to be in. He was our six-year-old black stallion and a Tennessee Walking Horse. As Mr. George, a local farmer, said, "The life's rising up in him again."

I saw him rearing up and stomping down on the ribs of one of my Hereford cows, over by a row of cedar trees, next to Jess Morton's silo. Then he'd reach down and bite the poor old cow viciously. They were flesh-tearing bites. This was not the first time he'd done this. Last weekend, Shocker had a two-day-old calf in his mouth that had wandered off from its mother and had squeezed into his corral. If I hadn't seen him, he probably would have killed it.

"Shocker, QUIT THAT," I screamed, violently MAD.

I looked around for a dead branch to break over his head. He just kept on, as if he'd never heard me. When I got near him he took off running and started chasing after another young cow that Rebekah had named Nancy. I knew she was within days of having her first calf. She was so pregnant she looked ready to burst. I felt like I could have killed that crazed horse if I could have caught him, but this was a thirty-five-acre pasture and he could easily outrun me.

The only thing to do was get his bucket with some "sweet" feed in it and try to entice him back to the barn. I started shaking his red bucket and from almost a hundred yards away he heard me, even though he'd pretended he hadn't noticed me before when I was yelling at the top of my lungs. He trotted over looking regal and graceful, his black muscular body highlighted against the new green of the grass covering these fields. His mane sailed in the wind. When he got close he walked calmly back into his fenced-in lot behind the barn and daintily munched his grain.

After he finished I saddled him up and rode him to the back of the farm, to the "hayfields" that covered about fifty acres. He made me so angry sometimes, but in some ways I understood him. It felt so good to both of us to be galloping. I often felt like Shocker. If I was kept penned up and not allowed to run, my energy built up to the point of an explosion.

I ate dinner alone as everyone had gotten hungry long before I got back to the house. There was a plate of smothered pork chops, green beans, corn bread and coleslaw, one of Barbara's great southern meals. I was exhausted tonight even before I read the kids their story. It had all piled in on me this day, being so consumed by my China trip, plus the stresses of everyday living, not to mention the horse attack. There was no way I'd be watching any of _Late Night with David Letterman_ tonight. The children's bedtime story turned out to be my own.

Our bedroom faced Alberta and Walter Kinnard's little white house, which they kept immaculately clean. As I lay still I could see Alberta walking around, cleaning, I guessed. Alberta seemed to work day and night, inside and outside. Before I knew it I was asleep and far from my bed and quiet little Spring Hill, Tennessee.

_I was at a campfire on a flat plain. Sitting next to me was a Mongol nobleman. His name was Strong Wind and he spoke a strange language, but I understood. "My people," he said, "came out of the forests of the north, looking for fertile pastures and hungry for war. None of us then knew of this thing they call writing. We'd tell of our history around night fires. . . ._

_"One of my family, far back, was Temuchin. The Mongol woman who carried him was Mother Cloud. When Temuchin was born he clenched a lump of clotted blood in his tiny wet hand and it was prophesied that he would be a warrior all the earth would bow before. Later he would go by the name of Genghis Khan. At his most great power, his empire would begin at the Mediterranean and span all the way to the Pacific. It would take all the Himalayas and touch Siberia. We, the Mongol people, ruled the world."_

As I dreamed, I knew that I'd read the story before in an old book. I could recall the morning I read it during "Library," back in the sixth grade at Julian Curtis School in Greenwich, Connecticut. It wasn't that the story was so incredible that I couldn't forget it, it was the adventure that happened while I was reading it. It was a minor adventure compared with taking over the world, but it sure got my attention. That day, my friend Walter Ritch dared me to throw a library book out the window. Maybe I was filled with the spirit of Genghis Khan that day, but no matter, I did it. Instead of stopping with one book, I threw a bunch out, ten, maybe fifteen.

I thought I'd gotten away with it except that as we were leaving, the principal, whose office was directly below the library, was standing in the doorway, blocking my escape.

"It appears to be raining books," he said very sternly, "and I want to know which one of you threw them out the window."

I admitted what I'd done, knowing there was no escape, and had to stay after school that day. I read all about Genghis Khan during detention.

Before I got out of bed that next morning I knew I had to go to Mongolia. Looking at a map that afternoon, I learned that China had taken for itself that part of Mongolia now called Inner Mongolia. I must go there, whether it was open to me or not. Reaching the lands of Genghis Khan would be my Mount Everest.

# *Packed for Chomolungma*

The last few weeks before leaving were wild. I hardly slept, and when I did my dreams exhausted me. Normally when I go on a three-day business trip I pack an hour before I leave for the airport. Preparing for this trip strained my nervous system. I had to plan so carefully, and not just for what I'd need; I also had to think about things that I couldn't be without if they were broken or lost or stolen. There was no way I could take just one camera. Two camera bodies were a must. I'd need to take twice the amount of film I intended to use and keep my stashes in several different places. For the first time I was going to try to record everything I saw and felt and learned on cassette tapes. I planned to take double the amount I thought I could possibly need. Ran Ying had assured me that, unlike many foreigners, the Chinese will very rarely steal anything.

I planned carefully about the clothes I would take, but if something bad happened, I figured I could always dress like a Chinese. I couldn't even imagine how many tons of food and equipment and personal things the team would be shipping over by boat, months before we'd be leaving the States. I got a letter from the team suggesting what I'd need. It said:

## Recommended Clothing And Equipment

For Travel in China (*2 weeks, hot and humid weather*)
Packed in a JanSport Great Escape travel pack:
    2 or 3 pair of jeans or light cotton pants
    4 to 6 T-shirts, shirts, blouses
    1 pair running shoes
    1 pair sandals
    4 to 6 pair cotton socks
    Underwear
    Lightweight jacket
    Lightweight sweater
    Sunglasses
    Sun-lotion
    Sun hat
    Toilet articles
    Personal first-aid kit

For Travel in Tibet (*2 weeks, possibly hot days, cold nights*)
Packed in a JanSport duffel bag:
    Lightweight hiking boots
    4 to 6 pair of wool socks with silk or Polypro liners
    Long-john top, wool or Polypro
    Long-john bottom, wool or Polypro
    1 pair pants, wool or pile
    1 sweater or jacket, wool or pile
    Rain jacket and pants
    2 pair gloves or mittens
    1 warm parka, down or fiberfill
    1 sleeping bag, down or fiberfill
    Glacier glasses with side shields
    High altitude sun lotion

2 one-quart water bottles
Potable aqua
Eating utensils (bowl, cup, spoon, fork, knife)
2 bandannas
Toilet paper

I made a thousand notes to myself of things to do before I left.

### Things For Peter To Do Before Trip

CAMERA:
1. Camera cleaned before leaving
2. Purchase film:
    A. 80 rolls slide film ASA 25
    B. 90 rolls ASA 64—36 exposures
    C. 10 rolls ASA 200
3. Get 5 lead-lined bags
4. Get lens-cleaning solution and antistatic spray

My friend Dr. Fuqua, a local cardiologist, suggested taking the following to serve as my own first-aid kit:

Malaria medicine
Gamma globulin
Upper-respiratory medicine
Medicine for diarrhea and constipation
Dust masks
Medication for virus and bacteria infections
A & D ointment

I also needed:

Traveler's checks to exchange for Chinese money
United States postage stamps for token gifts
Business cards to look official if needed
Mennen Speed Stick, Old Spice scent
Sugar-free gum (cinnamon), 30–40 packs
Batteries—3 AA alkaline Eveready batteries
8 pkg. C Duracell (for tape player)
Fifty 90-minute tapes
3 fat notebooks
Medium pt. Bic pens, fifty

Food was our fuel on Everest. I'd heard from Skip that we'd be taking tons of the stuff. You just don't take a quick spin from base camp and head for the closest McDonald's. If you did go looking for the nearest McDonald's and you headed north from base camp at Mount Everest looking for a Quarter Pounder, large fries, and Coke, you'd have to go through Tibet, middle China, Outer Mongolia, central Russia, and across the North Siberian Lowlands. Once there you'd go over the top of the world, through the Arctic Ocean till you started down the other side of the world through the frozen parts of northern Canada. Surely you'd see a golden arch soon after getting to Canada.

If you wanted to go west from Mount Everest, it would be a couple of thousand miles at least, to Saudi Arabia. To get your large fries and Big Mac, it would be a long and death-risking journey over Everest, down through Nepal, across India, Pakistan, and into Iran. The last thing I'd say to any Iranian was that I was looking for a McDonald's. My head might end up on the end of a righteous sword. Sneaking through Iran, I'd catch a boat across the Persian Gulf, landing in Saudi Arabia, happy and starved. Anyway, it's a long way to fast food no matter which direction you go from base camp.

On the historic 1963 American expedition to Everest from the Nepal side (where Lou's twin brother, Jim, became the first American to make the top of the world's highest mountain) the team brought twenty-eight tons of equipment with them. Our expedition shipped four and a half tons. The '63 team had a budget of $400,000, which would be equal to at least one million 1984 dollars. Our '84 team's budget would be closer to $200,000.

The successful '63 team used 850 Nepalese porters to carry all those 28 tons of food and gear. We would use 38 yaks, and they could carry our equipment only partway up the mountain. Past 21,000 feet, they couldn't function, even though they were the only animal beasts of burden that could carry anywhere near this high. The 1963 conquest took 300 bottles of oxygen; we took only 30. In those days each bottle weighed 28 pounds; now they weigh 15. Then each bottle had a pressure of 1,800 pounds per square inch. Now they have 4,000 psi and last much longer.

Sherpas were used on the Nepal side of Everest as guides and climbing companions. They were born and raised in villages in the high regions of Khumbu, in narrow emerald valleys walled by the stone-gray of the seemingly endless mountains. These devout Buddhists, who consider the mountains spiritual beings, call Everest

_Chomolungma_ (pronunciation Chó-ma-lung-ma), "Goddess Mother of the World"; they know the mountain Makalu as goddess of destruction, and Taweche is the mountain where the heavenly horses gallop, sometimes leaving hoofprints in the rock. The Sherpas would make their assigned climber his morning tea, often setting up the tents, cooking, carrying the life-giving high-altitude equipment needed. They did these things and more and saved climbers incredibly precious energy high up. Often they saved their lives as well. Once any human gets much over 18,000 feet above sea level, the altitude has a degenerative effect on the body that can't be reversed by normal rest and food.

There would be no Sherpas for our team, for there were none on the China side of Everest. This sacred place had been closed, off and on, to the outside world for a couple of thousand years. The lamas who ruled Tibet did not want foreign adventurers in their Shangri-La. The Tibetans themselves, living a primitive existence, had no reason to try to climb any of the holy mountains of their Himalayas. When they did get up high, it was in the summer when a grazing bull yak might wander off looking for greener pastures. Sometimes, in the light-headed heat of a snow-leopard hunt, the leopard's tracks would take them into the soft snows, higher than the highest temple. The Tibetans have hard bodies and sun-toughened skin as well as metabolisms for climbing at extreme heights, but no climbing skills. There is talk of someday training the Tibetan villagers to function like the Sherpas. Today, they do nothing but guide their supply-loaded yaks.

The following is a sample from a computer-generated inventory list of the amazing amount and variety of food and equipment we took with us to Mount Everest.

### China/Everest Expedition Food: A Sampling

48 rib-eye steaks, in foil pouches
24 6 oz. cans chunk chicken
24 tins deviled-ham spread
6 6 oz. cans smoked salmon
4 tins sardines
48 foil pouches Mexican omelette
111 2 qt. pkgs Kool-Aid
630 single serve pkgs egg nog
480 single serve freeze-dried coffee

200 1 oz. tins raspberry jam
36 servings Pop Tarts
12 16 oz. boxes Grape Nuts cereal
24 single serve pkgs CornNuts
50 foil pouches strawberries
6 12 oz. boxes Ritz crackers
12 jars Grey Poupon mustard
24 bottles Tabasco sauce
2 10 lb. cans hash browns
48 boxes macaroni & cheese
144 Snickers bars
144 Hershey bars
72 Baby Ruth bars
24 Kit Kat bars
200 single serve pkgs wet-wipe towels

*The Equipment Inventory: A Sampling*

2 spools 7mm climbing rope: 800′ each
2 Sequoia tents
2 JanSport Everest tents
2 Ultra Light tents
144 AA batteries
4 Bleuet 206 stoves
5 folding chairs
6 20-cup coffeepots
6 frying pans
24 size D batteries
30 Hefty plastic bags
4 JanSport D-2 packs
24 Bic lighters

All together, not including each member's own luggage, there were 175 boxes, weighing around 4.5 tons. My three "packs" were only ninety pounds. After much research and planning, I decided to fit all my stuff into three "soft luggage" bags. One for my back, that I'd fit about forty to fifty pounds into, and one for each hand. That way I could balance out the load. I decided on a Yak 6000, by JanSport. It had an internal frame, was turquoise blue with a black bottom, and could be thrown into donkey carts, cargo planes, and jeeps, even roll down glaciers, without getting torn up. Plus it was padded enough to protect whatever was inside. I also used a travel pack called the Great Escape. It was made more for the traveler cruising around Europe who might do some backpacking, some hitchhiking,

PETER JENKINS

The young Tibetan woman who sold me the turquoise, coral, and silver necklace in the Lhasa bazaar

Tibetans surrounded us
in the Lhasa bazaar. What
fascinated them most was
the hair on Skip's chest.

PETER JENKINS

A scripture reader "for
hire" at his table on a side
street in Lhasa

PETER JENKINS

The stone walls of the Potala, some ten feet thick

The Potala and its 999 rooms sit above Lhasa. It "smelled of a thousand years of musty tapestries, rancid yak butter, and monks' sweat."

A lone jeep kicks up dust between the "wilderness" of Xigaze and Xegar.

The once-in-a-lifetime views through the windshield of our tired bus never ended in Tibet. We went around countless corners and over many mountain passes before getting to base camp.

PETER JENKINS

My friend the holy man
of Xegar

A Tibetan woman and
her dog keep a protective
eye on the holy man as he
shows me around her
compound.

PETER JENKINS

Xegar, my favorite village in Tibet

A grouping of Tibetan homes

"Himalayan Hysteria": The great joy of a beautiful Tibetan day

A young Tibetan mother cools off in the shade of the city of Xigaze, halfway between Lhasa and Mount Everest.

A dusty-faced little nomad girl on the road with her family

A lady "appears" on a narrow road in a rock gorge near the Tsangpo River.

Some of the high roads between Lhasa and Everest were cut out of rock and seemed as narrow as yak trails.

and a lot of train travel. It had back pads and a belt that tucked inside a pocket. I would be able to cram 4,300 cubic inches of needed equipment inside it. This kind of luggage was very flexible and incredibly tough.

One of the greatest equipment discoveries I made became my third bag. It was a Lowe Pro camera bag, a Compact 35. Inside were foam panels that could be moved to make an assortment of different pockets for lenses, camera bodies, film, and whatever. I fit into it two Nikon camera bodies, an F-3 and a Nikon FE. The F-3 was considered a more complex camera. Also, I brought three Nikon lenses: a 180mm, a 35mm and a 105mm. I'd been told that the 180 telephoto would be a necessity in the mountains. It was the only way to get up-close pictures of the wild animals, shy people, far-away mountains and anything else I couldn't get near. I'd use a 35mm wide-angle lens and a 105mm lens for portraits.

There was extra room in my Lowe Pro for lens-cleaning solution and paper, and twenty to thirty rolls of slide film taken out of their boxes. I also used this as a giant wallet and kept my money and passport and other important papers in it. Normally, I hate carrying a wallet, so I figured that I'd put everything that was crucially important in one place. I always kept some extra money in another pack in case this one got lost.

The months since Skip's call were gone. Now there were only a few days left. It was turning out to be a suffocatingly hot summer here in Tennessee and the old house we lived in had no air conditioning if you didn't count the cracked windows and holes in the roof. Ran Ying would be leaving in a month for Beijing on a Northwest Orient Airlines flight. I wasn't sure how she'd get to Sichuan Province where we were planning to meet, but she'd have to worry about that. There was always an off chance that something would happen and she'd not be allowed to come meet me. I decided not to worry about it. If she got there, fine, and if she didn't, I'd figure some other plan of action. Tibet and Everest came first.

# Over the Himalayas____

Something was said in Chinese, very fluently, then it came over the loudspeaker in English. "Thank . . . you. Lady and gentlemens, for fly . . . ing . . . C.A.A.C. Airlines. . . ." C.A.A.C. was *the* only airline in China. We were now flying over Tibet; the sharp peaks of the Himalayas reached up from the brown ground below and seemed to pull us into them. We still had countless mountains to fly over before we landed in Lhasa.

This was my first time ever off the continent of North America. I was zooming inside myself with the potential for adventure. During my flight from Nashville to Seattle I'd squirmed and wiggled in my seat and paced the aisles. The next morning the team and I left Seattle for Tokyo. It was an overnight in Tokyo and then on to Beijing, capital of China, late the next day. I was in Beijing, China! But my mind was on getting to Tibet. Soon, we would breathe its thin air and feel the dry warmth of its sun. This was a day I'd never thought could happen. I'd be standing in Tibet in less than an hour.

On our C.A.A.C. jet, I sat between the two elders of our team, Lou Whittaker and Dave Mahre. Dave seemed to be feeling very emotional about seeing these mountains below. Lou was deep inside himself, which was unusual.

"Peter," Lou blurted out, "a lot of us wish Marty could be on this plane with us, right now." Dave nodded his head in agreement. "Marty was one of the first people chosen for our 1982 Mount Everest team, the team that didn't make it."

"Marty worked for me as a guide on Mount Rainier," said Lou. "There were few things that held Marty back. She got what she wanted." Marty was from Washington, from a little town of maybe a couple hundred people on the peninsula. She was raised more or less by a single parent, her mother. She had a brother and a sister who had died. One died of some unknown illness during the night and the other one had some kind of accident. Marty was the last child left alive.

"Marty was a local northwestern person, the type of girl who enjoyed the outdoors, who rode horses, who was raised in an outdoor environment," Lou continued.

"Every guy fell in love with Marty. I thought, 'Man, here goes the guide service!' 'cause they all fell in love with her and she picked this one guy. She'd go with him for about a year and the next summer, she'd pick the next guy, who was delighted. The guy that she left wasn't jealous, which was an incredible thing to me. Age didn't make too much difference. From the age of eighteen to thirty-something, Marty seemed to trap each of the guides and become their girlfriend for a season.

"Well, about every team member had dated Marty at one time," Lou said. "Maybe Geo . . . but Phil for sure. Yeah, she was an attractive gal and had a lot of charisma.

"Phil always said, referring to Marty, 'She is mine and I'm going to marry her!' Everyone on the team said that Phil loved Marty more than any woman he'd ever known. "Phil was determined to marry

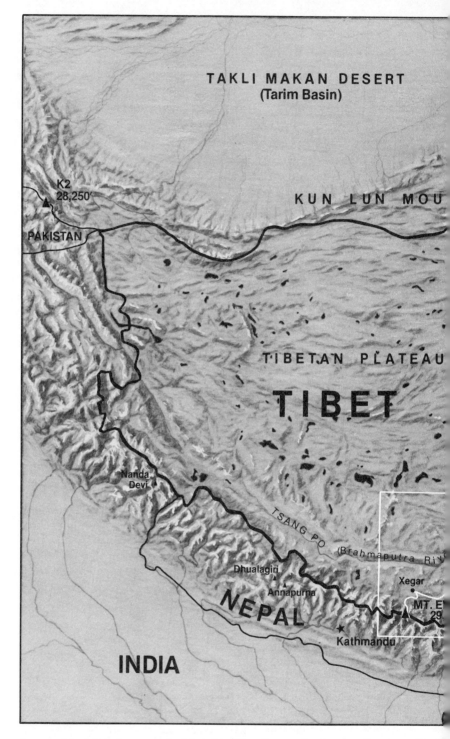

Its southern border guarded by the Himalayas, the home of many of
the world's highest and most magnificent mountains, Tibet has an
average altitude of about 15,000 feet. Tibet was conquered by China
in 1951, but not before the Dalai Lama left his palace, the 999-room
Potala, and escaped overland into India.

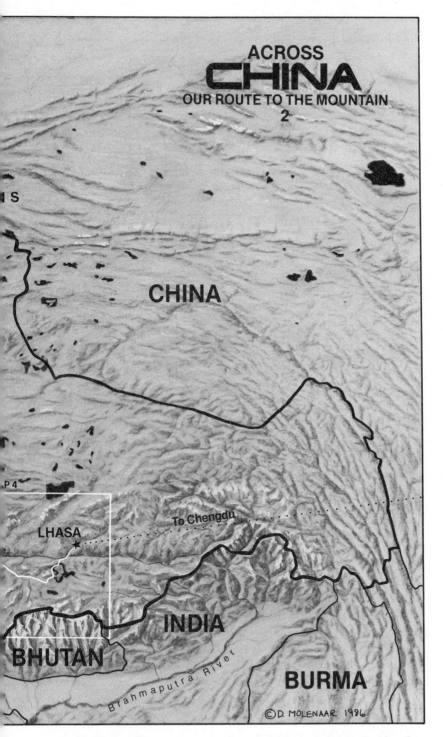

ACROSS
# CHINA
OUR ROUTE TO THE MOUNTAIN
2

CHINA

LHASA

To Chengdu

P 4

INDIA

BHUTAN

Brahmaputra River

BURMA

©D. MOLENAAR 1996

We landed in the city of Lhasa and soon attracted hundreds of
Tibetans as we wandered around the dusty open-air bazaars. They
were amazed at our skin color, beards, and different color hair.
After acclimatizing, we began our journey into the interior of Tibet.

her," Lou said. "But she wouldn't get married."

Phil Ershler, thirty-four, usually had his very dark sunglasses on, even inside, masking a sometimes critical eye. His nickname was Boy-King. He walked with his powerful chest, pumped up from lifting weights, inflated, sometimes strutting stiffly like a male dog about to fight. Phil was five feet six inches tall and weighed 150 pounds. Most experts believed Phil had as good a chance as anyone to be on top of Everest.

"She started out as a cabin girl, just a cook on the mountain." A "cabin girl" was all a woman could be in Lou's Mount Rainier guide service, until Marty became Lou's first female guide.

"One day she said to me, 'Look, I'm cooking the meals and I'm also climbing the mountain. I want to be a guide.' Marty used to get up about one in the morning, get the water going, cook the breakfast, feed the clients, stack the dishes, go up the mountain with us, come back down, fix soup or something, clean the dishes, and then hike down with the climb back to Paradise, the lodge at the bottom of the mountain.

"She was pretty tough." If Lou called someone tough, you better know they were. "We'd call her Thunder Thighs, she was so strong. She had a beautiful body, was real smart. Marty was a beautiful person.

"She became a great guide, too. Both the men and women loved her when she guided the rope. She got complete confidence from them. Even when she was at the age of twenty-two or so, she could just tell them what to do. She'd say, 'Jump that crevasse,' and they would do it. She would be tougher on the women than on the men because she wanted the women to be just as good as the men.

"On our '82 expedition to Everest she was the one who held the group together. When we lost her, it was devastating. She was climbing with Wickwire and they'd stopped to rest. They were high up on the mountain, at around twenty-six thousand feet, and Marty leaned back on the rope and her waist harness suddenly came undone. She fell onto her back and made a vain attempt to grab the rope. But, she was falling fast. Marty fell thousands of feet to her death."

There are things in everyone's life they never get over and there was no doubt Lou would never get over Marty's death. It was as if her death two years ago gave the men who loved her more drive to make this expedition a success.

"Most of the guys had gone with her and still were in love with her. Phil is still in love with her. Everybody was just completely devastated when she died. Marty used to say, 'Lou, I'm just never going to live beyond thirty.' She would have been thirty-one three days after the accident."

# 10

## *What Legs*_____

Maneuvering our plane over and through the tightly packed snow-capped mountains that surrounded Lhasa took a very calm and skilled pilot. I wondered if our pilot had such skills as our plane dipped and swerved on our descent to the runway jammed between three rows of mountains. We landed, without a crash.

Tibet was instantly captivating. On our arrival in Lhasa (pronunciation "Lá sa") we were confronted almost immediately with women trading forbidden wares, flashing smiles that made us feel welcomed in the bazaar, an open-air market.

I hadn't been at the Lhasa bazaar ten minutes when a Tibetan woman stopped me. She smiled the whitest smile, opened her wrap-around type "dress" and pulled out a beautiful necklace made from turquoise, coral, and pounded silver. She grabbed my hand and wrote something. Surely she wasn't selling herself? . . . No, not in the holy land of Tibet! She beamed her bright white teeth again and pushed the ancient necklace closer to my face. I wondered if I was in trouble as Tibetan men crowded around me, their black cloaks weathered by dust and rough wear. Out of their cloth belts stuck the handles of curved daggers. So far, these people _seemed_ very friendly and innocent and curious. What were the daggers for?

The young black-haired woman seemed to be writing a number on the palm of my hand. I tried to make a gesture that said I didn't know what she was doing. She grabbed my hand again and very slowly wrote what seemed to be a seventy. I looked at her and said slowly, "Seventy yuan." A yuan is the Chinese version of our dollar. We got two and a half yuan for each dollar. That meant she was asking about twenty-eight dollars.

I shook my head dramatically and wrote down "Thirty-five."

She acted very upset, and smiled slightly while she wrote down on the palm of my hand "Sixty." She acted as if that was as low as she was going.

I glanced up into the deep blue Himalayan sky and wrote down "Forty." By now there were one hundred Tibetans gathered around us.

She shook her head sadly. That must have been her way of saying the deal was off, as I heard the sounds of jewelry clanging together underneath her clothes. The dusty black cotton dress highlighted her gleaming turquoise and silver jewelry and rainbow-colored threads woven through her braided hair. She looked a lot like a Navajo.

I began to walk away, which was hard to do since there were at least a hundred and fifty curious people now surrounding me. The main bazaar of Lhasa, Tibet's biggest city, is where all peddlers of snow-leopard skins, raw yak meat, and bright-colored wool fabric, come to sell their wares along narrow stone streets. The dry, blinding blue air served as their roof, here in one of the world's most isolated cities.

The woman with the necklace walked after me, grabbed my arm from behind, and almost spun me around to face her. She reached for my hand and wrote down "Fifty-five." The Tibetan men thought her aggressive approach was funny and they laughed. These Tibetans have the most joyous, free-flowing laughs and laugh often.

I grabbed her warm, callused hand and wrote "Fifty," and we made a deal. When I pulled out my Chinese money, the by now huge crowd of people squeezed in even closer, just to get a look at all that cash. Most of them would not see that much money in a year and they acted as if watching this trade was the most exciting thing they'd done in ages. Being in Tibet was easily one of the most thrilling things I'd experienced in my life. It was hard to believe I was more than ten thousand miles from home.

The beautiful young Tibetan woman had sold me her necklace on the street, and we were both pleased with the deal, but what I didn't know was that our transaction was illegal. She walked away quickly from the crowd and disappeared down a narrow alley. There were Tibetan rugs of bright red, shocking pink, black, and all kinds of other bright colors hanging on a whitewashed wall she passed. The odor of yak butter, which smelled like the world's most aged cheese, made its way through the bazaar. Fortunately all the yak-butter and yak-meat vendors stayed off to themselves a few alleys over. A bicycle passed us with a yak head tied to the back of it.

Ahead of us was a small table, about the size of a card table, with a crudely painted sign behind it with a picture of a tooth in red and blue. Beautiful Tibetan writing was advertising something on the sign. Since everything else was out of doors here, could the dentists be too? Maybe eating nothing but yak products stained their teeth blue. I couldn't read Tibetan.

There was a man sitting in a ragged chair, and someone was bending over him with what looked like rusted pliers. I pulled my camera around quickly, and focused on the "mad Tibetan dentist." Click. What happened? The dusty man having his tooth pulled leaped up from the low-tech chair and ran down the road. I guess the dentist didn't want to get beaten out of his tooth-pulling fee so he ran after his patient and wrestled him to the street, littered with horse and donkey dung. The frenzied dentist placed his foot on the man's chest and continued pulling the tooth.

Before I could make my way through the crowd, an old, stooped-over woman with the mischievous grin that most Tibetans wore, blocked my path. She pointed to my bare white legs and started laughing. Lou, said that being at such high altitudes brought on a behavior pattern he called "Himalayan Hysteria." It made you act crazy, laugh uncontrollably, and sometimes make irrational decisions. And before you got used to the altitude you had another symptom, "Himalayan Sick-to-Your-Stomach." There was also the severe "Tibetan Super Migraine Headache," which was impervious to whole bottles of aspirin. Maybe living all their lives at this altitude made all these people naturally high. Maybe they smiled constantly because of their Buddhism or because they were so isolated from all the world's tensions. Tibet's average altitude was a fortress-like 17,000 feet above sea level. It was 12,000 feet here in Lhasa.

Once the old lady hemmed me in, pushed closer by the crowd, she leaned down for a close-up inspection of my legs. She ran her fingers over my calves. Surely Tibetans were not cannibals and she wasn't hungry for a big, juicy leg-of-man! The more she rubbed and played to the crowd, the more excited everyone became.

The next thing she did drove me wild. Maybe she couldn't see very well, but it was as if she had a revelation when she noticed that I had hair on my legs and arms. She began pulling at it, which was hard to do considering that it isn't very long and was blond from a Tennessee summer's sun, which made it hard to see. She seemed to think the hair was glued on to my arm and proceeded to tug at it. Since Tibetans have almost no body hair, I was something of a sideshow attraction here in the middle of Lhasa.

If she was perplexed by the downy hair on my arms and legs, she really became concerned when she reached up to the red hair of my beard and tried to yank it off my face. I may have been the first redheaded, "red-skinned" foreigner she had ever seen, much less laid hands on. She jabbered more excitedly than ever in her Tibetan language and got a firmer grip on my beard. Gently I took her hand and tried to counteract the force with which she pulled.

The old lady's bold innocence was a character trait of Tibetans. Skip, who had been buying his own necklace and had his own crowd circling him, was also being studied up close. A young Chinese soldier, who was watching all this, spoke Tibetan and Chinese and a fair amount of English.

He squeezed his way toward me and asked me a question that the Tibetans were debating among themselves. "Please, most polite man. May I ask of you a most personal question?"

"Yes . . ."

"These very gentle and most inquisitive people are wondering," he said very slowly, "which color hair, yours of red or his of white is the most pure?" The Tibetans listened in total silence as if our communication was magic. Maybe they thought our coloring made us more holy.

I looked over at Skip, a blond, who was still surrounded, and said, "My red hair is given only very rarely to those that God smiles upon. Those of us with red-color hair can fly."

The soldier, dressed in wrinkled Chinese green, with the red star of the motherland on his hat, translated into Tibetan. He was obviously thrilled.

They all stared at me as though they were looking for some feathers somewhere.

"Please, sir," I said quickly, "tell them this is only an American joke. This color hair is very common in our country." The Chinese acted confused, but the Tibetans thought it was a great joke. They patted me on the back, as they went back to their shopping or selling. I realized that my kind of humor was appreciated here. Later that afternoon, after having bartered for a couple of bone-handled daggers and having watched trained monkeys perform, I made it back to our room at the compound where we were housed.

# Chris

The door was open to our room. A Chinese man was standing there in a blue shirt and blue pants, the typical Chinese look. He pulled up his shirt and started rubbing all over his body. He rubbed his face, his arms, all in a fast motion. "This guy is weird," I thought.

Maybe he was talking about us taking a bath. Someone had mentioned we could take one today. We followed him down several alleys, past a couple of buildings, to an old building. All of a sudden we were in an old-fashioned bathhouse with tubs surrounded by their own partitions. We floated in a blissful state and talked to each other like a bunch of cousins at a family reunion. These were probably the only bathtubs in Tibet, and this was to be the team's last bath for two months.

Lou was in the tub next to mine. Back in the state of Washington, Lou was famous for the large parties he had in his hot tub that held over thirty people. A hot tub relaxes the mind, even in Tibet. Lou and I started telling stories. He told me about the young man who was responsible for us getting to climb Everest. His name was Chris.

"Chris Kerrebrock had sandy-blond hair, he was an up-type person, a very easygoing guy," Lou said. "He was a very muscular fellow about five ten with the most muscular legs I've ever seen," Lou added. "If it hadn't been for Chris we wouldn't have been here in 1982, or now.

"His dad is a professor at MIT and an astronautics engineer. He used to work for NASA. On an exchange, he was asked to go to China to do a study to help teach the Chinese astronautical engineering. Chris suggested to his dad that if he went to China, perhaps he could get permission from the government for Chris and some friends to climb the north side of Everest." At that time, in 1979, no American had climbed Everest from the Tibet side.

"One afternoon Chris and I were sitting up on Camp Muir, which is an advanced base camp for Mount Rainier, where Chris worked as a mountain-climbing guide for me during his summer vacations. He was a brilliant, prep-school kind of a guy, and was going to graduate school at Columbia in New York.

"Chris said, 'Lou, would you do it? Would you lead the expedition and pick a team?' I said, 'Yeah, if you get the permission.' I told my wife and she said, 'What do you think the chances are?' I said, 'About one in a thousand.' During that time China was not open, which was in 1979. Chris started working on it and his dad took the papers over.

"A year or so later Chris said, 'Lou, it looks like we might have broken through, we might have a chance of making the climb!' I said, 'This is incredible!'

"Chris was unusual because he was talented in so many things. He was an Ivy League student, an excellent climber, he could play the trumpet well enough to be in a symphony. He loved the big city and loved the mountains as well. He was from a nice family.

"He liked to party, liked girls. He was one of the more well-balanced young people I knew, with a terrific future." I thought I could hear emotion building in Lou's voice as he told me about Chris. I wondered why he was telling me so much about him and I was almost afraid to hear the end of the story.

"Once we got permission, it was time to start raising the money for the climb. Chris arranged a meeting with the U.S. Tobacco Company in Connecticut, to see if we could raise some funds. We got a handshake agreement from them for fifty thousand dollars. Chris set it up, so I met him there. After that he was leaving in a week for a climb of Mount McKinley with Jim Wickwire.

"It was raining as I dropped him off at the train station. He was going back to New York. It was pouring down rain and about eleven o'clock at night. Instead of just standing there, or sitting there in the car, I shut the thing off and got out. He dropped his bags and we gave each other a good hug. I told him that his friendship meant a great deal to me." Lou looked far past me.

"Many years ago, I lost one of my closest climbing friends," Lou continued. "Well, since I started climbing I've lost a lot of friends, but one of the first ones was a fellow back in the sixties who was a really good friend. He died on a climb and I'd never had a chance to tell him how much I thought of him and that he was a great guy.

"The same thing happened when Dusan Jagerski was killed up in the Fairweather Range of Alaska. He was one of my guides. The fall was over four thousand feet so there was little doubt he died. We never retrieved the body. That was in the late seventies and at the time I hadn't really told Dusan how I felt about him, either.

"While I was hugging Chris in the rain by that train station, I said, 'Chris, this has been a great day, you've got a great expedition coming up, and you're the greatest guy.'

"I was the one who introduced Chris to Wickwire. Wickwire said he'd like to climb to the summit of McKinley so I suggested that he and Chris go up together, get to know each other. I told Chris before he left, 'Whatever you do _don't_ ever totally trust anyone you're climbing with! No matter how good they are, anyone can make a mistake. Even Wickwire can make mistakes.' Chris was a little intimidated, going up with Jim for the first time. He knew that Jim had a world-class reputation as a climber.

"I went on to tell him, 'Hey, Wick's not a mountain guide, he's an expert climber. A guide is a climber who's learned how to take care of people. That's something a guide learns from the first time he ties on to somebody. He learns to treat everybody as though they're inexperienced because even the good guys make mistakes. In thinking back, I can honestly say that the same accidents that have happened to Wick could have happened to me. There are so many things that are unpredictable. The fact is I'm still climbing with my good friend Jim Wickwire.'"

"They were climbing Mount McKinley, just the two of them. Chris was tied awful close to the sled and Wick was close too, only twenty feet apart, *really* too close on a big glacier. But that's hindsight."

Lou stopped talking. Everyone had left the bathhouse and the only sound was water draining through the pipes. Then Lou said, "Chris used to play his trumpet on our ranch at Mount Rainier. It sounded great ringing out over the lake at night. As he lay dying, Chris told Wick he wanted us to put his trumpet mouthpiece at the top of Everest. We had it in the '82 expedition and we've got it now. I expect someone will be leaving it there."

Later, much later, Wick would tell me of what happened to him and Chris. The telling of it was not easy for Jim either, so he gave me a copy of a statement he'd submitted to the National Parks Service. It said:

On the approach to Kahiltna Pass, we each had pulled a plastic sled loaded with gear but decided that one sled would be enough to transport all our gear to the foot of the Wickersham Wall.

Early afternoon on May 8 we began to encounter hidden crevasses [cracks in the surface of the snow] on the glacier at about the 7,000' level. Despite being able to observe slight sags in the snow, which meant the presence of crevasses, we still fell into small crevasses only with a leg or up to our lower torso on five occasions.

Chris led, pulling the sled by means of a nylon sling. I followed, tied to the rear of the sled by the same means. Between the two of us was a separate climbing rope not more than 20' in length. The rest of the rope was coiled on Kerrebrock's pack. There were occasions when Kerrebrock had to pull the sled up over a rise, or when I would have to brake the sled in descent, or when the sled would tip to one side or the other because of bulges in the snow's surface.

Unlike the crevasse area through which we had come, the way ahead appeared free of crevasses. We could not see any of the telltale sags that had meant crevasses behind us.

Kerrebrock led down a gentle hill at the edge of the glacier. We were walking at a fairly rapid pace down this hill when the accident occurred. I did not see Chris fall into the crevasse because I was watching the back of the sled and working to keep the climbing rope between us from being snagged under the sled. My only clear recollection is falling through space with the thought that Chris, the sled, and I were falling into a crevasse and that "this was it."

Instinctively, I knew the fall was likely to have fatal consequences. Oddly, a diary entry made the next day states that "as the slope was downhill, I recall a brief moment of trying to get set to try to stop us, but there was no chance." Despite this entry, I have no recollection of seeing Chris break through the layer of snow covering the crevasse, seeing the sled follow him in, or being jerked off my feet.

The crevasse was slightly more than 3' wide at the surface, and we fell to a depth of 25'. Chris fell first, then the sled (which weighed about two hundred pounds), and then I fell, one on top of the other. [Chris fell in the diving position, headfirst.]

I managed to get my pack off and set it to one side. The crevasse was extremely narrow where we landed, only about 18 inches wide. (Being wedged in that narrow crack was like having your body stuck in a vise made of ice. Unmelting ice. This vise was bigger than a football field.)

I had difficulty shifting my body and could only move freely when directly facing the crevasse wall. . . . I could not see his head or upper torso, but we could talk. He was highly agitated about his predicament, and I told him the only way that I could help was to attempt to climb out of the crevasse and then pull him free from above. We were wearing snowshoes at the time of the accident so I had to remove them, and awkwardly put on my crampons to climb back out.

My left arm was numb from the shoulder down and extremely weak from the injury to it from the fall. I could not lift it without great pain, the arm was virtually useless. It was later determined that I had broken that shoulder in the fall. I managed to retrieve my ice hammer from the top of the sled and then began the delicate process of climbing out of the crevasse.

Due to the narrowness of the crevasse, it was not possible to penetrate the ice with either the front points of my crampons or the pick of my ice ax. Instead, I used the ice hammer to chip away very small edges in the ice upon which I was able to stand with the crampon front points. With my back against one side, I gradually made my way to the surface. [It took Jim about an hour to climb 25 feet of vertical ice.]

From above, I placed an aluminum stake about three feet long across the opening of the crevasse and looped the rope around it. Then I pulled the slack in from Kerrebrock's pack where the other end of the rope was attached. Pulling from above, I was not able to dislodge Chris.

I then descended into the crevasse. For the next several hours, I made repeated efforts to free Chris from the crevasse. With my injured shoulder and arm, and because of the narrow confines of the crevasse at his level, I was at a decided disadvantage. I attached the rope to the cross straps of his pack at different points and pulled repeatedly with my arms. Later, I did the same thing using the force of my legs. This did not work either. I attempted to cut off his pack with my ice hammer but that was unsuccessful.

After my very frustrating efforts to free Chris, I climbed back to the surface and attempted to make radio contact. I was not successful. I then returned to the crevasse and made further futile efforts to get Chris loose. Finally, we recognized the inevitable. Exhausted from my own efforts of several hours, I left him at about 10:00 P.M., climbing back to the surface with considerable difficulty, as my left arm was useless. When we parted, he was close to death from exposure to the ice and frigid cold. It was probably not more than three hours later that he died or at least lapsed into unconsciousness.

What Jim did not say in his statement was the following:

"We had our last words together at about 9:30 P.M., six hours after the accident. With a broken shoulder and exhaustion from sustained efforts to free Chris from his trap, I barely made it out of the crevasse the last time. He said, 'Take care of yourself.' After a tearful departure, I spent the rest of the night inside a nylon sack near the edge of the crevasse. It must have been shortly before midnight that I heard Chris singing. The words were garbled, but the melody seemed to be that of a school marching song or 'fight' song. It was deeply moving because in the face of death, Chris's spirits were soaring.

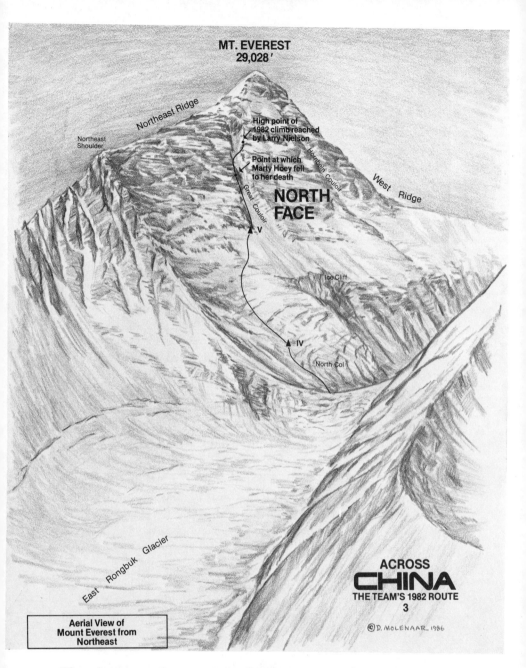

MT. EVEREST
29,028′

Northeast Ridge

Northeast
Shoulder

High point of
1982 climb reached
by Larry Nielson

Point at which
Marty Hoey fell
to her death

Hornbein Couloir

West Ridge

Great Couloir

NORTH
FACE

▲ V

Ice Cliff

▲ IV

North Col

East Rongbuk Glacier

ACROSS
**CHINA**
THE TEAM'S 1982 ROUTE
3

© D. MOLENAAR 1986

Aerial View of
Mount Everest from
Northeast

The adventurers I accompanied to Mount Everest in 1984 had been
here as a team once before in 1982. (Their unsuccessful route shown
above.) Other historic Mount Everest climbs are 1953: British—1st
ascent—Hillary (New Zealand) and Tenzing (Sherpa)—Nepal Side;
1960: Chinese—Kongbu (Tibetan) and Chu Yin-mua and Wang Fu-
chou (Chinese)—Tibet Side; 1963: American—1st U.S. ascent—Jim
Whittaker (American) and Gombu (Sherpa); Also—Unsoeld and
Hornbein—1st ascent West Ridge and 1st traverse; 1975: Japanese—
1st woman—Junko Tabei—Nepal Side; 1978: Austrian— 1st ascent
without oxygen—Messner (Italian) and Habeler (Austrian); 1980:
1st solo without oxygen—Messner— China Side.

"Chris asked me to stay in the immediate area to wait to be rescued. He thought that I would fall into another crevasse trying to
get out and that no one would ever know what had happened to us.
In the morning, both of my arms were in great pain, apparently
from the prolonged effort to free him. I did not move from the area
of my nylon sack until four days later. On the morning of May 13,
very weak and almost completely out of food except for a few sticks
of beef jerky, I decided to climb back into the crevasse in an attempt
to get some food from the sled. All I could get to was some jam,
honey, and crackers. This helped me to survive the next ten days
until I was rescued.

"On May 15, I moved back up the slight hill we had descended
just prior to the accident. I thought that I would have better line of
sight for making radio contact with the pilot who'd dropped us off
or some other passing airplane. The morning of May 16, a major
avalanche off the Wickersham Wall threatened me. Although the ice
debris did not hit me, the wind blast did. I then decided to begin a
careful effort to make my way back up the Peters glacier.

"For the next three days, I managed to pass safely through the
dangerous crevasse zone. On May 18, however, a major storm developed from the south. I was caught in the middle of the glacier without any protection other than my nylon bivouac sack. The winds
were so ferocious at times that I feared the sack would rip apart.
With my half bag and down parka, however, I was able to live."

The storm blew itself out the evening of May 21, thirteen days
after Chris and Jim had fallen into the crevasse. On May 22, two
weeks after Chris died in the vise-grip of ice, Jim was rescued, near
death himself.

It's not easy to place a phone call from Tibet, but I managed to
get through to home. Barbara had gone shopping and Rebekah answered the phone. "Daddy," she said. "Do you remember it's my
birthday on Saturday?" That hit me like a hammer in the face.

"I love you," I said.

She said, "I love you too, Daddy. Please come home soon."

"I'll be home as soon as I can, honey. Give Mommy a big hug for
me, okay?" I hung up and stood out under the blackest sky I'd ever
seen and cried.

## Bad Boy_____

It was August 14, 1984, and about time. Today we loaded our supplies, over 175 boxes, into old army trucks, which would go to base
camp ahead of us. Living in Lhasa at 12,000 feet above sea level
wasn't easy, but those of us who had been throwing up in the bushes
were holding down food now. Several of us had popped so many
aspirin trying to rid ourselves of the intense altitude headaches that
it was about like eating popcorn. Finally it seemed that my body was
getting used to the altitude here in Tibet.

Early the next morning, before the sun shone on the ancient

streets and before the fat dogs started to bark, we headed out. We were driving toward Mount Everest, toward Chomolungma, Goddess Mother of the World.

We all piled into an old bus and Lou passed out paper dust masks. On our way out of the "city," donkey carts scattered and we spooked some young nomads as they ambled slowly down the center of narrow stone streets, as if they didn't know what to make of these loud metal things, (trucks) that headed for them. The arid valley in which the city of Lhasa rests is only a few miles across from mountain to mountain. There was no need for moats or a Great Wall in Tibet; their gods took care of fortification when they made this place. It had more natural protection and was more isolated than any other land in the world.

The road that headed out of Lhasa was being widened by Chinese decree, our interpreter explained, because there were plans to bring more foreigners into Tibet. Most of the road building is done by hand. Construction begins when a big rock is blasted apart, then the pieces are broken into smaller pieces with sledgehammers. Next, hundreds of Tibetan workers sort the rocks into piles of similar sizes. Then layer after layer of hand-cracked rock is carefully placed to build up a roadbed. It takes years to build a very few miles of road.

Until recently Tibet had never welcomed strangers. Conquerors have made their way here a few times through a hundred mountain passes during the thousands of winters of Tibet's isolated history. Of the few individuals who came to Lhasa, the heart of Tibet, only some had conquest on their minds. Some were the princes of Genghis Khan on holy pilgrimages, some were wind-burned traders coming up from Nepal and India, and there was a handful of white men with mountains in their eyes. For me to be here was a dream come true. Strangely, I felt comfortable and at home in this exotic land.

Our bus sputtered across the bridge of the Tsangpo River. Once over the river, the road narrowed dangerously. The roads were gravel and in many places barely wide enough for two passing trucks and a feather. There were no guardrails. But how many Tibetans would fall off the road walking or riding one of their surefooted shaggy horses? I lost count of the drop-offs. They seemed to fall down till they went to the center of the earth. Lou said it would be this way for several days till we got to base camp. And then the "real" mountains would begin.

The mountainsides were barren and covered with a gray shale-type rock. Far below us were a few small round fields next to the banks of runoff streams. The fields that were the greenest of green were barley. A few dark yellow fields were flowering mustard. The mustard is used to make oil. I saw small bent-over human figures, five hundred feet below our road, cutting bundles of wheat by hand. If this land were a giant quilt there would be many squares of gray and gray-brown with occasional patches of pure yellow and strong green.

Most of the climbers had retreated inside themselves and that's where they stayed. They were trying to hibernate with their eyes open, conserving every gram of energy for the climb. After they climbed Mount Everest, on their way out, _then_ they'd look around Tibet. Their portable cassette players, headsets, Vuarnet sunglasses, and dust masks hid anything they might be thinking.

George Dunn was sitting in the front of the bus across from me listening to Beethoven. Everyone called him Geo. He was thirty and looked like a tall surfer; blond, tan, lanky, and easy. If anyone on the team looked as if he might have been a former "space cadet" from the hippie days, it was Geo. He was also valedictorian of his high school. He was so addicted to mountain climbing that things like putting his degree in urban planning to use, marriage, and a fast new car would have to wait, maybe forever.

Sitting behind Geo was Peter Whittaker, the youngest on the team at twenty-five, and Lou's son. Peter was rocking hard to a tape by a new-wave band called The Meat Puppets. He was lean, tan, had thick wavy brown hair, and stopped the girls dead in their tracks at home. In the winters he worked at Snowbird, a great Utah ski area, as a glamorous helicopter ski guide. Skiers are flown to slopes filled with "virgin powder," a term for snow that has never been skied through. The guides then ski with their clients through the calf-deep powder. In the summer he served as a guide for his father on Mount Rainier. Peter is one of the hottest young talents on the American mountain-climbing scene.

Our bus crawled as it struggled toward another of the countless mountaintops we would have to cross. Prayer-flags with tattered bits of cloth reached out from piles of rocks at the top of almost every mountain. A prayer-flag is a prayer written on a piece of cloth or rag tied to a stick. The incessant winds flap the prayer-flags and the Tibetans believe this continuous motion keeps their prayers always going forth to their mountain gods. We passed two Tibetan women on a road that went up across a barren mountain that invented the name "the middle of nowhere." Each carried a baby wound tight in bright woolen cloth and strapped to her back.

On our way down the mountain we passed a solitary, barefoot teenage boy. He was standing at the side of the road looking out over a valley. Was he wondering if he would ever leave this place without a name, thousands of miles from a city and centuries back into time? At the bottom of the mountain the sun was almost straight up. Here we began driving along a mighty blue lake. There was a small village at one end of the lake. Rugged Tibetan women were working up on the rock hills with picks, digging out scrubby bushes to burn in the winter. The women gather these while herding small herds of goats. Young children were out and around collecting yak dung for fuel. The dung cakes were stacked, neatly on their sides, like records, on top of the walls that surrounded the stone house. Fuel is a rare and precious thing in Tibet.

Once past the mountain-bordered lake of "heavenly-skies" the bus began climbing again. Our driver ground the gears, double-clutching. It sounded as if the transmission on this bus would disintegrate into a pile of metal shavings. The angle of the road was so steep it was a tense few moments while the driver tried unrelentingly to get the bus into the next lowest gear. If he couldn't, and the brakes gave way, we would roll back, crashing off the cliff.

He finally crammed it into gear and we sped off, up to the top of another mountain. At this altitude, where all engines lose power, we sped along at a fast walking pace. A few flies flopped about inside. Here they fly slow or they don't fly at all.

The bus overheated and stalled. The driver took a bucket and walked to a mountain stream, came back and poured water into the overheating radiator. We stood around outside and waited till it cooled down. When we took off again, John Roskelley, the rebel, a superstar among a busload of mountain-climbing stars, was not inside. He was sitting on top of the bus! "If this mental midget of a driver is going to kill himself and us by running off the snaking roads, I'm going to live" was John's philosophy. He could always dive from the top of the bus if we headed down a ravine. John didn't mind risking his life when HE was in control of it, but he hated for someone else to. Especially if that someone else was a "foreigner." Few people had risked their lives as much as John.

Three miles down the road, the bus overheated, sputtered forward a few feet, and stalled again. The driver, a tall and bony, hyper Chinese man, had turned too hard, and I got what I thought was a last view of the cliff, which went almost straight down, over a thousand feet to a foamy river. I could see the black specks of some grazing yaks, finding food from an occasional patch of wild grass.

The bus scraped the cliff's edge, straightened out, and came to a full stop. Again. With the motor killed there was no escaping the full blare of our driver's favorite tape, a shrill, staccato song accompanied by instruments that writhed and screeched. We called it Chinese Torture Music and it fit our mood. Tension among the climbers was high. They thought of nothing but Everest now, and this fool driver in this piece of junk, which cost good American dollars, could stop the whole show. The climbers would lose the mountain if they couldn't get themselves and their gear to base camp on schedule. They looked as though they wanted to commandeer the bus and throw the driver over a cliff.

Everyone kept to his place though, except Roskelley, who had got back in the bus. He tore out of his seat and lunged down the aisle. Roskelley grabbed the handle that opened the door but the driver grabbed it too, trying to keep John inside. John pushed his hand away, jerked open the door, and jumped off the bus. He started walking. I wondered if he planned to walk all the way to Everest.

John was walking mad. You could tell by his stride he was furious. John Roskelley was used to people doing things _right_. He was known for his hot temper and he'd just lost it, but he was also a member of Lou Whittaker's team. Lou did not put up with "star" foolishness. Usually outbursts of temper and egocentric behavior were extinguished immediately. And Lou didn't allow more than a few screwups from anyone. The worst penalty would be to get sent home; the next most severe punishment was never to be invited on another expedition.

I wondered how Lou would treat this Thoroughbred, who was flinging his high-spirited head against the reins of his lead. The fact that Lou even invited John was a surprise to many. Lou'd never climbed with him before and Lou never judged a man or woman till he'd climbed a mountain with them, a killer mountain. Having Roskelley on our team was an indication of how BAD Lou wanted the top of Everest. It was no different from the wealthy owner of a professional football team paying millions for the finicky quarterback who could bring him a world championship. John was one of the few superstars of world climbing. Mountaineering stars can be swarmed by fans in Japan and Europe, while in America they're unknown.

John was out of sight, around a sharp corner. Lou stood outside the door of our cooling bus, looking down the gravel road. Was he angry? Was he going to boot Roskelley off the team? What was Lou going to do with him? Lou was known for not showing anger when he felt it. We all waited and wondered, especially the guys who'd been led by Lou for many years, who probably knew what he was thinking. The bus slowly began rolling down the road again. We picked up John and he quietly made his way back to his seat and sat down. As far as I know, Lou didn't say anything to John. John seemed sorry he'd lost it. He was known as the "John McEnroe of mountaineering."

# 13

## *So Daring*———————————

Across the narrow aisle from John Roskelley was his probable climbing partner, Jim Wickwire. The lawyer, our lone Yuppie, had that
Kennedy look: handsome, well-dressed, with button-down, white
and blue dress shirts. But today he wore a bandanna around his
neck and had on shorts. Jim Wickwire, father of five and founding
partner in Wickwire, Goldmark and Shorr, a prominent Seattle law
firm, was actually beginning to relax. Even in Beijing, Jim had worn
his blue blazer, and that was in a city where "formal" meant an
ironed shirt.

A few months before we'd left for this adventure, I'd seen a segment about Jim, now forty-four, on *60 Minutes*. Climbing had been a consuming passion for him for over twenty years. The TV segment told about Jim being the first American to climb K-2 in 1978, the world's second highest mountain, which sits on the China-Pakistan border. During that climb he lost some of one lung and some of his toes. K-2 was just eight hundred feet lower than Everest. This was Wick's second attempt at Mount Everest and probably his last.

Wick was listening to Vangelis's *China* album. I went over and sat with him. His black head had only a few gray hairs. I found myself wanting to talk to him about why he kept climbing. He'd been involved in three major climbing accidents in which four dear friends had died, not to mention the fact that he could have been the one killed in each situation. I wanted to ask him about it real bad, but I felt embarrassed. But being on the verge of death is part of a mountain climber's life, so I asked him, "Jim, what does your wife think of the dangerous things you do?"

"Well," Jim said, "she knew I was a climber when we got married and on our honeymoon I took her on a climb. She had problems with her legs, they were kind of rubbery, so it was a real struggle getting down. After that she wasn't very interested in climbing."

Wick paused to think. "One time on the way into the Alaskan mountains, we pitched our tents right under this big ice wall. We had chosen a place we thought was really protected. We'd stopped there because we were worried about avalanche danger. Our two tents were side by side. . . . At about seven in the morning I heard this tremendous crashing thud and the ground shook. A second later it was all quiet, and nothing had happened to us.

"I looked out the tent door and saw that an entire section of the ice wall, about thirty feet high and about fifty feet across, had collapsed. It had ended up about five feet from the tents. So here was a tower of ice—the rubble was about twenty feet high. If it had hit us we would have been buried there, forever. We all looked at each other and said—'If that can happen and we didn't get it, then this climb is going to be a good one.' Later in that climb my two friends in the other tent died."

The bus horn blew and four Tibetans on horseback scattered down a bank. Is our belligerent bus driver in a bad mood, or what?

"When someone dies like that, what does it do to you?" I asked.

"It isn't the same every time. It's a shock to see a close friend die

This elderly Tibetan woman got up from a doorway to the Jokhang Temple in Lhasa to take a closer look at my legs.

The haunting ruins above the village of Xegar are a constant reminder of my friend "The Holy Man."

A pilgrim spins his prayer wheel at the Potala in Lhasa.

Mountainous Tibet is a tough land in which to survive. Yet Tibetans are a people of great joy as is evident by this child's greeting.

A rare view of a shrine inside one of the Potala's 999 rooms

The God-centered spirit of these two monks lives even under Communist rule.

Golden Buddhas sit inside the Tashilhunpo Monastery, begun in the fifteenth century, which overlooks Xigaze.

Our yak caravan works its way along the East Rongbuk Glacier between Camps 1 and 2.

John Roskelley introduces a puzzled yak herder to "American-type" music.

JIM WICKWIRE

Mount Everest always looms large. Our base camp at night.

Jim Wickwire holds pages of his diary, as John Roskelley reads at the frigid Camp 5, elevation around 25,000 feet.

PETER WHITTAKER

JOHN SMOLICH

The only ladder the climbers used was on these steep ice slopes below the North Col at 22,700 feet.

Members of our team make progress toward the North Col between Camps 3 and 4 while Everest watches. *(overleaf)*

right in front of you. I remember when I walked out to get help the time those two guys fell and died, it was like a motion picture repeating itself over and over again as you walked along. It was that vivid. I think you're up there knowing there's some risk attached to it, knowing something could happen, but I don't think you'd be up there if you thought it would happen to you." I'd heard Lou say many times, "There are two kinds of climbers. Old climbers and bold climbers."

Wick continued. "The risk can be much greater in a Himalayan climb because you have not only the normal risks of rockfall, icefall, avalanche, storms, and winds, but you have the factor of altitude.

"Altitude is probably the most hazardous of all because it affects your mental capacity, your ability to make the right decisions," Jim stressed in his firm yet sensitive way. "I'd say the majority of mistakes on any mountain are tied to human error, either in the form of a direct act or lack of an act, or a judgment error that puts you into a situation where you get creamed by an avalanche."

Jim glanced out toward a chain of peaks and said, "When you're in the Himalayas it becomes more of a mental problem. You have to endure tremendous amounts of physical discomfort, boredom, and frustration. Many days turn into weeks, and the expedition doesn't go forward. It takes weeks and months to 'get Everest.' It takes a special mind-set to adapt and function so that when your moment comes and it's time to go to the top, you're ready for it. . . . I've been on expeditions where by the time you get to that point, you're down to just a very few people of the total group. Everyone in this bus thinks that he will be the one on top, but we'll be very fortunate to get one of us up there."

Lou had told me that Wick gets stronger and tougher the longer he's in the mountains, while many other guys, who may start out meaner and leaner, get sick and weaken. Jim's about five eight and normally weighs 170 pounds. Many climbers think it's not a bad idea to go on one of these long sieges a bit heavy, to have some reserve of fat. Jim had a reserve that would turn to muscle and fuel.

"Just look around, Peter. Some of these guys will become physically sick. Some could lose it, mentally. I don't mean go crazy, although that's happened before. Sometimes climbers lose the reason they're here. Their goal becomes blurred and they want to be back in Seattle, eat some good Italian food, be with the family.

"Many times the most successful climber is not the most talented or strongest physically. But he is the most driven. The same thing is true for life. It's unfortunate that being a driven person has become a term of derision. The world used to admire people who were driven." A light-gray owl was scared by our passing bus and flew over the tundralike ground with long, rythmic wing beats.

"The climbs of the really big mountains sometimes bring out-of-control, suicidal behavior in people you'd never suspect," Jim said thoughtfully. I wondered if anyone from our team might lose it.

"There was this guy from another expedition. He was an American legend. He did the first winter ascent on Mount McKinley in 1967, and later became the leading guide on McKinley climbs. He probably climbed it twenty-five times. This guy was incredibly strong. People thought of him as a superman," Jim said.

"He had made the summit of Everest. He insisted on camping at twenty-seven thousand feet on the way down instead of retreating as his climbing partners suggested. Maybe he thought that after Everest there would be nothing, so he took his backpack and threw it over the side of the mountain.

"He's still up there," Jim related. "He refused to descend further. There were two Sherpas and the wife of the leader with him. According to the one witness, one Sherpa came down and one stayed as did the woman, thinking maybe he'd be more sane in the morning. But at dawn he was dead. The woman was very weak and the Sherpa badly frostbitten. As they started back, she went a few yards, collapsed, and died. The Sherpa came down by himself."

I still could not totally understand what drove these people to the mountains. What crazy power does Everest have to make sane, powerful people act in such a suicidal way? What happens up there? Would any of these men snap from the pressure of making the top? Or of not making it to the top?

It was obvious to me that Jim Wickwire would be hard to beat back from making the summit, this time. Right before I moved back to my seat Jim glanced at his watch, which was still on Seattle time, and said, "Well, my family is getting ready to go to bed right now."

# 14

## Daddy's Girl_____

Since leaving the seemingly 'gigantic' city of Lhasa we'd traveled for many, many miles, most of it on roads that had never heard of the words *straight* and *level*. We'd passed through Tibetan communities almost as old as these mountains. Gyangtze. Xigaze. Tomorrow would be a brutal bumpy ride to our last stop, before base camp, the tiny village of Xegar (pronounced "Sha-gaŕ"). As we all felt stronger, the slow pace of this worn-out bus became more aggravating. Was Everest squashed in among the thousands of peaks that we passed all day long, every day? Was one of those Everest?

Less and less were we looking around and seeing what was in front of us. More and more our minds chanted: EVEREST . . . EVEREST . . . We continued down the incredibly scenic roads, past some of the most fascinating people I'd ever seen, yet they began to lose my attention. EVEREST. Will we see you on top of the next mountain, or around the next corner? After we pass the ruins of the next temple? Will we ever get to you?

Next stop was the top of the highest pass we'd driven to yet, over 16,000 feet. For the past hour or two I'd been enduring altitude headaches again. They felt like a red-hot knife in my brain. The driver stopped for all of us to catch the view but my head hurt so badly my vision was blurred. I didn't care about the view; I felt like dying. If this, and much worse, was how these guys would feel 10,000 feet farther up, I didn't see how they could do what was required of them. I wobbled once past three or four piles of stones that held many prayer-flags and went back to the bus. My eyes pounded.

I hadn't thrown up more than five times in my whole life, the last time being my first frat party at college. But the second I hit the ground I knew what was coming. My stomach felt like it was made out of overstressed rubber. I ran up to our interpreter, Fang, and said, "Tell bus driver to wait. I must go behind rock."

I felt like I was throwing up my brains. Could I be getting pulmonary edema, a deadly form of altitude sickness, where your lungs fill with fluid and you slowly drown if you don't retreat back down to lower altitudes? I decided I was going to try to forget how sick I felt and keep on. An hour or two later I felt a bit better as we went lower and entered the widest, most fertile valley we'd been in since Lhasa.

Here there were ancient irrigation canals and old, stunted cotton-wood trees clinging to their banks. In the courtyards of their isolated homes Tibetan woman beat clumps of wheat on the ground, separating the grain from the stalks. Whatever wheat they got would have to last them and their families through the frigid Himalayan winter.

Every time Tibetan children saw our bus and they were within a mile of the road, they dropped what they were doing and ran toward us. They ran gracefully and fast. It was as if we were the only parade they'd ever seen! Some of us would throw sticks of gum and candy out to them.

We bounced into Xegar. Elevation over 14,000 feet. How could

anyone live that high? There would be one more day here of acclimatizing. Then on to base camp if the river we had to ford wasn't
too swollen with glacier runoff. One more day of gag-a-minute food.
We'd stopped making jokes about it, and stopped eating most of it,
except for the small bowls of roasted peanuts. The other stuff, raw-
dough rolls (that's right, uncooked rolls the size of large apples), and
fried strips of old yak meat, stayed mostly uneaten. Every time we
ate, a crowd gathered standing within view in the "kitchen," waiting
for us to leave our tables full of food. The moment we were gone
they attacked our food and cleaned up our table. To the Tibetans it
obviously was delicious. They'd probably gag at some of _our_ delicious
food, like potato chips, mayonnaise, and burgers.

It was in Xegar that I got to know one of the team's most fascinating members, the only woman, Carolyn Gunn. Carolyn had been a
Muir maid, an Okie, a veterinarian, a goat roper, a veterinary surgeon, a ski-lift operator at Snowbird, married to a Wyoming cowboy,
a cook, a hootch mama, a daddy's girl, a mountain climber, a
painter, a quail hunter, and more. Carolyn could do anything she set
her mind to. On this adventure she would be base-camp manager, a
very important job, possibly do some support climbing if any major
tragedies hit, and keep her "brothers," as she referred to the team,
pumped up with thousands of calories.

She was deeply respected by the entire team, without exception,
for she pulled more than her share. Not even Roskelley could say
anything about Carolyn. If anyone on the team was romantically
linked to Carolyn, I didn't know about it. She was a very private
person. We sat on a rock porch and talked.

"In high school (class of '68), I weighed ninety-eight pounds and I
was five five, so I was this real string bean," Carolyn began. "To be
popular in high school, you had to be voluptuous. I was just ignored. I spent a lot of time studying and riding horses. In junior
high I was skinny and terribly shy. I started to hate school and didn't
do very well in it. I got a warning slip. That warning slip turned my
life around because I was so mortified that I started to study. In my
junior and senior years I finally worked my way up to the National
Honor Society.

"All the other girls—the voluptuous ones—started going to group
parties in the seventh grade. I never had a date until the senior
prom. And that was only because I was president of the German
club and they needed someone to take Hans Mueller, our blond

German exchange student. I was real excited at first, but then I was bored stiff. I made my own dress and bought gold slippers."

Two Asian ravens, considered by Tibetans to be powerful reincarnated spirits, landed near us and acted like they knew more than a raven should know.

Carolyn's voice, normally very controlled, like many intellectuals I knew, became filled with emotion. "My dad was an insurance agent. . . . I was All-American tomboy. . . . I have one sister and no brothers. Although Dad never said he wanted a boy, he always enjoyed having someone to go hunting, fishing, or change the spark plugs with. I was always with him. My sister was an indoor type, she stayed inside all the time and read.

"We'd go hunting in the hills in eastern Oklahoma. I had a twelve-gaugc and hc had a bcautiful, double-barreled sixteen-gauge shotgun. The twelve-gauge would bruise my shoulder when I would shoot. My father was always my idol."

Carolyn "had the greatest pair of legs in Tibet," said Peter Whittaker. Carolyn often wore small, nylon runner's shorts when we weren't in snow country. Her legs were an inspiration to the team, but her brains and ability were much more appreciated and important. No one got by here on legs alone.

"I went to Oklahoma State and got a B.S. in animal science. Halfway through my senior year I married a cowboy from Wyoming. His father had always been a cowboy and he had four brothers. The father is still cowboying at sixty-nine; he still rides a horse every day. My husband, Fred, never went to college; I met him at a rodeo. In college I was in the National Intercollegiate Rodeo Association. I was a goat tier.

"I met Fred, and I think I was in love with the idea of being married to a cowboy and living in a little town; it has a certain romantic aura. It was fun for a while. After three years in Wyoming, being a housewife in a cabin with no electricity or heat, it started to wear thin. I started to feel like my brain was mildewing. There was only one other person in town who had a college education at that time.

"Fred and I got a divorce and I went back and applied to vet school." As Carolyn talked about her former cowboy husband, there was none of the detectable emotion in her voice that was so strong when she told me about her dad. "I got accepted and went to school at Oklahoma State for four years, straight through. I'm in small-animal care.

"I did an internship at Angell Memorial Hospital in Boston for fourteen months. I loved Boston. From Boston I went to the University of California at Davis and completed a three-year surgical residency. My father died before I finished vet school. . . . I finished up at the University of California and I was burned out. I just wanted to be outdoors and go live in the mountains and do a job where I didn't have to do a lot of thinking. I didn't want a lot of pressure or responsibility. The job that popped into my head was a lift operator at a ski area. Didn't pay much more than minimum wage. Well, that's what I did. I went to Colorado, got a job at Purgatory in Telluride. It was an outdoor, mundane job and a lot of good, physical work, shoveling snow and skiing.

"During the summers when I was in California getting my surgical residency I had gone to Washington and Oregon for the first time in my life. I fell in love with Mount Rainier. Finally I climbed Rainier. I thought it would be really fun to work for Lou, at Camp Muir, so I wrote to RMI applying for the job as Muir maid and I got it. They called us Muir maids, hootch mamas, cabin girls." Carolyn started with the same job Marty Hoey did.

"In vet school dating had been a problem. More often than not, I'd have a guy over for dinner and he'd have to get it off the stove and eat it alone. I'd be on emergency call and half the time I'd get beeped. I wanted to get away from the academic life-style to become just Carolyn, instead of Dr. Gunn, and enjoy people at all levels rather than just the isolated academic world. I didn't want to climb the academic ladder any further because I felt like I was getting out of touch with the world. I said, 'Hey, stop the world! I want to get off!' and I did."

Lou came to the door of his room, listening to Pavarotti on his Walkman, and singing and waving his long arms around mimicking an opera singer.

Carolyn was surprised she'd said so much. Right before she left I asked her some personal questions about a couple of the climbers. She answered, "When I was a kid I wanted a brother. I feel like all these guys are my family. I love 'em all like brothers." We had one more full day in Xegar.

0          25          50          75

0          25          50          75          100

TSANG PO (Bra

Xegar

SEE MAP 5

Base
Camp

MT. EVEREST
29,028'

NEPAL

Kangchenjunga
28,168'

SIKKIM

After spending some time in Tibet's holy city we loaded almost two
hundred boxes of food and equipment in old Chinese-built trucks
and took the high road out of Lhasa. Only a few thousand
foreigners have been allowed into Tibet's interior and about the only
way to explore beyond Lhasa is to be part of a mountain-climbing

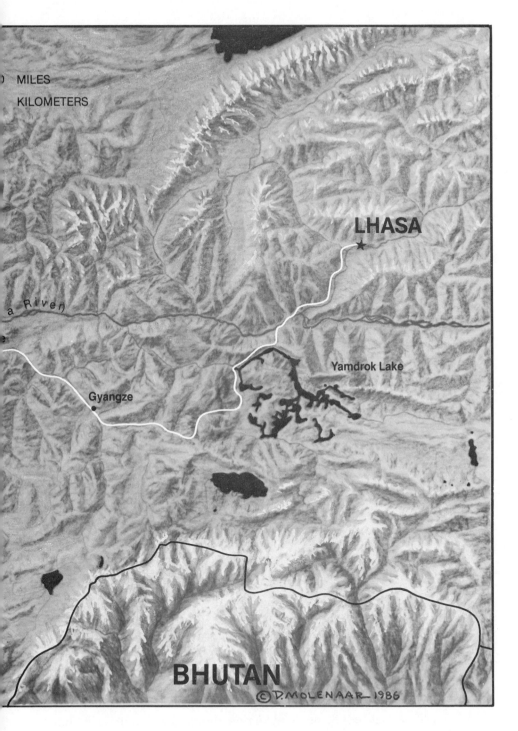

MILES

KILOMETERS

a River

LHASA
★

Yamdrok Lake

Gyangze

BHUTAN

© D.MOLENAAR 1986

expedition. On our way we passed nomadic herders tending their
yaks and crossed boulder-cluttered rivers, some having no bridges.
Finally, after enduring Parnelli Yak's outrageous driving on Tibet's
shockingly narrow roads, we made it safely to base camp.

# 15

## *The Holy Man*_____

This day was ours. I took my camera and headed for town. To the wandering Tibetan herder coming down from the hills, Xegar was a chance to see someone, anyone. Maybe even a group of young Tibetan girls who would be sticking out their tongues welcoming him.

In this village in the middle of the Himalayas lived a few hundred people. The stone houses, huddled together at the base of the cliffs, were connected to each other by the walls of their compounds in which the villagers kept dogs, drying dung, goats, and small children. Some of Xegar's houses were whitewashed, decorated with black and red brush strokes as bold and free as any you'd see on a canvas in the Museum of Modern Art. A few houses carried painted swastikas, a religious symbol meaning eternity and truth. Often these swastikas were inlaid in turquoise into the floors of Tibetan temples. Thousands of feet above the village, perched on the edge of the cliffs, were rows of ruined stone forts and temples. How could anyone have ever built anything that high up on such steep rock?

On the east side of this thin valley were the barley fields, nearly ready for harvest. These rich, dark-green fields offered the only vivid color here. The rest of the rocky land was a dull shade of gray or gray-brown. The only other color was the blasting blue of the Himalayan sky.

On a pile of rocks by one of the courtyard walls sat an old Tibetan man, his face so deeply lined he looked as ancient as the mountains. He sat propped up on an old cane, spinning his prayer wheel. The prayer wheel was shaped like a brass can covered with graceful designs, and spun on a wooden handle. The Himalayan people believe that prayer does not have to be spoken, it can be thought and then offered to the gods by the constant spinning of the wheel.

The ancient-looking man motioned to me, reached out his smoke-blackened hand, and pulled me to him. He pointed to my camera, wanting to look through it. The few "funny-colored" (white-skinned) people that he had seen had obviously shown him their cameras before. The way he held the camera up to his ear, after clicking off a picture, made me think that some climber had taken a picture of him with his "magic" Polaroid. He listened for the sound of the instant picture coming out of the camera. Many of these people had never seen themselves before, except in a meadow in some still pool of rainwater.

No picture came out of my black Nikon F-3. He made funny "pushbutton" motions. He wanted me to take his picture again. Holding it backward and upside down, he clicked off another picture. Then he excitedly pulled me next to him and made me sit down. He smelled of decades of smoke and wet wool. His red-brown, thick, and wrinkled skin glistened with oil. When would my mystical machine produce his image? "ZZIIP! Out it will come any minute," I could almost hear him thinking. I shook my head no, and he seemed to understand.

Then the old Tibetan put his arm around me. This man radiated understanding and I could feel between us that warm vibe of love that has no certain dialect. He had the sad lines of a hard life in his face, and his body was slightly stooped. He tugged at me to go with him, somewhere. I didn't even think about *not* going. I followed him at once.

He led us through narrow alleys closed in by stone walls of thin, crumbly rock. Women peeked out of holes and cracks in doors to watch us pass. Where could we possibly be going? The old man spoke the beautiful-sounding Tibetan language as if I understood. He'd stop and point to a particular door and start telling me a story, I supposed, about who lived behind it. I smiled and nodded. But I was so frustrated because I could not understand Tibetan. Thank God, Ran Ying would be meeting me in Chengdu to help me understand the rest of China! The old man gently eased me through a gateway. His prayer wheel spun constantly.

When the narrow path that wound through the village of Xegar got closer to the mountains, the gentle old man stopped me. He pointed upward. He put his hand on my shoulder, and as his voice got louder and faster, his grip on my shoulder got stronger and stronger until it actually began to hurt. He spoke passionately but I couldn't understand. When he first began to talk to me his voice was gentle, as soft as spring. Now his voice was agitated and upset. Had I done something wrong? He grabbed me by both shoulders, turned me toward him and shook me. Were those tears in his eyes? Had some white man once hurt him or his family? Two lounging mastiff dogs sensed his anger and stood, the hair on their backs rising straight up.

The Tibetan again began pointing to the rocky forts and temples on the cliff overhead. His hand shook as he tried so hard to tell me something. Finally he accepted that I couldn't understand him. He pushed down hard on my shoulders, forcing me to kneel in the dusty courtyard. He got down on his knees too and gathered up some small stones. He began to arrange the stones in the shape of a building. In the dust he drew the shape of the steep peaks that surrounded the village and drew dots to represent other buildings. Then he grabbed some bigger stones and dropped them on the rock buildings he had made, smashing them. He made "crash BOOM" sounds, in a Tibetan accent.

What did this mean? He dropped the stones with a sneer. He put his fingers beside my eyes and pulled my eyelids to each side, making them go slanted. His face tensed with hate. His smile changed to a vicious squint. Could he be talking about the Chinese? Were the rocks he was dropping symbols for dropped bombs? Is _that_ why there were so many mounds of stone and rubble on the hills and cliffs of Tibet? Is that where the thousands of monasteries at one time perched?

The holy man took my hand and led me out of the courtyard up a slim trail toward the forts and temples. After almost an hour of walking and walking and winding our way up the mountain, we came upon a huge pile of shattered rock and strewn, splintered timber. Though the old man's eyes were reddened from so many years of dust and smoky fires, I thought I could see tears filling his eyes. Yes, he was crying.

If only this holy man could have talked with me! He had such a tortured expression on his face, I wondered what kind of experience could have caused it. Yet, within the sadness I could see his survivor's soul, still lit with love. Perhaps if he could have spoken English, or I Tibetan, he might not have dared to tell me all that had happened to his homeland. Fear might have stopped him. His tears flowing before me now were risk enough.

It was getting dark; I should have been back for dinner. I had certainly not missed any food worth eating. I had been sitting and walking and "talking" with the holy man for hours. When I got up to leave, I pulled out an extra picture I had of my stallion, Shocker. I gave it to the holy man and he put his gnarled, bony hands on my shoulders and pulled me close to him and hugged me. He'd spoken about another world. And I so wished that I had been able to "talk" with him. It was frustrating me more and more that I had to stay with a group and keep a tight schedule. I found myself wishing that I could be traveling through Tibet, alone, with a few saddlebags on a good horse, stopping when I met someone like this special man, living a season in his village.

Later that evening I asked Wick what he knew about Tibet. He gave me a book that he'd brought with him. It was called _In Exile from the Land of Snows_. The book told what the Tibetans had experienced since the Chinese took them over in 1951. No wonder the old man had cried. Reading this book I felt that all of Tibet could cry and cry and never stop. It's been reported that before the Chinese Communists conquered Tibet there were almost six thousand monasteries. Nine were left standing. After the rage of destruction took place, the monasteries were stripped of their gold Buddhas, which were inlaid with jewels. Next their gold and turquoise roofs were dismantled. Irreplaceable hand-carved wooden blocks used for printing their scriptures were burned in army fires or shipped out. Brass bowls, Tibetan rugs, altars, anything, everything valuable, were stolen, pillaged, sold, or melted down.

Before Mao took over Tibet, one quarter of all men in Tibet had been "holy men," monks or lamas, approximately 120,000 of them. Now, there were fewer than a thousand and none were allowed to practice their religion without working at other jobs. And that's how the Tibetans were "liberated" by the Chinese. It had never hit me so brutally how words describing a government's actions can be so abused—"liberation," "education," "for the people's good. . . ."

Maybe some army had swept into the holy man's village and never left. Sure they blew up places his people had worshiped in for centuries. Yes, they stripped his nation of its gold, but he had not forgotten his gods. *They* could not be bombed or sold or burned. And, in the quiet long nights of many Himalayan winters he would tell the young people how it used to be. And they would tell their children as they grew old and keep on telling each other far into time, centuries after the holy man was dead. It was obvious their souls could not be crushed by any conqueror.

# 16

## *First Sight*_____

"This day we climb higher in truck, see tall mountain you seek. We cross river. Find American base camp." That was the stuttered attempt of our Mongolian liaison officer, who was trying out some of his primitive English. Normally Bao let our interpreter speak for him, but he seemed to feel comfortable with us and was now beginning to talk himself.

It was August 20. We were told to throw all our personal gear into the back of an old truck and then lie, sit, or stand on it. We would travel like this till we reached base camp. The truck looked like a

1943 model. Our bus and its driver would be staying here, but unfortunately our new driver was a Tibetan wild man we called "Parnelli Yak." He was so named in honor of the famous American race car driver Parnelli Jones. That's what the guys called him during stretches of the ride we expected to live through. When he drove like a maniac with a frontal lobotomy, he was called much worse. If we survived the drive, today, *finally* we would see Everest.

The roads leaving Xegar were the worst yet. Some of them weren't much wider than a goat trail blasted out of the rock cliffs, just hanging there in the middle of the sky. Some went through fields of jagged stone. They were all curved for danger. This particular road up the mountain wound back and forth, back and forth, its switchbacks so curved and frequent they would have made an astronaut dizzy. A quarter of the way up the road, the truck appeared to be dying. Every hundred yards or so it would jolt violently, then it would recover and go a bit farther. Parnelli had a picture of the Dalai Lama hanging from his mirror, as if this godman would take care of this lunatic, no matter how he acted. Parnelli seemed to be confident, but I was certain this high pass had stressed our truck so badly it was sure to explode, and then there was the Rongbuk River still to cross, the river without a bridge.

I'd never experienced so many mountains. There seemed to be a million of them. The farther we went into Tibet, the more they showed themselves. Over every pass, around every cliff, and through every narrow valley arose more and more mountains. We passed several clusters of Tibetan homes with smoke fluffing out from the tops of their flat roofs. It was the dead of summer and a chilly high forties this morning.

Our two trucks jerked us around as though we were trapped inside a crazed washing machine stuck on the spin cycle. At the bottom of one mountain we passed another village with a dozen or so stone houses. Young men in the mustard fields were removing stones that blocked the flow of irrigation water. Several shepherds herded their sheep out from the stone-walled pens for a day of high grazing among the mountain grasses.

As we climbed upward we strained, struggled, sputtered, and prayed that the steering wouldn't snap or the brakes dissolve. "Please God don't let Parnelli get his eyes distracted by a rich meadow or some other Tibetan temptation and go off the road!" After what seemed like forever we approached the top of the 17,000-foot pass we yearned for.

When we finally arrived at the crest we looked out over a wide valley, the widest we had seen in days. A mountain range ran in front of us looking like the world's biggest and most beautiful postcard. The king of all mountain views lay ahead. Before us was the largest concentration of tall mountains in the world, and just beyond those towering giants were the countries of Nepal, Bhutan, India. There was a reverent silence among us all, the kind of silence one feels in an ancient, holy cathedral. At last we were looking at Everest. Even this far away Everest pointed higher and reached farther into the cloudless sky than anything around it.

Mount Everest had sounded like a fine name in America but here in the holy land of mountains the name Everest seemed too spiritless, too ordinary, too WASP. CHO-MO-LUNG-MA was a name to fit its awesome mystery. It looked as though only the mountain rose out of the earth and everything else was an afterthought. Its power was overwhelming and fear of it struck in my heart. Imagine trying to get to its top! The spoken sound of its Tibetan name, Chomolungma, seemed to say to me "Human, you can go no farther. _I forbid you._" I could understand how these mountain people who gave a spirit to everything from rocks to ravens would be awed by the goddess who lived in this, the world's highest mountain.

Lou and his son Peter stood together and I could see Lou point toward the mountain, moving a long finger from its left side to its summit. This would be the direction the climbers would take when they went up Everest. For once Peter Whittaker made no wisecracks. He was humbled by the mountain. Everyone was. Wick stood with Carolyn showing her where our base camp would be set up. Steve Marts, our movie cameraman, shot some film, for this was a blessed-by-the-gods-of-the-sky view of Everest. Few foreign people had ever seen the mountain so clearly from such a distance, since it was often hidden by a cloud cover. Phil stood off alone. Was anyone thinking about Marty, who was buried where she fell, forever a part of Everest? Geo and Dave Mahre talked excitedly about the team's possible routes. They had been thinking of Everest routes every day of this trip. The Goddess Mother was a sharp slab of rock and snow that had been easy on no man and destroyed many. Climbing her was a very serious business.

Roskelley had a lot to think about. He stalked around like a captured panther. Out toward Everest, he'd risked his life hundreds of times in these Himalayas in the last eleven years. He'd probably spent more time out there than any climber in the world. The world's highest and most famous mountains were in front of us or just over the hill, so to speak. This was THEIR neighborhood. There were others no one but a mountain fanatic or a world-class mountaineer would have ever heard of. They, too, were some of the world's most difficult and highest peaks. Some of these were first climbed by the man who was gazing in their direction now. John didn't care about the peaks he'd already conquered; he could not take his eyes off Everest. He'd been to her before and was shunned. What was he thinking? Did he think he might be punished by the goddess of this mountain, not allowed to make it? Would Everest open herself to John, finally? What would he do if she didn't?

None of us were the types to have our pictures taken for the scrapbook, we'd all been to so many exotic places, but today, standing on the top of this pass with Everest graciously showing herself to us, was a chance no one could pass. Could this be a "sign" of good weather to come? We all had our pictures taken, standing with Chomolungma.

Parnelli Yak had grown up in the Himalayas herding goats and hunting wolves. It was not a big deal to him, seeing Chomolungma. He was in a hurry to race down the other side of this mountain, to the long valley below and our river crossing. The later we got to the Rongbuk River, the higher the water would be. The more water, the more chance we would not be able to drive our truck across. The trucks could drown out and stall, or worse, flip over. If we couldn't cross the river there would be all kinds of trouble. It could set the expedition back beyond recovery. Already we were making one of the latest attempts ever. Passing a prayer-flag, I thought of Barbara and the baby soon to be born, of Rebekah and Jed and the farm, of Tennessee, of America. I pulled out a photograph of my wife and children. I couldn't think about them for long without feeling overwhelmingly sad.

# 17

## Jin Mie, Head Yak Man_____

The horn beeped and a yak herder dressed in black dove out of the way. He'd been standing in the middle of the road, around a blind corner, about the thousandth curve we'd spun around and lived. Passing a few brilliant-green fields far below, I was told that this was the village where most of our yak herders came from. Their lives were spent within sight of this mountain, and our expedition would be only their second experience with a climbing team. Tibetans, unlike the Sherpas of Nepal, are not professional mountain climbers. They go only as high as their herds lead them.

The head man of our yak drivers was Jin Mie. He lived in a stone house just like the ones below. He would tell me much about himself and the lives of his fellow villagers. Some of his men have never seen a "white" person before. For a few decades on the other side of Mount Everest, on the Nepal side, Sherpas have been helping men and women from faraway lands, like England and America, climb Everest. Only in the past few years have the Tibetans begun to use their yaks to help climbers get their gear up the world's highest mountain.

Everything Jin Mie said to me was said in Tibetan, translated from Tibetan to Chinese by our Tibetan cook, and then translated from Chinese to English by our chain-smoking Chinese interpreter. So in a roundabout way, this is what I understood Jin Mie to say:

"My village now called commune, Colla Commune. It's about three and a half days' walk with yaks to base camp.

"Our yaks. They are strong now because it is fall. They not as strong in spring because then grass is short. Now grass long, they get more to eat. All our yaks are male—all are steers—no bulls. If you don't cut bulls, it is difficult to control them. They might hurt people." Jin Mie made a motion with his arms like the jabbing of a yak's long horns.

"Most yak are easy to control when they are cut; you throw stone, hit them, then they go. But some might bother the people even after they be cut. When cutting the bulls, we do not cut some of the strong ones so they can give the next generation."

Although the head man was only forty-four, he looked more like sixty-four. His hair was black and thin for a Tibetan, and his braid was wound around his head. His skin was very oily. His voice had authority, yet it had a very soothing tone, no louder than the sound of a Himalayan mist.

"Our winter is three months. In winter the local people here collect some grass and wood and also water the land. The winter is snowy sometimes." The weather in the place where he lived was warmer than base camp, but compared with other places it was still much colder. It surely got way below zero, since it could be forty below zero on Everest in the "summer."

"What is your favorite food?" I was dying to know, hoping we might discover that we were missing out on some local gourmet treat.

"Meat is first and second is yak butter. Sheep, goat, and yak meat. Most like."

"Is it hard to milk a yak?" I asked, hoping for some great answer for a new yak joke.

"Who milks your yak when you away from your village?" he wanted to know.

"My wife, Barbara, does; she enjoys milking our yaks," I said, grinning. He believed me.

"Oh, most normal. My wife, or her mother, very strong. Milk yak, too." I didn't have the heart to tell him we didn't have any yak then. I even had a picture of UFO, my Brahman bull, in my wallet. I thought I'd show him later.

He said, "Because we are different people, this must be reason why Tibetans have little hair on their legs or arms, and why you have on legs and arms so much hair. This very interesting," he said politely. "So like to see."

I pulled my pants leg up and he stroked my calf muscle. My leg was fairly tan. He took off his mukluks, traditional Tibetan boots, and pulled up his pants.

"Most odd. My leg skin more white than yours." This excited the head yak man greatly.

I had been dying to know what the inside of their homes looked like. I asked him.

"The kitchen room is very big. Parents and young children stay together in the kitchen room. The big children will stay in another room or with the daughter-in-law, if married.

"We have custom—one son marries a girl, they will still stay with the parents together, so no new home. The grandparents also stay together, the whole family." He remembered that the oldest person he knew in this last valley before Chomolungma was eighty-three, very old for this area.

"When do Tibetans normally get married?" I asked.

"Most Tibetans are married when they are twenty years old. This is normal. Women who reach thirty never marry."

"How do they meet the one they are to marry—do parents choose?" I wondered.

"Some of the young ones meet each other by themselves, and some are decided by the parents—the girl and boy don't know each other before they meet."

Knowing there was no way for any of these people to get to a hospital in less than a few weeks' yak trip, I asked, "Who delivers the babies?"

"Just the family. We don't need help."

"Do you hunt for deer, birds, bear, leopard, or anything?" I asked, noticing that many nomads and villagers carried rifles as they traveled.

His eyes narrowed to a squint. "Sometime we shoot the wolf because wolf sometime eat sheep, and sometime shoot wild goats. Few snow leopard here and wolves are bigger than dog. I shoot several leopard west of Chomolungma."

"What's the biggest city you've ever been to?" I asked.

"Went to Lhasa. 1959. After that never been to Lhasa. Saw city and monastery and was very big and everything is good."

"Are the girls prettier in the city or the mountains?" I asked straight-faced.

He answered laughing, pulling up one sleeve, which revealed a long scar. "The girls in city not have so much work to do and they have more time to dress themselves. But girls in mountains have to do much work—to drive the ox, pick rocks. So compared to girls in city, they are not as beautiful."

The Chinese interpreter burst out in wild laughter. He said the same goes for Chinese women. "Tell him," I said, "few women drive oxen in America. Some drive cars, some drive planes."

The shy, whispering leader wanted to ask something. "Do your women name cars?"

"Some do. Some name cars after boyfriends, like Willie," I said.

"Do you give your yaks names?" I asked.

"Yes. According to yak's color. The head yak's name is Ren Jiu. The whole body is black and the tail is white."

"Why is Ren Jiu the leader?" I was curious.

"He work very hard, not lazy. This yak always walk in front. Also he can smell person's tracks. He very smart."

Jin Mie volunteered, "Certain yak also hurt people but never hurt to death. Maybe broke the clothes or hurt the skin." I wondered if that was how he got the scar on his arm.

"Where do you find the beautiful turquoise and silver to make your jewelry?" I asked. I was expecting some great story of how they gathered turquoise in some sacred field.

"We trade for the silver and the colored stones but we not know where these things come from." He had turquoise beads woven into his hair.

He seemed so tough and must have had such amazing endurance. I asked, "Do Tibetans have any kind of sports?"

"Yes. Traditional sport is they carry rock to see who is strong. They also do running, and shooting.

"What's a running race like?" I asked. He seemed to be enjoying my curiosity.

"When I young, in school, they run about twenty kilometers. You wait and see. You run from this end of valley to top of mountain, then come back. The fastest one is named Jan Du."

"How big a rock do they try to pick up?"

"The weight about one hundred fifty kilos. Also in Tibet is riding and bow and arrow. There are different activities with horses. Then another one is while the horse is running, try to pick something up from the ground, also shooting bow and arrow from horse."

The elder Tibetan lit another nonfiltered cigarette and we chewed some cinnamon gum I had. He'd never seen or tasted gum and it was funny watching him trying to eat it. "Do you have any children?" I asked.

"I have three children. They are all girls, ages twenty-nine, twenty-six, and twenty-three. The oldest is married; the other two girls still stay with me."

I thought I'd try to make him laugh so I said, "In America, when we look for a wife, we like one who has nice figure, good body, good worker, healthy. What do you look for?"

He answered with a subtle smile. "First people try to find the beautiful one, second try to find the strong one, third try to find the girl who can do some home work." He was unruffled.

"What does 'beautiful' mean in Tibet?"

"We think a girl, her hair must be good, not so thin, and a full face, not hollow-cheeked." He continued, "We wish to invite you to be guest to our family. We serve beer. You sit together and drink, have food, sing, dance."

"Thank you so much. I would love to, maybe next time I come visit you." I found myself talking like he did.

"Good, then," he said. "You come back my favorite time of year. It is winter because we have already planted and we will kill the goat, the sheep—we can have the meat, not so much work to do. Winter is best. On the weather, spring and summer are the best.

"My family now own four yaks," he volunteered proudly. "They will plow the land we grow. There are five persons in my family and we have more than one hundred sheep.

"Yak cost three hundred to four hundred yuan [about one hundred fifty dollars.] We always buy big ones, not small ones. My wife name Son-Nan Toma."

We had a great talk. I asked the interpreters to ask him if he wanted to ask me any questions about America. The Chinese interpreter acted nervous about what his questions might be.

"No questions to ask you," answered the interpreter. We shook hands and I wondered why this Tibetan with the probing brown eyes would ask no questions. Was he afraid to?

Well, I better ask a few more things. "Have you ever seen television?" I wondered.

"Never saw television." I hadn't seen it for weeks and hadn't missed it a second.

"Have you ever driven an automobile?"

"No. It's allowed if you have money, but for me not like to buy a car."

"Do you know every pass and know how to get around everywhere here?" I asked.

"I know very much about the place where I stay, but I don't know about Chomolungma base camp."

I gave him a lighter that my dad had given me before I left, to thank him. He tried to strike it as he held it upside down. He couldn't do it and kept trying to strike it. Finally it lit. His face lit up with the magic of technology. What a proud face he made watching the small flame from his new lighter. It was magic and our talk had been a great blessing to me, I told him.

# Booming Out
# of the Darkness_____

When we came down from the top of the mountain where we had
seen Everest, Parnelli began to drive like a normal person who
wished to live to an old age. I found out later that this was the road
that led to Parnelli's village, and everyone walking on that road,
man, woman, and child, was Parnelli's close relative.

The road was the narrowest we had ridden so far. It was as curved
as a snake curled around a stick. We passed by some brutally beautiful land. Most of it was rock, yet over by the red cliffs with the
yellow streaks of rock in them, a small spring seeped out and a cou-

ple of orange wildflowers bloomed. Beside them grew three dark-green, stunted bushes.

We crossed over a primitive log bridge that spanned the river, passing four teenage Tibetan girls who giggled and stuck their tongues out in greeting. The rushing gray-colored river joined the Rongbuk, a larger river cutting through the center of the broad valley. Few nonnatives had ever set their eyes on this particular scene; glacier-covered mountains, prayer-flag-covered homes, and handsome Tibetans with red thread woven in their hair, with their quick white smiles and stuck-out tongues. I could see the base of a glacier running out between the two mountains across the river. This was the closest I'd ever been to the continent-moving ice that flowed down from the top of the world.

The bright sun deeply warmed our bodies and I was in a heightened state of Himalayan Hysteria, the euphoria caused by the altitude, the purest of sunshine, the most vivid of blue skies, the sparkling Tibetan faces. Carolyn and I had decided back in Xegar that the ultimate sign of a people's ability to survive was their sense of humor. No one smiled more than the Tibetans.

I felt a great sense of peace here. The pace of life was Tibetan-time. There was no hurrying. The rocks and sky and yaks and dark-skinned people, even the air, *everything* looked especially beautiful, especially pure today. If these villagers could see how we live—our cities, our traffic, our rushing crowds—what would they think? They probably grew up here, seeing the same few hundred people all their lives, most of them never leaving this valley.

A young powerfully built Tibetan boy was whirling something over his head. It was a rock sling, like the one David used to slay Goliath. He let a rock fly and it hit a rebellious goat that was straying too far away. Farther down this heavily rutted road, we spotted some young children playing in a series of muddy, barren fields. They would run, all of them nude, and slide like otters on the mud. Tibetans as a people reminded me of otters. They were beautiful, strong, healthy, graceful, and made hard work into laughing play. This valley had a Shangri-La feeling. When the children saw our truck, they all jumped up, waved and ran toward us, laughing and dripping with mud, hoping for some candy and ready to make instant friends with strangers.

Skip and I decided that we would stand up in the open back of the truck because sitting down made our insides feel they would jerk loose from whatever held them together. The dirt road angled closer to the river, which was capped with white water. Parnelli was yelling that the water level was too high to cross, furious that we were late in getting there. If Tibetans had swear words in their vocabulary, he was using dozens of them. He was very mad!

Parnelli was driving angry, which was stupid of him since our old truck felt as though the force of the vibrations from the rock-infested, hole-eaten road would snap it in half. He slammed on his brakes at the bank of the swollen river. I muttered to Skip, "Well, there's no way we're making it across this thing! That white water will flip this Chinese wreck right over and wash us and all our gear away. At the very least it'll drown out in the middle of the river and that will be it!" I was thinking that the nearest pay phone was back in Japan. If we stalled out here, we were done for. It was a long yak ride back to civilization.

Parnelli waited at the riverbank trying to get his courage up. He revved the engine, ground it into gear, inched forward, and stopped. He backed up, stopped, and stalled. All of us screamed for him to go ahead. Finally he drove into the current. The truck moved forward bravely for the first ten feet, till it hit the main force of the rushing water. The potent current shifted the truck sideways. It felt as though we were going to be flipped over. I got ready to jump clear, hoping to land in water where I would be carried past the truck and be able to swim over to the bank—if I could swim at all in this killer current. All my camera, gear, money, and food would be gone. There was no way this rapid, runoff river would hold back anything as powerless as a backpack or a camera bag.

Somehow Parnelli got us going straight again and we progressed a few more feet. The truck choked, jerked, and rocked like a boat about to break open in a pounding sea. We made a few yards. We were halfway across the river when the current seemed to lift us, moving our back wheels forward, turning us around full circle. Parnelli crammed the truck into a lower gear, which I thought he was crazy to do. What if he couldn't get it back into gear, and we began floating away? We shrieked encouragement to him. I was worried about what some of the hot-tempered climbers might do to Parnelli if he couldn't get us out of this river. They had been saying _they_ wanted to drive across the river anyway. They might drag him out and take command of the truck. They hadn't come this far to have Parnelli screw up their expedition.

We finally lurched and bounced our way across to the Mount Everest side of the river. The truck sat in the sun and drip-dried like a soaked dog. We pulled out a few boxes of food and waited for the next truck to appear. The truck didn't show, and didn't show. We sat on the riverbank, refusing to leave till everyone was there. An hour passed. Lou went off for a walk with his wife, Ingrid. Lou had decided back home that it would be good for the team to have non-climbing companions along to provide relief from the intensely serious business of scaling the world's tallest mountain. Ingrid, Skip, Russ, myself, and a couple of others would be leaving the team after we helped them set up base camp.

The other truck came into sight far off in the valley. We learned later that they had gotten stuck in a deep mudhole. Their driver made it across with no problem. Maybe he was more afraid of mud-holes than raging mountain rivers.

The road to base camp was a single lane of rocks, dirt, and ruts. Now that we'd made it across the river, the jolting effects of the ride seemed worse. My face burned like fire. The ultraviolet rays of the sun this high up could cook your skin fast. And all you needed for proof of this was to look at any thirty-year-old Tibetan. His skin looked a hundred years old. We kept our faces greased and protected as much as possible.

We passed piles of prayer-stones. Tibetans gather flat, slatelike rocks or rounded river rocks and spend time during winter carving prayers on them. Then they pile the carved stones along the road as an offering to their gods. They also carve prayers on yak horns. Over the years these piles of prayer-stones get very large. In places where there are no foreigners to carry them away, they can grow as tall as the Abominable Snowman the Tibetans believe lives around Chomolungma.

The road went up steeply and the lush, green valley disappeared. Here there was nothing but rock; rock mountainsides, rock mountaintops, rock and more rock. I don't know what got into Parnelli, but he acted as though he'd win a prize if he could get us to base camp in ten minutes, instead of the three hours it normally took. He drove as though this road had no thousand-foot drop-offs, and he missed sending us careening down the cliffs more than once, with just an inch to spare this side of death. Never, never, never had I risked my life so often in a moving vehicle! I positioned myself in the open back, standing up the whole time, ready to jump clear. We were on the highest road system in the world.

The closer we got to Chomolungma the less we could see of the mountain and the smaller it seemed to get. I felt as though we were traveling across the surface of the moon, it was such a barren landscape. We stopped at 16,500 feet, at the ruins of the Rongbuk Monastery. There was nothing left of this place, which for centuries had been sacred to the Tibetan Buddhas, except some dissolving mud-and-stone walls. A few beautiful paintings remained on a crumbling wall, almost peeled away.

Out of nowhere, which is the way these mysterious Tibetans often appear, came two weathered women clothed in baggy, dusty black robes. They were gray-haired nuns who had returned to build this place of worship back again, stone by stone. Like so many other temples, it had been ruthlessly destroyed in the mid-1970s. The nuns offered us some tea. The nuns had probably not bathed in months, and surely ate only what people brought them here, so far from even other Tibetans. Their zeal to rebuild this highest temple with basically nothing but love and energy was evident. They'd offered Skip and me tea, but we needed to get to base camp. They waved like they hoped we'd come back again. Then the two old women returned to their work amid the ruins.

3:45 P.M. Base camp for the China/Everest '84 team was a stony area the size of several football fields. Chomolùngma was our dead-end sign, and our inspiration. It was also our predator, always looking down at us, the invaders, mere specks on a hard gray ground. She whom we came seeking was covered with glistening snow.

The first thing the climbers did when they arrived at base camp was to look up at a nearby knoll. Lou looked. Wick looked. Geo looked. No doubt, Phil looked. Dr. Ed looked, and so did Papa Dave Mahre. They were looking up at the stone piles that memorialized people who had died trying to climb Chomolungma. Their eyes sought out Marty Hoey's stone pile, a pile that they themselves had built. The memorials to Marty, to two great English climbers killed that same year, and to some Japanese, were always in our view. Everest was in front of us, our front door. The memorials to the dead were behind us. There was a chance that there would be at least one more stone pile next to Marty's before our team was finished here.

We'd get no closer to Everest because a few hundred yards off was a monster glacier, the Rongbuk. It stopped us, rising a few hundred feet. The trucks with our supplies, enough to last the team over two months, were waiting to be unloaded. Based on the equipment inventory there should be over 175 boxes, each weighing about 55 pounds. Lou organized everyone and we formed a human line of box movers. Some boxes were marked food. They were being checked in by Carolyn, base-camp manager, and Geo, who'd been in charge of arranging for all the food back home, a job that took thousands of hours.

The boxes labeled tents, ropes, crampons were piled near Phil Ershler. Phil was in charge of all equipment and stood there with his list. I was surprised and impressed with the team's organizational skills, for the loss of one or two crucial boxes, oxygen bottles, climbing ropes, severe-weather parkas, and certain medical supplies could spell doom for the entire expedition.

Dr. Ed Hixson was in charge of all our medical supplies. Ed, a general surgeon from Saranac Lake, New York, had taken three months off from his practice to join the team. "Mount Everest General" would be our emergency room, intensive-care unit, in-traction room, recovery room, and, God forbid, morgue. Ed was here to monitor the climbers' health, to keep anyone from losing fingers or toes or from collapsing with pulmonary edema. Our hospital would be an oversized tent. We all hoped it would never be used.

Lou chose the location for the main cook tent and told everyone to pitch their tents in a circle around it. The Chinese liaison officer and our two Chinese interpreters would camp a little farther away, close to the memorial knoll. The team's Tibetan cook and the cook for the Chinese set up their tents by the side of a small river-born glacier. We were surrounded on three sides by mountains. Everything man-made looked out of place here. Our colors were too bright. The shiny metal poles seemed too straight. Being in the presence of Chomolungma gave me a feeling I was unprepared for. I felt very insecure and totally unimportant. Also, here at 17,000 feet, I felt very light-headed.

Skip, Russ, and I pitched our tent. Lou and Ingrid would be in one, till Ingrid left. Peter and Greg Wilson, a recent graduate in English lit from the University of Washington, would be in a tent with John Smolich. John was the strong, silent type and a loner, yet considered to have the strength of a bear. Wick and Dave Mahre were trying to set up their tent, jabbering like a couple of old ladies. One thought the support pole should go here, and the other thought it should go there. They fiddled around and after several attempts, and a few squabbles, finally got it set up. And these were guys who had decades of experience in high mountains? I wondered who made their beds back home.

The team seemed to be contented for the moment. We'd accomplished one more goal in a long line of challenges. So far we'd all made it through the intense physical training required for this expedition. We'd gotten the permits from the sometimes impossible Chinese government. The few hundred thousand dollars needed to pay for everything was successfully raised, even though it's always harder to raise money for an expedition if you've failed the time before, as the team did in '82.

The team had purchased and organized the equipment and food needed to get to the top of the world's highest mountain. They had said good-bye to the people and places they loved. Thai Airlines Flight 741 went without a hitch to Tokyo; China Airlines Flight 928 went okay from Tokyo to Beijing; our flight from Beijing to Chengdu, and from Chengdu to Lhasa, spectacular as far as the scenery went, was otherwise uneventful. We had survived a ride through the world's most beautiful mountains at the hands of one of the craziest drivers in Tibet.

This time Lou had planned for the expedition to spend more time in Tibet adjusting to the extreme altitude before reaching base camp. For that reason everyone was healthy and had lost very little weight. The team was meshing well, much better than most, and there seemed to be no ego clashes brewing so far. Often ego duels tore expeditions into little pieces. No group severely divided by ego battles can get to the top of Everest. And one more thing was ready. Lou carried Chris's trumpet mouthpiece with him. Someone here would leave it at 29,028 feet, on the top.

Everest stood before us, much more mighty than I'd ever expected it to be. There was no escaping it. It always ripped your eyes away from anything else. The only way to avoid the sight of it was to hide out in your tent. Even at night its snow-covered rocks reflected the slightest moonglow or starlight, and there it was, BOOMING out of the darkness. It _stood_ before us. It seemed to make a kind of noise, a deep bass noise, the lowest and deepest of sounds, reverberating like an everlasting note across heaven's roof. BOOM . . . BOOM . . . It was strong enough to make my whole body shiver. It drew me, and scared me away. "Come to me," it seemed to say, "I will carry you higher than any mortal was ever meant to go." There was nothing left for us now but to get our bodies, minds, and spirits ready for her.

Our leader Lou had kept mostly to himself all the way from the USA to base camp. There wasn't a lot he needed to do. Lou was the kind of leader who was one of the guys, whether climbing a mountain, soaking in a hot tub, or partying—until he was needed to be a *leader*. He was beginning now to assert his control over the team. Everything was discussed quite democratically, but it was Lou who made the decisions.

Lou told us his ideas of what made a great climbing team:

Find nine athletes with enough confidence and strength to accept a high-risk sport, ones proud enough to care for their bodies and develop them.

Find those whose parents encouraged them as children to climb stairs, chairs, trees, walls, ropes and never discouraged them from trying new adventures.

Find climbers who attempted the major peaks like Baker and Rainier and Hood at an early age, or joined scouting to learn camping and hiking and living in a mountain environment.

Find skiers who knew about deep snow conditions. Let them guide and climb in the summer and be ski patrol and avalanche patrol in the winter. And give them full first-aid backgrounds.

Have those nine athletes experience and survive avalanches, icefalls, rockfalls, diarrhea (a problem), and one hundred mile an hour winds with diarrhea (a bigger problem).

Find a team doctor who has 'been high,' gotten sick from the altitude, and who still wants to go back.

Find a base-camp manager who is a veterinarian to care for the animals (another word for team), who can also climb and cook and live above 21,000 feet for weeks at a time. Who can give an IV, and hopefully keep the climbers' weight loss down by cooking delicious meals.

Lou continued, saying he assumed that the team knew how to live in a sub-zero, high-altitude environment and could cook and sew and mend and repair and remodel or make anything we might need—headlamps, recorders, cameras—splice rope, repair stoves. We had to know how to dig caves, build igloos, put up ladders, modify oxygen regulators and masks, sleep in hammocks on walls, or sit on ledges in bivouac. Lou reminded us of the important ability to leave our loved ones for three months, fully committed to getting someone to the top of the highest mountain in the world.

Lou closed with this quote from British poet C. Day Lewis:

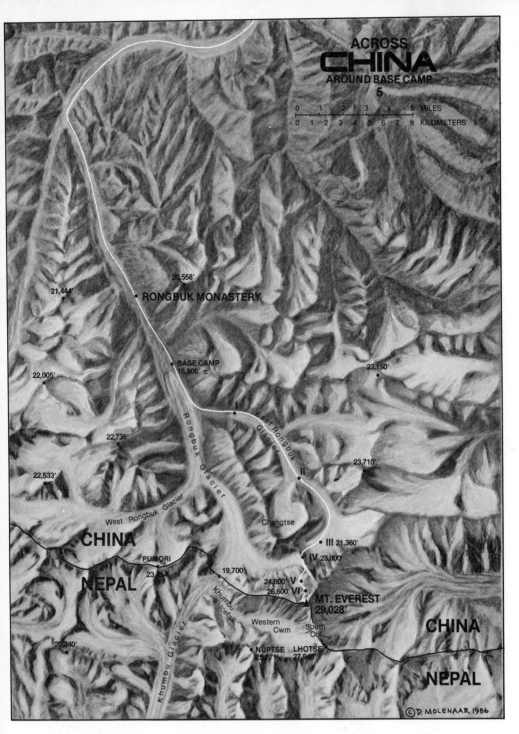

0    1    2    3    4    5 MILES
0  1  2  3  4  5  6  7  8 KILOMETERS

21,444'

20,558'
● RONGBUK MONASTERY

22,005'

● BASE CAMP
16,900' ±

23,150'

22,736'

I

East Rongbuk Glacier

Rongbuk Glacier

22,533'

23,710'

II

West Rongbuk Glacier

Changtse

CHINA

III 21,360'

PUMORI

IV 23,000'

23,494'

19,700'

24,800' V

NEPAL

26,600' VI

MT. EVEREST
▲ 29,028'

Khumbu
Icefall

Western
Cwm

South
Col

CHINA

Khumbu Glacier

20,240'

NUPTSE  LHOTSE
25,771'   27,940'

NEPAL

©D. MOLENAAR 1986

The last river we crossed was filled with glacier runoff. The raging
current felt as if it would flip our truck. Once on the other side we
headed up the Rongbuk Valley toward the largest dead end on
earth, the ultimate one, Mount Everest. The barren, narrow canyon,
which occasionally widened into a rocky valley, housed the ruins of
the Rongbuk Monastery, now being rebuilt.

*Those Himalayas of the mind are not so easily possessed.*
*There's more than precipice and storm between you and your Everest.*

When I looked up at the soft, misty grays of the sky, I saw razor-sharp cliffs covered with snow. Fingers of unmelted snow shot down the gray-green rock below the coated peaks till they melted and turned into a tiny mountain stream. The sun broke through and reflected pools of gold on the water's surface. The farther down the mountains my eyes went, the less dull the rocks became. They glowed with soft yellows and tans. There were natural pillars of stone and more often than not there were the remains of a temple perched there. It was a gentle scene at the base of the mountains, but always my eyes returned to the Goddess Mother, cold and white in her pristine snows and higher than anything else in the world.

# 19

# *Living in the "Death Zone"*

We'd taken our time through the 12,000-foot zone in both Lhasa and Xigaze. There my head beat like a drum, but otherwise I felt about 75 percent normal. At the 14,000-foot zone, my mind slowed down considerably, and although I certainly didn't feel like running anywhere, I felt I was functioning at about 70 percent.

But here at base camp, elevation 17,200 feet, everything changed again. We'd passed into another significant zone of adjustment. All the time we'd spent getting our bodies used to the oxygen-starved altitudes of Tibet seemed wasted. At first, it was hard to carry on a conversation of more than a few words at a time because just talking required too much oxygen. The first days at base camp I had to strain and breathe deeply to get enough oxygen to keep my head from feeling as though it would explode. I was even afraid to go to sleep. At home, I never thought about the fact that when I'm asleep, my body slows down. The heart beats more slowly. Breathing is slowed. All this means less oxygen in a body that's hungry for more, not less. I was worried that if I dozed off, I would black out and, who knows, maybe never wake up again.

Lou said that this altitude was a piece of cake. Higher than 18,000 feet he called the "Death Zone." No life could long sustain itself in the death zone. One of the most important characteristics of a climber's ability was how fast his body could adjust to altitude. Wick and Roskelley were known for their ability to adjust. Fang Ming, our young Chinese interpreter, who'd never even been out of Beijing before this, threw up violently for days before his body finally could function at base camp. Every hour or so you could see Fang's body doubled over, his face bone-white, throwing up. Dr. Ed said that if Fang hadn't recovered when he did, he would have been evacuated.

It was impossible for me to imagine myself going 12,000 feet higher to get to the top of Everest. That any of these climbers could do that humbled me and gave me an intensified respect for them. For the first time in my many adventures I had to force myself to admit that I did not have what it takes, here and now. I could never get to the top of Everest. That admission was one of the hardest things that I'd ever had to cope with.

Climbing mountains to these men was no weekend adventure, it was an addiction. It was what they lived for. They could live without some things, but not without the MOUNTAINS. With almost every one of them, their addiction began when they were young, on weekend trips with the Boy Scouts or with high-school friends. By the time they finished college the mountains had them. Like addicts of all kinds they became more isolated from "normal" people. They associated more and more with those who spoke their language; a lexicon of risk, snow conditions, blind rappels, and mountains named in foreign tongues in bizarre corners of the globe. Although most of them were dashing, sleek, and attractive, even women were a diversion, no matter how wonderful. You could not be addicted to love and mountains, both.

I also understood why these normally off-the-wall, cutup, joke-a-minute guys now seemed so serious. There were few things in this world that required more focused attention and such a continuous flow of survival instinct than climbing Mount Everest. Also, I now understood why so many of these climbers had a difficult time working at "regular" jobs. Once you get used to living at intense levels, always with the possibility of death close by, it's hard to check back into normal life again.

The definition of a "normal, mature life-style" was to these men about the same as it is for most of us: After school's over you get a conventional job (banker, teacher, salesperson, Boeing factory laborer) working a forty-hour week. Then you marry, have a few kids, buy a place to live, and cut a lot of grass. There are piles of bills to pay: electric, phone, rent or mortgage, car, clothes, credit-card charges, and on and on. There are the adventures to the grocery store. There's often church on Sunday.

All this normal living restricts the mountain climber from what he's addicted to . . . climbing . . . the summit . . . the superhuman feat of _getting_ to the summit, knowing he's one of only a handful of people in the world who can achieve this, and who are brave enough, or crazy enough, to risk their lives to do it. How often could anyone risk his life buying a pound of hamburger at the grocery store? Choosing to risk your life is probably the biggest natural high. The requirements for normal life are not only too safe for them, they would keep them from the mountains.

If anyone "lived on the edge," it was these extreme climbers. They lived on the edge literally, often spending weeks looking thousands of feet straight down. They lived on the edge of human survival by stressing their systems at altitudes the human body was not designed for. They spent more time living at a level of "maximum vitality" than any businessman, athlete, or creator I'd ever known. Except for Wick, the lawyer, and John Smolich, who worked during the off-climbing season as a surveyor, all of them were trying to make it full time in mountain climbing. Only Lou was making a comfortable living from the mountains. The others were basically getting by. There were no new cars for them every few years. There were few hopes of a dream house. Financial security and fat retirement plans were not part of the package.

Every one of them was keenly intelligent, attractive, obviously physically gifted and abundantly blessed with extraordinary stamina. All of them would look SUPER in three-piece suits. Surely, they could have hooked up with some other big-bucks business. Dave Mahre, the father of nine children, found out about his addiction when in the midst of fatherhood. He vowed he would not get into "extreme" expedition climbing till all of his kids were old enough to take care of themselves in case something like death happened to him. Fortunately for Dave, he was the one in a million who still had the body and mind for extreme climbing in his fifties.

Lou, our leader, had the capability of making each climber feel that he was here because he had the ability to make it. Some of the guys had just been paying their dues longer. Lou considered each member of the team equally important. No one would make the top, for instance, if John Smolich, the quiet loner, couldn't carry food from Camp 4 to Camp 5. The yaks could go only as high as Camp 3. If Carolyn couldn't keep the team filled with thousands of calories a day, there would be no strength left for the last half of the mountain. If Papa Dave wasn't ready to do whatever he was called upon to contribute, the team would fail. The thoroughbreds, Phil and Geo, although they'd paid their dues for years, would have to work just as hard as anyone else on the bottom half of the mountain.

And what about Roskelley, a world-recognized mountain-climbing superstar? He would have to put it all on the line throughout the entire expedition. None of this prima donna jive with Lou and the boys from Rainier Mountaineering. Lou couldn't stand anyone on a team who didn't pull his own weight. And John couldn't either. He'd been known to scream at teammates for sloppy work or laziness. I'd heard stories of some expeditions escalating from shouting fits to all-out brawls, fistfights, and breakups. Immediately after we got to base camp, John was off at his own initiative building us a rock outhouse. Someone even left a *Time* magazine to read. Everything about the magazine, especially the ads, seemed unreal. It was hard to relate to troubles in Iran, swimsuit fashions cut up to the model's waist, and U.S. defense-budget overruns.

Wickwire, another long-established star, would do all that was asked of him and more. It's imperative in climbing high that a team not rely on one star. Competition is great and Lou knew, expertly, like a brilliant coach, how to set up the players. When you have a number of leading men to choose from, you're more secure. If Wick couldn't hit the home run on summit day, Phil might. If not Phil, then Geo. If not Geo, then John. Then there was always the chance that something unfortunate could happen to all of the big boys and someone else would capture the glory. One of the "mature" climbers, Lou or Dave, could be pressed into service if everyone else fell apart. Or one of the young bloods, John Smolich, Greg Wilson, or Peter Whittaker, might end up being the hero. Peter was acting as confident as ever, even though he had no idea how he'd do here in the Himalayas.

A very interesting phenomenon began to take place among the team when we got to base camp. First of all, it was as if those of us who weren't climbers weren't even there. The climbers were like boxers before a world-title fight. Each one was totally consumed with his vision of the fight, the battle in which someone much more powerful would do anything to knock him out. THE SUMMIT, and LIVING were their two goals, and each became increasingly possessed by it. I WANT THE SUMMIT. I MUST LIVE. I MUST HAVE IT. I WANT TO LIVE.

Each member of the group with "first team" or "summit team" ambitions began to pair up with the guy he thought offered the best chance for success. Phil and Geo were mentioned as probably the first summit team, because they had the talent, but also because they'd done so much work as food and equipment managers, getting the team this far. Wick and Roskelley began spending a lot of time together.

# 20

## *Pure Sound*

The pure sounds around Chomolungma are many. The wind had many voices and it came from many places. Some days it whipped down the Rongbuk Glacier from the direction of the peak, sounding like a thousand horses running. On a calm day it could be as quiet as a baby breathing in a crib. Rocks were our drums. They slipped from high above on all sides and fell: falling, falling, falling till they stopped, slamming into the river at the bottom of a steep gorge or wedged under a giant boulder. Sometimes I could follow the clatter of a single, small rock as it tumbled along, building up speed.

When the ground became unstable because of rain or melting snow, the big rocks fell free. They would strike a chilling fear in anyone below imagining what a four-hundred-pound boulder could do if it dropped on a tent, falling from three thousand feet! Fortunately, base camp was in a wide-open rock field and was not susceptible to being hit by falling rocks. Later, in a higher camp, climbers would listen for that most horrifying sound on any mountain, the surging explosions of an avalanche wiping away everything in its path like so many pebbles in a tidal wave.

This was the only place on earth I'd ever been where there was no chance of hearing anything but the sounds made by rocks or rain or wind or rivers. Even in Alaska, a bush plane or chain saw could interrupt the chords of the wilderness. Here there wasn't even a chance to hear a far-off jet. No possibility of sirens. No car racket, or the clangs and bangs of office builders. There certainly were no people standing on a corner with ghetto-busters wailing reggae. The only soul sounds were the occasional moans of my homesick heart.

When my head hurt from lack of oxygen I would put on my headset and turn up my tape to drown out the maddening, supernatural stillness. The rocks sounded as if they were falling inside my head.

Far-off, behind me, I thought I heard something. I'd been looking above the glacier at two eagles, crisp black shapes in the dark-blue Himalayan sky. I turned for a second, not wanting to lose the eagles who were spiraling higher. I saw nothing down the silver-colored stone fields toward the Rongbuk valley. There was no chance of the neighbors coming for a visit here! The eagles were smaller when my squinting eyes found them again.

Then I caught the distant echoes of bells. Way down there, as far away as my eyes could see, was a line of black dots. Had our yak herders finished the fall harvest or was it some renegade group of escaping Tibetans, heading for asylum in Nepal? Our team was waiting, waiting for the "yakkers." There would be no telegram saying, "Will arrive with 28 yak, 12 yak herders, 10:15 A.M. on the morning of the 25th." The yakkers knew nothing of electronic communication; their arrival message was given when you saw them coming.

The bells grew louder and more beautiful. The brass bells rang to us on the hot, thin air, bouncing from rock wall to rock wall, their jingling becoming more and more distinct. THE YAK CARAVAN was coming! Was it ours? The black line moved slowly. The men were dressed in black. Most of the yaks were black too. By now the whole team was watching excitedly, hoping these were our yakkers, standing together at the biggest dead end in the world.

As I strained to watch the caravan, I thought of how it must have been for a pioneer family homesteading in Nebraska to see a far-off wagon train approaching. "Break out the best food and pull out your fiddle and take a bath," they must have yelled. I felt like running down to the caravan, but I didn't. The normal pace of the yaks on level ground was two miles per hour. They'd be allowed a two-day rest at base camp, Wick said, before the all-out assault was begun.

It was a three-and-a-half-day walk to here from their village. The most important thing for the yak herders was not our climb but their harvest. Harvest meant having enough food for another year of life. They prayed for a good harvest and they prayed for the safety of their yaks. Carrying our equipment up a mountain was nothing more than a side job to these full-time villagers and farmers.

The team's strategy for climbing Mount Everest was to establish camps ascending beyond base camp and gradually work their way to the top. First, equip base camp, which was the team's home base, hospital, and recuperation center. Then move fast and efficiently, letting the yaks carry as far as they can. Once the yaks can go no farther, members of the team take over the gear, hauling it up the mountain. Climbing teams are like runners in a relay race, I heard Lou say many times. The guys who do a lot of the earliest climbing are sacrificing their chance to cross the finish line so that some other guy on the team can. On major expeditions the climbers not considered prime summit-team candidates go first, breaking trail through deep snow and ice and carrying the heavy loads of food and supplies while the summit team carries as light as they can (their own clothes, sleeping bag, etc.). This way the summit boys conserve energy.

Dave Mahre, who was already beginning to grow a salt-and-pepper beard, stood next to me and said he was looking for his favorite yak from the 1982 expedition. He'd named her Alice, although Alice was a steer. Alice had probably saved some fingers and toes of Larry Nielsen, one of the 1982 team. Larry, a high-school teacher, had attempted the summit by himself in a daring shot at the top. He'd left two team members behind, when one was injured, and gone on alone. He froze his feet and hands and Alice carried him over ten miles off the mountain. Larry, not the type to be refused, went back to Everest in 1983 with another team and this time became the first American to climb Everest without oxygen.

Only yaks with tranquil personalities can carry people and they are few and far between. Dave said Alice had mostly white hairs, with some black mixed in, so that she looked almost silver. "You could walk up to her and pet her," Dave said. That's slightly less surprising than being able to walk up and pet an alligator. As the caravan got closer he thought he recognized her. Dave often played a big role in mountain rescues and climber evacuations. He was also a very emotional and sentimental man and could cry easily.

The line of black yaks and black-haired Tibetans circled just below the rock knoll where Marty's stone memorial stood. They would pitch their black tents there. Sometimes these tents, which looked like a low-slung version of a desert nomad's tent, were so heavy they required two yaks just to carry one. I noticed that the herders wore their smoke-stained sheepskin coats with the fur in. Based on the rough looks of these men, I thought they could have cut our throats and cooked and eaten us for dinner. But the Tibetans are gentle people. Because of Buddha, they are consumed by a reverence for all life, down to the squirming worm. They even believe that the surface of the earth has a spirit, a life, and to drive over a meadow in a jeep that makes ruts, is cutting the earth and will harm and release its spirit.

# Heated by Men

"The tent was heated by yak dung and the warmth of men. Their faces were red-brown, mine was white," Carolyn wrote in her diary at base camp. While most members of the team ignored the Tibetans, Carolyn befriended them.

"Most of the yak-men sat on goatskins, cross-legged in front of smoke-blackened pots and their handleless cups. Six men, from several in their late teens to the oldest, a small, wizened man of about 60 years, lined the tent." As I read Carolyn's diary, I thought that surely the eyes of the yak herders danced with excitement and curiosity over this woman, perhaps the first Western woman some of them had ever seen. Carolyn herself was excited to be with these gentle yakkers, so different from any other men she had known.

"The Tibetan men wore goatskin pants, coats with the fur inside, and various ornaments. Their hair was in two braids with red-thread fringes braided in. Also, in their flyaway hair were rings, coins, ivory and safety pins as decorations. They were quiet, shy, and friendly.

"I felt as though I were being transported to the Great Plains of the American Indians, so identical were some of the features of these men. To me 'savage' has always had connotations of primitive rather than beastly, and surrounded by what therefore could be savages, I felt frail but not in danger. Rather I felt a comfort, a closeness, especially as I saw the men huddle next to each other against the chill. They put their arms around each other and laid their heads on each other's shoulders. One of the older men lay at the opening of the tent on his stomach listening, and soon a younger yak-man of about 20 came and lay right on top of him, for there was no more room."

Carolyn next recorded a conversation centered around one of the most important things in a yak herder's life, his yaks:

(To the Tibetans there are few things that matter as much as their gods and their mountains. But the yak is one. The yak provides them with milk, fuel, and hair for weaving into cloth. The yak gives meat, and marrow from its bones. It gives power to plow their sacred barley land. The yak carries things humans can't. Salt . . . Trading goods . . . It can pack tents for a nomad's survival. A man can cross the yak with a cow and the yak gives its strength to that bloodcross. The yak is much more important to them than cars are to a Californian.)

"Yaks are a sign of wealth. The more a man owns, the greater his riches. A good, healthy working yak is worth four hundred fifty yuan.

"Baby yaks are born after six months in the belly, and at four to five months they begin to eat grass. 'If cow yaks bear baby every year, then very good. God blessing family,' said one of the men's leaders. 'Every other year only OK.'

"Calves are weaned by putting on them a carved wooden muzzle, which contains several sharpened spikes. The mother will not let them nurse with the muzzle on," Carolyn wrote.

"'At two to three years old yak trained for plowing or packing.

Training period last till they learn, sometimes only three days. Yak very smart. Sometime. In summer we take them to high-mountain pasture, they feed. In winter they eat dry range grass, sometime dig through snow to live.' One of the yak-men was holding a lovingly woven collar of red, gray and blue, with a special bronze bell. Their bell collars rang all day and night as the yaks worked and milled around camp, throughout the night. It was a special way to drift off to sleep."

"'Yaks work for people till fifteen to sixteen years old, then usually live about eighteen years. A yak's fur has long stiff guard hairs, and their undercoat most soft and fine to touch. Guard hairs woven into rope. And undercoat spun on a drop spindle, used for clothing. Hide used for soles of traditional shoes.' I couldn't believe it but a few of the younger guys actually had crudely made high-top sneakers on.

"'Yaks are never dehorned. No portion of the yak is sacred in this area. However, in some areas, some fat is burned in lantern on the day of slaughter for good luck. Plow animal very special, receive red and white tassels in ears, on tail. Non-pure-blood yak receive no tassels. Red or white prayer-flags often attached to yak, too.' The Tibetans' voices were so soothing and soft, as relaxing as a cooing baby. Yet they themselves were so incredibly tough. It was confusing.

"'Nursing cow yaks milked once a day, kept inside at night. Make no cheese. Make yak butter. Boil milk, let stand overnight, then add soda, then churn,' the yak-man said. For the herders to talk about their yaks was a special honor. They were pleased a foreigner would be so interested. Yaks were life to them."

Carolyn continued her journal of her evening in their tent: "The dung fire blazed and gave off an amazing amount of heat on this frigid Tibetan night. Their brown faces glowed and the red light from the flames burnished the soot-blackened tent walls."

The yak-men liked this young woman, Carolyn. Their custom was not to talk much to women, or to answer questions from women, but they thought, "This woman different, very fine. Very smart woman, and wise." Carolyn thought the yak-men very fine and wise also.

And so, Carolyn and I learned much from the yakkers. They would be a major and irreplaceable part of the expedition's success or failure. And now, finally, they were here. The climb could now continue beyond base camp, toward the top of the world.

The plan was: When the yaks arrive, allow them two days' rest.

Load approximately twenty-seven to thirty yaks with about one-hundred pounds each. Loading a yak is done very politely. You cannot hold down a yak, they have to stand still to be loaded. Yaks will carry gear from base camp to Camp 1 (18,300 feet) on the first day. On the second day they'll carry from Camp 1 to Camp 2, (19,700 feet), which will be the longest and toughest haul for them. Day three calls for a tough haul between Camp 2 and the advanced base camp (21,300 feet).

The first day, we helped the yak herders drive the yaks on their trip from base camp to Camp 1. The technique is similar to driving cattle on foot—you've got to be easy and gentle with them, never crowding them. Only if they break out do you run after them, as we did a couple of times when they made a break for the water. Running after a yak at 18,000 feet is not fun. Your lungs feel as though they are going to blow up. Yaks looked to me like small buffalo. They were very surefooted and could carry about 55 pounds per side, for a total of 110 pounds.

Before the climbers got fully acclimatized they had trouble keeping up with the yakkers. One time a caravan got ahead of two climbers who were to show the yakkers where to drop the gear, and they deposited their load three or four hundred feet lower than they should have. There were many negotiations in English, Chinese, and Tibetan trying to get that one fixed up. The yakkers had to go back, reload, and take the equipment where it belonged. Without them, every bit of equipment would have had to be relayed by the climbers. A totally draining, probably defeating torture.

Besides driving the yaks up the mountain the younger Tibetan men had to carry on their backs bundles that looked like some kind of straw. This was feed for the yaks because the mountains provide no grazing. To indicate how much they would carry, each herder chose a rock and that rock symbolized the load they would take.

The trail from base camp went by the left side of the glacier, then up onto the base of a neighboring mountain. There the trail was high above a river that came shooting out of another massive glacier closer to the base of Everest. The narrow trail went fairly straight along the top of the river canyon until it dropped back down into the canyon again. At the bottom men and yaks had to cross the icy water to finally arrive at Camp 1.

# *The Party*_____

A white goat showed up in base camp, mysteriously. It was tied to a stake near the river born under the glacier. It moved around the rocks looking for a bite of some stunted plant. After the Tibetans arrived with their yak caravan, the reason for the goat was made known to us. The yakkers killed the goat, cutting its throat and draining all the blood into a skin bag to be mixed with other things to make sausage. They were not sacrificing it to any mountain gods, though. IT WAS PARTY TIME!

This afternoon we would transform base camp into the world's highest circus. Goat luau. Singing lesson. Break-dancing exhibition, disco, and blessing of the beer. The team, our Chinese interpreters, and the Tibetans were throwing a party for those of us who were leaving in the morning. Two huge crows appeared like spirits materializing, the way most life showed itself in Tibet, suddenly out of nowhere, and acted as if they were supervising the event. It was the yak team's job to slaughter the goat. They performed this by the river, reverently. The small medicine man with the twisted scars on his face and small leather pouch of magic objects tied to his hair was in charge. He made most of the important cuts with his gleaming knife. First the Tibetans skinned it, then they laid the skin down and carefully cleaned out the intestines.

Each one had his job. The younger ones took the scraped intestines to the river to wash. The middle-aged yakkers, the ones in their twenties, cleaned the bones and kept them for the marrow. The few older men (they were in their thirties, looked in their fifties) cut the meat in small, bite-sized pieces and placed them in a big metal wok. Throughout the morning as they prepared the goat we joked and swore we would never eat goat, and we wondered how they could possibly eat the stuff they did. At lunch, Lou informed the team that there would be a party late that afternoon, that the Chinese and Tibetans had provided us with a goat, and that we should all respectfully eat some of the goat. I felt like saying, "Yes, Daddy," but I thought, "No way am I going to eat any of that thing after I saw what they did to it!"

The two giant crows hovered about. Tibetans believe that crows, native to these Himalayas, are the spirits of reincarnated life, and as with all life, they allow them their place. They would never scare them off or shoot them. Our yakkers shared a few treats with them, though not much since they saved practically everything. The crows were perched on a close-by boulder when the yakkers began cooking the goat. Lou walked through camp and said for everyone to come on, the party would soon begin. There was little excitement. A party, with no roof, standing on an endless floor of rocks, having to eat goat, possibly dance with other men and gasp for breath. I didn't get dressed up.

Skip and I strolled slowly over by the Tibetans' cook tent. The rest of the team walked over obediently as well. The cook had stuck some shish-kebob-type metal things in the wok filled with goat pieces. He also poured a sauce of who-knows-what over the meat.

Everyone stood around, acting polite, making small talk, glancing up at the mountain. The sun was not shining here, but it was brilliantly lighting up the main peak of Chomolungma, highlighted above the shaded peaks below. All the Tibetans were here, as well as the Chinese, and every one of us from America.

Lou and Dave politely tried the goat. They put a few of the smallest pieces on their metal cooking forks and held them over the fire. When they rushed back to get as many goat pieces as they could fit on their skewers, a few of us tried it. It was delicious. Incredibly tangy. Bite-sized. It almost melted in my mouth. I thought, "Peter, have you been breathing Tibetan air too long? You're scoffing down goat like it was the best BBQ in Texas!" I didn't think about it long because I was back filling up my skewer, though this time I had to compete with a bunch of the guys. We had fast become marinated-goat lovers.

Peter Whittaker headed in the direction of our cook tent. He brought with him base camp's cassette player, which he called a Third World Briefcase. He put on the sound track to *Footloose*. The Chinese had already begun chanting, "Disco, disco," which seems to be one word a lot of the younger Chinese know. A few yaks had strayed high above us searching for a few bites of grass. The enchanting sounds of their beautiful bells were drowned out. The crows flew away right about the time Peter cranked up the tape player.

Everyone stood around in their own groups, like at most any party. Then Lou broke out some beer. He gave a bottle to one of the yakkers. He carefully carried it to their elder along with a metal cup. He poured some, and dipped his thumb and first finger into the beer, flicking it into the air. He did this four times, in the direction of north, then south, east, then west. We were told that they offered everything first to their gods, to show their thanks. I found it interesting that they would offer a god beer. Then each yakker took a drink, in the order of his age. It was ceremonial and very special the way they shared.

By now Lou and Ingrid were dancing, their last chance to dance for no telling how long. Lou lifted up his long legs and strutted like a stork, performing. Ingrid, who'd had a bit of trouble with the altitude early on, was having a blast. She soon was dancing with Bao, our Mongolian liaison officer. Bao's wide, darkly handsome face was both thrilled and embarrassed. Rebekah's favorite song, "Maniac," came on and I danced one for us. For some strange reason I thought back to what my father used to say when I was in high school and I would complain about there being nothing to do in my hometown of fifty thousand people. He would always say the same thing. "Peter, you've got to make your own fun happen." Here I was at the end of the world, about to dance with Mount Everest.

The Tibetans stood in an orderly line, all dressed in black. They stared at us cutting loose, and asked Fang many questions about us.

"Why do these white-faced people all look different? Some are red-haired, some blond, and some balding. Some are very tall and some short."

"Why they dance like they're having a mad fit?"

"Why they listen to such weird-sounding music? What is mountains like in their country?"

"Why do they come so far just to climb Chomolungma? How can they take off so much time from raising their crops and yaks?"

"Who make their bright-colored clothes and their purple and orange climbing ropes? They are very beautiful."

"Who take care of their yaks, their women, their fields?"

"Has their country ever been taken over by Chinese like ours has?"

They seemed very pleased to see us acting so goofy! These strange people from far off could have fun and laugh, just like them. Come to think of it, they had seen very little laughter out of our camp. Mostly, there was building tension.

The Chinese guys, being from Beijing, were a bit more worldly, but they came unglued when Peter Whittaker and Carolyn started doing the bump. Maybe the Tibetans thought that was some kind of American mating dance. Dancing at 17,000 feet above sea level stressed the whole body. After two dances I felt as though I'd run fifteen miles, but I didn't care. Lou, the entertainer, stood out in front of everyone and began pointing to his nose, showing how big it is. The Tibetans couldn't understand why Peter, Lou's son, was not "born of Ingrid." Lou told them that Peter was by his first wife, so they thought then he had two wives, and they liked that. "Different American custom." In Tibet, where there used to be a shortage of men because one quarter of all men were celibate monks, women used to have more than one husband. Often a woman would marry three brothers.

Trying to stir things up even more, someone asked Fang to tell the

Tibetans that Skip had one hundred girlfriends back in the USA. The reason his hair was blond was because he tried to keep up with all those women. All the yakkers broke out into spontaneous applause! Most of them came up to Skip and touched him, hoping some of his powers would rub off on them. Skip waited awhile before asking Fang to tell them, "All this a joke." They laughed and laughed.

We all tried hard to get the yakkers to dance American-style, but they would not. Maybe they thought it was evil, which wouldn't have been the first time someone thought that of dancing. They definitely thought it was "most unusual." Especially when big Dan McConnell lay down on the rock-covered ground and started break-dancing. Dan, a Seattle-based PR man, was the person who would be receiving all news from the team (good or bad) and passing it on to anxious family, friends, and the media. He would be leaving with us in the morning.

Finally the Tibetans were ready. They asked Wick to turn off our music. Maybe it was hurting their silence-tuned ears. They all lined up, arm in arm, like the Rockettes, and began chanting, and side-stepping and kicking up their legs in unison, superbly. Their hauntingly beautiful "song," sung with no accompaniment, except for the slight breeze off Chomolungma, fit perfectly here. They stopped and motioned for us to join them. We all walked up and put our arms around the yakkers. The line was twice as long now as we tried to learn their intricate steps, while singing their song at the tops of our voices. "Heyyyyy-ya—Sha-ma-soooooo." English words can not convey the beauty of their Tibetan words in song.

We wore bright red parkas, jeans, flannel shirts, mirrored sunglasses, and they wore their black clothes, woven from their own sheep. The dancing line of Americans and Tibetans didn't move perfectly, but we had soul. For me, it was the most moving experience yet.

We sang three or four more Tibetan songs all at different dance speeds requiring different steps. Their voices sounded as pure as the winds of the Chomolungma and I'd take their dancing, arm in arm, stepping in unison, to our jerky steps, alone, any day. After their beautiful singing we felt compelled to do a few tunes ourselves. The yakkers sang as if they had been learning from the moment of birth. We sounded like some lonely bellowing yaks. We began our concert with "She'll Be Comin' 'Round the Mountain When She

Comes," and paused a moment before we broke into "God Bless America." We couldn't sing in tune, but it was obvious we all loved our homeland, even if emotion was a bit awkward for a lot of these rock-tough climbers. I was surprised that everyone sang because back home in the nonconformist spirit in which they lived, some of these climbers would have looked away while others sang. Here at the base of their mountain they belted it out passionately. We wound up our concert with "Jingle Bells." After our selections, the Chinese sang two of their favorites. Our encore was "Old Man River." We begged the Tibetans and they sang us another song too.

Then Peter and Lou started entertaining us with circus-type acrobatics, Lou lofting Peter into the air for some backflips. Then the whole team lined up and made a four-tier pyramid for the audience. They loved it when Papa Dave climbed to the top! The party broke down many of the cultural walls that kept us apart until now. It was too bad we had to leave in the morning.

By now, only the top of the mountain that had brought us across the world to dance and sing before her was lit by the sun. Skip and I made it back to the tent and flopped down on our down sleeping bags. We had formed a close and open friendship over the years and we talked to each other about everything, the way I'd heard some women say their friendships were. "Skip's uptight tonight," I wrote in my journal, "because it's 8:14 P.M. and the trucks that are to take us back to Xegar in the morning are not here yet. Skip normally wouldn't care about being on time, but he was worried because he had to get to the Greek Island of Santorini to marry Susan."

Skip had originally planned to be married right here on Everest and he'd shocked me some months before when he'd asked me to perform the ceremony. Deeply touched, I told Skip I would, if I could. However, Susan and Skip decided the wedding would be more romantic on their gentle island in the crystal-blue Mediterranean. It was a long way between here and Santorini, and Skip was beginning to pull his mind off Tibet and apply it to Susan. I, too, was beginning to think about the rest of China, which I was hoping to see and experience. I wondered if Ran Ying had made it to China OK. Some hours later it began to snow, a wet, heavy snow that almost collapsed our dome tent. The trucks pulled in after midnight.

That next morning, our last next to Chomolungma, I definitely didn't need coffee to wake me up. Standing next to the truck, which looked like a retired Chinese army vehicle, was Parnelli, the wild demon of Tibet's back roads. He smiled devilishly. I figured surely he would be a good boy on the way back. Skip and I would ride in the back of his truck again ONLY because we had no choice. For a long moment I contemplated walking back.

The climbing team would soon be alone; we would be gone. Skip, Russ, and I, "The Fun Seekers," would make them laugh no more. Ingrid would return home, via her homeland of Germany, and hopefully sleep well while Lou was gone, always awaiting the phone call from big Dan about the team's progress. Lou and Ingrid grabbed each other and didn't want to let go, in the same unspoken way men and women do when the man is going off to war. Big Dan hugged Wick and Roskelley, his good friends. I shook hands with Peter W., and John Smolich, slapped Geo on the back and hugged Carolyn. The others climbed up. We were gone. All the climbers waved longer than I thought they would, expressing their appreciation for us, maybe trying to hold on to us. Now that we were gone, they knew the climb would begin, focused and unrelenting until they either were allowed by Everest to stand on top of her or were turned back.

# The Lunatic

The monster boulders were falling. They were loosened by the wet snowfall of last night, making the ground that held them unstable. Over the sounds of the truck we could hear them crashing down the slopes and that was bad. If a big one hit us, we'd be squashed like an ant underfoot. At this moment we were driving through some narrow, chilling canyons that were constant danger zones.

We'd gone about a mile from base camp when we rounded a corner and before us was a low place in the road that looked like a mudhole about seventy-five feet long. Parnelli gunned his engine, but stopped before he entered the mud. Instead of backing up, he eased slowly into the muck and was stuck almost immediately. Once he turned off the engine, the sounds of falling boulders and rocks of all sizes came at us, loud, from all sides. Somehow Parnelli was able to back out and try again. Instead of doing what he knew he should do, backing way up and gunning it full speed through the deep mudhole, he did the opposite. He crept up to the edge of the mud and, turning his wheels hard to the right, mired down in the deepest part of this wet trap. The worst thing he could have done was to turn his wheels. He should have kept them straight. Also, why did he turn into the deepest part? The guy was either self-destructive, wanted the Chinese to send him to prison, or he was a lunatic! There was no other explanation.

The Tibetan cook who was escorting us walked back to base camp to get the team. I guess Ingrid would get to see Lou one more time. An hour later they came, and Lou had all of us throw rocks into the mud to make for better traction. We threw everything we could get our hands on in this land of rock, making a rock and mud track for Parnelli to drive through. As usual the Chinese sat off to the side and endlessly debated what should be done. If we had waited for them we would have been there another week.

When it came time for the "maniac" to make another attempt, he screwed up again, getting stuck worse than ever. Lou kept emotions from running wild and us from stomping Parnelli. He got everyone to work digging out the wheels and putting more rocks under them. Dave Mahre, who was a grounds and slopes manager at White Pass, a Washington ski area, and had driven heavy equipment all his life, was ready to knock Parnelli out. Dave was MAD. Dave got more than mad. Dave shouted that we should yank the "idiot" out from behind the wheel and let *him* get the truck through. But Parnelli would not budge and, with a pathetic spin of his wheels, somehow powered the truck through with a bunch of us behind, pushing our guts out.

We said good-bye again and were off to the river. Skip and I had already decided that no matter how tired we felt we would stand up the entire way to Xegar, a ten- to fourteen-hour ride. A baby donkey, either wild or lost, began running in front of the truck down by the Rongbuk Monastery. It was too young to know enough to turn off the road and so it ran and ran till it just lay down. A monk friend of Parnelli's, whom he had picked up by the monastery, jumped out and lifted the baby ass out of the way.

# CLIMBERS, YAKKERS, AND "THE MOUNTAIN"

Lou and Phil pumped up for Everest

Lou struggles through unstable new snow that was enough to turn the team back below the North Col.

Our leader, Lou Whittaker

Lou's oldest son, Peter, a "rising star" in world climbing

Mount Everest, peak at top right, is called in Tibetan Chomolungma, "Goddess Mother of the World."

Phil Ershler

"Am I pretty enough?" "Geo" wonders. George Dunn, called Geo, and Phil were considered one of the "hot" teams to be first to the summit.

Atop another mountain pass, we're at the mercy of our crazed Tibetan truck driver, "Parnelli Yak." Here, with prayer-flags on either side, we paused to get our first view of Mount Everest (far left).

"Papa" Dave Mahre, fifty-six, oldest on our team and also father of Olympic-gold-and-silver-medal-winning skiers, Phil and Steve

John Smolich, "the strong, silent loner"

Carolyn Gunn, in charge of base camp, was the only woman on the team. A veterinarian, she would end up saving the life of one of "the boys."

Greg Wilson, twenty-seven, coughed so much high on the mountain, he broke some ribs.

"At Camp Three we looked out over a whole new sea of mountains," said Jim Wickwire.

JIM WICKWIRE

The team attemps to establish Camp 5 but is soon turned back by "man-moving" winds.

PETER JENKINS

John Roskelley: "the bad boy of American climbing"?

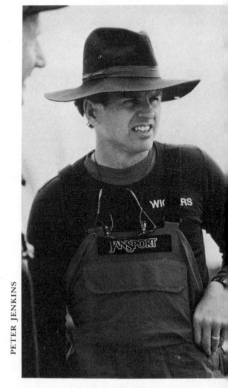

PETER JENKINS

Our lone yuppie, Jim Wickwire, survey base camp.

Ren Jiu, above, was the lead yak because "he work very hard, not lazy. Also he can smell person's tracks. He very smart," said one yak herder.

A yakker puts a hand-carved saddle on the yak and gets ready to strap on a load.

Jin Mie, elder of our yak herders, decides what each yak will carry up the mountain.

Next came the river. It was very muddy from the melting of last night's snow and the water level was a lot higher than before. Parnelli attacked it from a different angle. We spun and choked and gagged but got across. The sun was now warming the rocks and us. Past a cluster of rock and mud homes, there was another small creek to cross. Parnelli slowed to a crawl and almost stopped in the middle of it. Skip and I, normally slow to anger even in the face of his life-daring driving, began screaming at him, though he could not understand what we said. Lucky for him and his self-image he couldn't. We were stuck, again. This time we were hours from base camp. There would be no "team to the rescue." P. Yak pulled out a rope, hooked it to the front bumper, and we pulled the truck out. Maybe Parnelli had fallen on his head from a very tall cliff when he was a small boy.

We cruised happily for a few miles till we got to a crossroads that continued down the Rongbuk valley. The log bridge we had crossed coming in was washed out. Parnelli would have to drive across ANOTHER RIVER!!!! I thought about having a nervous breakdown but decided against it. Tibetans probably didn't know what a nervous breakdown was. I decided to laugh like a madman, instead. Parnelli eased around the swept-away bridge and attacked another swollen river. Many Tibetans stranded on either side of the river waited to see what would happen to the white adventurers in the back of the truck driven by one of their own.

Guess what happened?

1) He made it across with no trouble. _Wrong._
2) He made it across, doing a lot of brilliant deep-water driving. _No!_
3) He got stuck near the shore. _No!!_
4) He got stuck smack-dab in the middle of the river, AGAIN, driving like his usual STUPID self. _Right!!_

By now we were beyond knocking him out and taking over the truck. Too much time passed as we sat in the middle of the river. Finally a tractor came, hooked a chain to us, and pulled us through to the other side.

The rest of the way into Xegar we didn't get stuck ONCE! We did almost run off the road fifteen or twenty times. And we did stop for a tea break with Parnelli's wife and kids and parents in his village.

Also, we stood up the whole way, much of the time hanging one leg over the side of the truck, ready to leap for our lives. The others sat down, either trusting Parnelli's driving or too tired to care. Arriving in Xegar my arms and body felt like they'd been beat on with a tire iron.

That night we were wild with energy. Maybe it was the increased oxygen almost three thousand feet lower or maybe it was knowing that there would be no more Parnelli! In the morning we'd board another bus back to Xigaze. After our meal, Skip and I went for a walk. We'd eaten so little there was nothing to digest; we just wanted to stretch our legs. We found a bunch of excited young boys flying a homemade kite and watched them while they watched us.

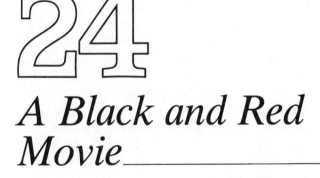

# 24

## *A Black and Red Movie*

I was distracted from the boys and their hand-painted kite by the sound of bells, often heard in these mountain valleys and narrow rock-cluttered passes. It was a caravan of yaks, their tails flicking, moving at typical yak-speed, which is however fast the yaks want to go. They, like the Tibetan people, move in an unhurried rhythm.

The nomad who was leading the herd might have been up in the mountain meadows all summer, away from his home village. He might be coming back down now for the winter, taking a week or even a month to get wherever he was going. His hands were blackened from the fires of yak dung he would light to heat his rancid yak-butter tea. A long turquoise earring stood out from his dark skin. He walked with his hands clasped behind his back.

It was getting dark and we fell in behind the yak caravan, walking back through the village on a single-lane street laced with mudholes. I noticed there was a crowd of people, maybe eight or nine, heading in the same direction we were. They all turned into a gate by a building that looked like an old school. The crowd walked quickly up the steps and into a dark room. What was going on? We'd been told not to go anywhere around here except for country walks, since this was a sensitive military area, being so close to India and other border countries.

We went up to the door and listened. I heard sounds unlike anything else we'd heard so far. It almost sounded like a scratchy soundtrack to an old movie. I looked at Skip, to see if he was game. Skip mumbled, "Can't we get in big trouble for going in here?"

"The worst they can do is throw us out. Let's go for it." We pulled out some small Chinese change, which we'd just seen others give at the door, and walked through a musty curtain into an old auditorium. It reminded me of an ancient gym in an American school. Whispers grew loud when the audience saw us walk in. We sat on the front row and immediately some little Tibetan girls came and sat with us.

It was a black-and-white movie. In the opening scene there was a view of a Tibetan home, with stone walls and smoke coming out a hole in the roof. It was in a beautiful valley, next to a stream. The feel was very pure and sweet, like a Tibetan version of *Little House on the Prairie*. An adorable little girl wanders off picking mountain-meadow flowers. Then cut. The scene switches to the little child, obviously lost, wandering scared and crying pitifully. She is in front of a temple. Surely there could be no safer place for a Tibetan child to find herself, I thought.

Inside the temple, peeking through a crack in a huge, thick wooden door is a wicked-looking monk: squinted eyes, greasy skin and hair, rubbing his plotting hands together. He takes on the hungry look of a vampire. The child is crying, obviously asking for help. The monk ignores the lost little girl, but does push the door open enough to lure her inside.

The scene switches to her frantic and beautiful mother, running in the wrong direction, up the mountain behind their peaceful little valley. The pace quickens now and we jump from one mountaintop to the next, to a tight canyon by a raging river, and our hearts tighten, wanting to yell out, "Tibetan mother, your baby went in the other direction!" I was amazed how well I could understand what was going on. The mother has run until she's ready to fall. She's on the verge of collapse, when we see a horse and rider approach in the distance.

The rider is a Chinese soldier. He is handsome, clean-cut, and his posture is heroic. He has the glow of a good Samaritan. He leaps from his horse at the sight of the crying mother and asks her, compassionately, what is wrong. She says her daughter is lost. The man gently lifts her onto his white horse and seems to say, "We will go find her." A blizzard hits them, and the brave soldier takes off his coat and hat and sunglasses and gives them to the grieving lady. He makes arm-uplifted signs of victory. He runs in front of his horse, leading them toward a valiant rescue.

Next, we flash back inside the temple. The music is grotesque and moaning and terrifying. The most simple optical illusion distorts the faces of the Buddhas and carved animal faces into nightmarish visions. The little girl screams at the sight of them. In the background the holy man can be seen laughing. He enjoys scaring the lost child horribly. Even I get scared watching the distorted faces of the carved stone "monsters."

Further inside the temple, the head holy man sits back on a sultry couch, smoking something powerful and sinful, while a sexy slave girl stands waiting for his orders. He slaps her for no reason. The whole audience gasps, like they've just seen the unthinkable. Of course, this _is_ the unthinkable for these most devout and isolated Tibetans. In this village, and in most villages in Tibet, there is no outside influence, no news, except that of the passing yak herder or truck driver. The movie must be shattering to their whole life's beliefs. This scene changes as the little dark-haired daughter screams.

A couple of the little girls sitting next to us begin to cry. I begin to feel angry. How can the Chinese show this garbage? Then it hits me. THIS is propaganda. The outside world hears that there is freedom of religion once again in China, while they practice their deliberate acts of brainwashing and confusion. The whole village must be here. What else is there to do on a Saturday night in Xegar?

In the next scene, the mother has now passed out from exhaustion and stress and is barely hanging onto the horse. The valiant

Chinese soldier staggers onward, down the narrow, stony paths still without a coat, lost in a blizzard, still looking for the missing child. The music is most emotional and heart-tugging and you can't believe that this soldier could be so long-suffering. He stumbles, falls down, gets back up, falls down, and the next thing we know he's walked back into the campsite of his comrades. Once there, he collapses, again. Why are these soldiers in Tibet? Are they guarding the Tibetan people from someone?

The soldier wakes up on a cot, near death. He has given all he's got and they've still not found the lost child. The Chinese hero leaves the unconscious woman in the warm tent of his fellow soldiers and strikes out AGAIN to find the lost Tibetan girl. The scenes skip fast now, as the soldier rushes from one mountaintop to another valley to another river crossing. He stops and asks Tibetan shepherds and farmers if they've seen her, and one says that he thinks he saw a small girl down at the temple.

The hero and his white horse come to a screeching halt in front of the imposing, deserted temple. He jumps off his horse and runs to the massive front door and begins to bang on it, beating his fists so hard that it seems they might start bleeding. The Chinese knight has finally arrived to save the lost girl from the evil, warped Buddhist "demons."

He forces his way into the temple, through an act of almost supernatural strength, and again the monstrous carvings inside the temple start "growling" and "moaning" and scaring the audience and even the Chinese hero. The evil monk hides behind a giant gold-covered Buddha, grinning slyly.

The soldier-hero makes his way, running and out of breath, into the lowest floor of the temple to dungeonlike cells, and finds the little child chained to a stone wall. The soldier beats the chains off with a spare rock, and carries her, tattered and filthy, out of the temple. There is one quick flashback to the head holy man, still smoking and now drinking liquor, as he and a few of his other monk friends are about to engage in some kind of orgy. They are obviously so corrupt and addicted to evil pleasures they don't care if one of their prisoners is escaping or not.

The soldier leaps onto his horse and gallops back to reunite the baby with its mother. They run to each other through a high-mountain pasture filled with wild flowers, in primitive slow motion. The Chinese soldier has done it all. He gets a spare horse for them and they all ride back to their home in the beautiful valley.

I felt stunned and then a raging anger began to build. How could they dare show this radical propaganda to these innocent and trusting Tibetan people? I imagined this film, and no telling how many others, making their way to every Tibetan village, over and over again. There was no critic on TV announcing that this was a shabby attempt to alter these fanatically religious people's attitude toward their beloved gods and Buddha. There were no critics doing film reviews here. There were no private companies making movies to entertain and enlighten, good, bad, or raunchy. All movies were made and paid for by the Chinese government, their prime purpose being to further the government's goals. Most Westerners know that Communists think that religion is the opium of the poor masses, that God is not only dead but never existed, that the government is God. I would never again complain about critics. If anything, I would push for _more_ criticism of our way of life, our media, our government.

Skip and I walked back to our tiny room with the dirt floor, stunned by our accidental experience. I felt a renewed and powerful appreciation for our government's laws enforcing everyone's freedom to believe and live as they so desired. . . . Freedom . . . I loved it and was beginning to understand how free I really was.

# The Dripping Ceiling___

The rain came down quietly all night, falling on the dirt roof of our room and eventually inside our room. Both of us were so mad about the propaganda flick that we just lay in our primitive beds, covered with two wool blankets, and stared for about an hour at the dripping ceiling, saying nothing.

I spoke through the darkness. "Skip, what would you eat right now if you could transport yourself back to Seattle?" I wanted to stop being mad so my weary body could sleep.

"I've been craving french fries, popcorn, and good beer," he answered like he was talking in his sleep. "I want some Better Cheddars, shrimp, smoked salmon, French onion soup, artichokes, deep-fried zucchini, and fettuccine on a tray for my appetizers."

Either I heard Skip's stomach growl or the Tibetan guard dog lying outside our room understood English and was also ready to head for the States.

"Then for my first main course I'd have some fried prawns, with lots of tartar sauce, fresh home-cut french fries, chilled prawns and horseradish sauce, a charcoal-broiled T-bone—medium rare with a baked potato with fresh butter, sour cream, bacon, onions, and corn on the cob right out of the garden. I'll have to think about dessert, later." Just the thought of the food Skip mentioned made my stomach crazy with desire.

Then I said, "I'd get me a thick, juicy hamburger, cooked medium well, covered with shredded, aged Cheddar cheese, topped off with a deep red slice of garden-fresh tomato. I'd put just the right amount of mayo on it, with some Vidalia onion sliced thin: all on a toasted, whole-wheat bun with some homemade sweet pickles on the side. Also, I'd want some roasted peanuts and a huge frosty mug of root beer, with four orders of well-done McDonald's french fries." It seemed like we were a hundred thousand miles away from our dreams that were never far away back home.

Skip put on his headphones and didn't talk anymore. I became horribly homesick. What was amazing to me was that I'd never felt like this before. I'd heard some of my friends at college say they got homesick. Not me. People asked me all the time when I was walking across America if I ever got homesick. I did occasionally but I never was more than a phone call away from my folks. And just knowing that if I needed to I could get on a plane and be home in a few hours made it a lot easier. But not here.

I wanted to look out across some rolling hills like I could do on our farm. I wanted to see huge, old maple trees, dark-green balls of leaves against massive splashes of light-green pastures. I missed seeing Shocker galloping across those lush pastures, his black mane flying behind his muscled neck. I hurt bad, wanting to get out of my car and have Rebekah and Jed come running out of the door toward me, yelling "Daddy." I wanted to take an early-evening ride in our Ford pickup, hearing the mockingbirds sing on a thousand fence-posts. I wanted to read a newspaper. I craved one of Barbara's incredible country-cooked meals of garden-grown green beans, country ham, and cornbread. I even wanted to see people I normally didn't even like. Where were MY people, MY tribe? Where were those Americans with that look of independence and freedom they didn't realize they had so much of? I even wished to change one of Jed's diapers. Hopefully, Jed and I would experience some of the world together, someday. And hopefully the world would be free for him to have a look around, if he wanted to. Skip was obviously thinking a lot, too, because he kept his headphones on a long time.

Our new bus driver was a dream. He looked very young but drove well. The only disturbing thing was that he had a rifle next to his seat. I wondered if there had been some kind of Tibetan uprising lately. But Fang Ming, the interpreter assigned to us, told me the bus driver carried the rifle with him to shoot rabbits while he drove to help provide him with some fresh meat for eating and trading. Fang all of a sudden pointed the gun out the window and began shooting at anything that wasn't owned by a Tibetan or *was* a Tibetan. Fang Ming said he'd never shot a gun before so the possibility of his hitting anything he aimed at was slim. One time as we passed a huge lake, Fang shot at the ducks and some fighting ravens.

There was much more snow on the mountains coming back from Chomolungma than going in. Some already had coated the high mountain valleys where the nomads spent their Himalayan summers. We passed huge herds of yaks. A lot of the yak herders were headed down from their summer grazing lands to the lower places where they lived "while winter passed."

About the only traffic on these roads other than yak herders, Tibetans on foot heading for market, and the very rare mountain-climbing team was Chinese army jeeps and trucks. One time we were stopped because there had been a head-on wreck between two army trucks.

Coming around the corner behind us were two nomadic men with faces that were used to living wild. They had some gold teeth, wore much turquoise and fur, and had on yak-leather boots. They carried rifles and long knives. Their peppy horses, more the size of long-bodied ponies, were loaded with supplies, plus some pelts. It was like meeting a couple of trappers in the early days of the American West, who were coming home with a summer's catch. Sticking out from under a frayed blanket on the back of one of the horses was part of a gray skin.

I walked over to take a picture and the meanest-looking one put his hand on his knife and shook his head. I walked up closer and while he tried to cover up the protruding skins, they slipped down. They were snow-leopard skins. We were in the prime habitat for the snow leopard, that rare gray ghost of the Asian wilds. To trap them, these men had to find the leopards' territories high in the deserted mountain ranges. Then they had to locate the trails the leopards traveled across narrow ledges. There the trappers had to place sharpened bamboo spears, coated with a horrible poison. Once the leopard broke its skin by stepping on the bamboo spear, it died.

If you're a Chinese driver assigned to drive the back roads of the farthest-back place in your far-back country, there's not a lot of thrills to go around. So the Chinese drivers decided that when they saw another truck or jeep coming they'd speed up and head right at them. They were playing Chinese Chicken. Whoever would slow down and get over in their "lane" first, lost. Going around blind corners, of course with no guardrails, all they'd do was beep their horns, lightly, and hope for a thrill in the road. Were there some young Tibetan kids playing? A herd of fifty nimble goats? Goats were fun because they did so many different things to escape.

Somehow the maniac-drivers must have known our bus was hauling foreigners because they left us alone. I was eternally thankful we never drove at night on these roads because all over China, the law says that when drivers approach each other they must turn off their lights!! Talk about crazy! Had they ever heard that headlight glare was better than a bumper in your face? We made it to Xigaze, and left early the next morning. Lhasa was a twelve-hour ride. It would take us almost fourteen.

# The Potala

For a Tibetan to see the Potala for the first time must be an experience that sends him to his knees. We were given the gift of experiencing this mighty Potala. You can't see it, only. You have no choice but to feel it. It overpowers you.

I've never been so overwhelmed by a building. It sat high above all of Lhasa, on a bare rock hill, all 999 rooms. Its glistening roofs of precious metal reflected the pure sun, as did its fortresslike walls of white and red stone. Some pieces of the stone walls were ten feet thick. It was a temple filled with 10,000 shrines and some 200,000 statues of gold, brass, wood, and ceramic, studded with countless jewels. It was a fortress bearing walls over a hundred feet tall, with a maze of hidden passageways connected by colossal wooden doors that seemed to take a giant to open. Since there are no trees in this barren land, and the wheel was not a part of the Tibetan's life then, trees used for the wood had to be carried from the forests of Bhutan on the backs of peasants for many hundreds of miles.

All the wooden pillars and window frames and doors were intricately painted in rich, glowing colors. Pink clouds flowed against brilliant red backgrounds. Cross-legged Buddhas were often the focus of paintings, meditating in the center of a lush valley, backdropped with jade-colored mountains, coral-colored fences, and floating holy men. Tibetan letters and symbols were carved precisely into the wooden doors. Gold inlay and overlay was everywhere. It was a shock seeing this Potala, surrounded by such a primitive lifestyle. It was almost like putting the grandest cathedral in Europe in the midst of the dustiest village in Mexico. The Potala was begun during the seventh century.

We were met at a creaky, massive bright-red door by a grizzled Tibetan who carried a flashlight. There was no electric light in this castle of stone and wood. He led us through many dark corridors illuminated only by a couple of little yak-butter candles. The stone walls dripped moisture and it was twenty degrees cooler inside.

We came to one room that seemed fifty feet tall. The guide's flashlight went out, and many of us bumped up against the wall. The place stank of a thousand years of musty tapestries, rancid yak-butter candles, and monks' sweat.

When my eyes finally adjusted to the deep darkness of a huge stone room lit with a few flickering candles, I saw it. A brass Buddha. It was three to four stories high. The hands were eight to nine feet long and shaped perfectly, the fingers graceful in the style of Asian art. Compared to the drab and dull-colored lands of Tibet, being in the Potala was like standing too close to a star. It was an overload of color. There was every shade of every color: red, blue, green, and so on. There were turquoise swastika signs inlaid in the floor. There was gold, brass, silver, and jade inlaid into the thousands of shrines, and white flowing scarfs draped over the altars. Offerings were given. They pinned to tapestries anything precious, like paper money, safety pins, bracelets, and keys. In another place we saw a tomb, forty-nine feet tall, shaped like a bottle covered with

100,000 ounces of gold. In it, preserved in salt, was the fifth Dalai Lama.

If the present Dalai Lama had still been ruler, maybe he would have invited us into his chambers at the Potala. But thirty-three years before we got here, the Dalai Lama, "the Living Buddha," had escaped on horseback to India, and has yet to return. At that time in 1951, the Chinese were spilling over the mountain ranges to the east, coming to take Tibet.

Just yesterday, returning from base camp, we'd driven through the small town of Gyangze, right at the crossroads of an ancient caravan route, where the Dalai Lama had escaped. I imagined seeing the fifteen-year-old Dalai Lama on his white horse, accompanied by a long caravan, single file, of monks and servants and royal cooks and fur-hatted bodyguards from Kham province, selected for their bravery. The fierce guards wore hats of fox skin and their rifles had fork rests. They were fleeing from Lhasa, across Karo La Pass, through a cut in the Himalayas to India.

As the Dalai Lama moved along the ancient trade route, long brass trumpets announced his coming as his caravan moved slowly over the windswept Tibetan tableland.

When his procession entered a hamlet or small town, there were clouds of incense and high officials pleading for a head pat (his official blessing). Their whole route was lined with small rocks to keep the evil spirits away while thousands of lamas lay flat on the ground, weeping, begging their master not to leave Tibet. As they feared then, the Dalai Lama, their beloved ruler, has not yet come home to the Potala.

For six hundred years this land was governed tightly by the lamas. Every family was required to give one of their sons to this ruling priesthood. There was once an ancient prophecy that this line of the Dalai Lamas, which began six centuries ago, would end with the thirteenth. The escaping Dalai Lama was the fourteenth. It was a prophecy that came true.

When we saw the Potala, only a few lonely caretakers lived here. It used to be a castle, a fort, a mighty temple, a capitol building. Now the Chinese said it was a museum, only recently reopened to the locals on Wednesdays for brief moments of worship. To the Chinese rulers of today the Potala was nothing but "relics of a superstitious past." My thoughts became near violent when I thought of some ruling government trying to tell me that my God, the Jesus my ancestors have worshiped for many centuries, was "now" dead. I couldn't imagine anyone turning our little brick church back in our small Tennessee town into a museum. Or more likely, since it's "nothing much" architecturally, blowing it up. Would they force our pastor Homer Kelly, to quit his "preaching" to start cutting weeds? I wondered how I would respond to being taken over, or "liberated," like these Tibetans had. Would I try to live within the "system" or die fighting? I'd probably be leading the underground forces.

As we left we saw a tall, gaunt man who wore thick leather gloves and had holes worn out of the knees of his pants. He held his hands together, praying, always. He would take about five steps and fall on his face, stretching out flat on the street. He was in an intense religious place inside his soul, doing a pilgrimage to the Potala. He was suffering to achieve a higher spiritual condition. I watched this man snake across the land. Devout Tibetans would "travel" like this for hundreds of miles from their home villages till they reached the Potala. Take a few steps, fall to the holy earth, pray without ceasing.

Today Tibetans live for the day when the Dalai Lama will come back to them from his exile. They will survive till that day or century. No oppressor, no government can kill their spirit by bombing their stone temples or by outlawing their gods. They will wait, silently doing what their oppressors demand. They will be ready. The light lit the rock walls of the Potala pearl-white. Whether I believed in their gods or not, I believed, as never before, in their _right_ to their gods.

# 27

## *"This Is an Adventure, Isn't It?"*

The mountain night is almost cold. We're leaving Tibet in the morning. Has it been a hundred years since I talked to Barbara and Rebekah and Jed? I felt a thousand years away from them. Compared to the base camp, Lhasa seemed much more "civilized." These wanderers of the streets had fewer coats of dust covering them than those nomads farther back in the Himalayas. I noticed pots of flowers in wide-open windows. It was August 30. A few days ago, Barbara had turned thirty-something. As far as I was concerned, someone could have nuked America and I wouldn't know about it.

The number-three baby could have come prematurely and I'd be a father again and the baby wouldn't have a name.

I wanted to call home, but I was afraid to. What if something bad had happened? To calm down I called a family friend, Pat, who had made me promise I would call her collect from Tibet. I got through surprisingly fast, sitting under the sky outside the compound manager's room. Pat was out to lunch but her assistant, Jennifer, accepted, thinking it was a crank call. (Pat said she never forgave herself for not being there when she got a call from Lhasa, Tibet!) I then called home. The static hurt my ears and I could barely hear the Chinese overseas operator. Above me were the stars of Tibet. They were as bright as a white neon bulb in a black cave. But here on the other side of the earth I could not recognize any of the constellations.

Barbara answered, sounding strong and independent. It was two A.M. here, about one P.M. there. "How are you feeling?" I blurted out. "Are Rebekah and Jed doing well? Have you heard anything from the parents? Is anything wrong?" I was coughing up a few weeks' worth of dust.

"The baby hasn't come yet. Remember the due date's not till mid-October." Her sweet southern voice was so soothing. Hearing it broke a dam inside me of repressed feelings of loneliness for them, home, our dog, Lacy. My lower lip quivered, something that had never happened before. Barbara sounded like she could run a country, she had everything so together.

I told her we were back in Lhasa, and that I would be leaving in the morning to meet Ran Ying in the city of Chengdu. She said that she'd heard that Ran Ying had left for China and that Ran Ying's in-laws, the Porters, had had Barbara over for dinner so that she could meet Ed and Ran Ying.

"Oh, that's right," she said, "Ran Ying mentioned something about having some problems getting her travel permits or tickets to Chengdu."

All during the phone call there were interruptions in the line like someone was monitoring the call. I found out later that all calls in and out of China are tapped, with an agent listening in every so often.

"Everything's fine here, honey," she said more than once. She said they had sent me a tape telling me all the news. I didn't get it in our one mail delivery at base camp, but that reminded me that I had a tape I made the night before I left of Rebekah interviewing me, acting like a reporter. I would listen to that soon. Barbara said that every night when she and Rebekah said her prayers, Rebekah pointed to a poster of Mount Everest that Skip had sent her and asked where I was on that mountain. She said she would point to a spot a bit higher each day. Jed was fine, although he'd pulled some of Rebekah's hair out this morning fighting over a doll. Barbara signed off by telling me that all our friends had been calling her, checking in on her and me. Mr. George, Larry Hughes, my folks and hers, Wally, Terri, Lamar and Honey Alexander . . .

"I love you," she said, as she was hanging up. I heard a crack in her strong voice.

"And I miss all of you more than I can . . ." I couldn't finish.

Our jet followed a wide river valley as we gained altitude to get over the Himalayas. The steepest mountains I'd ever flown over came straight down on either side of the river. I had a window seat. Skip sat next to me. The plane was jammed full and for a time I didn't think we would be able to gain enough altitude to make it over the mountains before the river valley ran out. These mountains were the youngest on earth, and tons of snow still lay on their vertical faces. The snow never stopped melting, but when winter came again, there was always a lot left. Some of Asia's great rivers were born below us in this eastern chunk of the Himalayas.

Now when I looked down and saw little round, bright-green fields at the bottoms of mountains, I knew I was seeing barley fields. The more fields I saw grouped together, the bigger the Tibetan village built around them. When I saw a group of black shapes in the highest, most distant meadow, I knew they were yaks. When across from them was a glacier that had only been touched by a few yak herders, I could believe it. When I saw enchanting stone pathways, following the barren riverbank, I knew they'd be used to take skins and other goods to trade at the markets that were weeks away in Lhasa. Before the jet got too high in the sky I could even see life-defying trails two feet wide, five-hundred feet above a wild gorge. I knew some Tibetans lived somewhere at the end of them. The whole time I'd been here in Tibet, I'd wanted to follow stone trails like these to wherever they led. But for now I couldn't.

What we now flew over was the most isolated part of Tibet, an area of nonstop mountains with no access other than by foot, horse, or yak. I looked down till I got dizzy. The land below was named "The Land of Great Corrugations." I scanned for a small light-gray shape chasing a wild blue sheep through a patch of green closed below the ice-covered peaks. It was my last chance to see a snow leopard.

At times in Tibet I'd been frustrated because I was traveling with the team, a group. I yearned to travel alone, stopping when I found someone fascinating, like the holy man back in Xegar, or the head yak herder, and immersing myself in their lives. Someday, I would come back to Tibet. Maybe I'd bring Rebekah or Jed to this most fascinating place of thin oxygen, massive mountains, and the flashes of the whitest smiles. I'd buy three of the toughest gray horses with the black muzzles (legend said they were strongest), pack our supplies on one and myself, Jed, and Beka on the others and follow these rock trails to whatever village they led to. We'd ride to places where they'd never seen white-faced people. I promised myself that I'd be back to Tibet, "my" mountain place.

We made our descent in Chengdu, hours after we'd taken off from Lhasa. I was worried about Ran Ying. What if she hadn't made it to Chengdu? How would I find her? How would she find me? If she hadn't been able to get this far into the interior of China, could she get a message to me? I'd worry about that if I got off the plane and she wasn't there. "This *is* an adventure, isn't it?" I whispered to myself.

# *A Certain Shade of Red*

We were about to come down into Chengdu (pronounced "Chung doo"), the largest city in Sichuan Province. This was the most densely populated province in the country. Looking down I could see rice paddies outlined by the darker green of bamboo. Many workers with round yellow straw hats were bent over in the fields. As we lost altitude, I saw pigs roaming freely in the dirt yards of the farmers' thatched-roofed homes. We flew over two boys herding a flock of white ducks. The ducks scattered at the loud sounds of our jet's engines.

On the roads I saw only a couple of trucks but many, many horse-drawn carts. There were very few poles carrying electricity or phone lines, and I saw only one rusty-looking tractor. Ancestors of these peasant farmers had been working this land for thousands of years. Every inch of available ground was farmed.

My clothes stuck to my skin and palm trees sagged under the hammer of summer in tropical China. I was standing on the runway at the Chengdu airport. Pale Chinese men in uniform watched us all get off the plane and at the same time kept relatives and friends from rushing in our direction.

I scanned the crowds for Ran Ying. Everyone I saw had black hair. No one stood off alone; they all crowded together. Ran Ying had been easy to spot the first time I met her back home in the country cafe in Spring Hill. Now I was worried I might not be able to pick her out from all the other Chinese. She wasn't with the first group standing outside at the edge of the runway. Almost everyone wore a similar type of wrinkled blue shirt and pants. The people shouted greetings to each other in shrill voices for the Chinese talk very fast.

We were funneled down a narrow walkway, between two primitive concrete buildings. It was about 95 degrees. A bright-green lizard leaped onto my arm from a huge green leaf covered with water droplets from an afternoon thundershower. Ingrid was greeted by a new special officer assigned to "take care" of us while we were in Chengdu. I didn't feel a part of "us," anymore. But where was Ran Ying? Maybe she would be waiting in the city at our hotel, which was for foreigners only. There were a few cabs in China, but the native Chinese people couldn't afford to use them. Maybe she had a problem getting to the airport. Was she even in central China? Could she be stranded in Beijing?

The officer in charge told us to put our bags down under some palm trees, which offered little shade from the humid, silver haze of the afternoon sky. If in fact something had happened to Ran Ying, what would I do? What _could_ I do? Would I have the courage to go on exploring without her? I wouldn't understand ONE WORD anyone said, but I could see a lot, maybe find someone who spoke some bits of English. I'd already tried getting an interpreter, but they'd said all interpreters were being used. I wished I was more gifted at picking up different languages. Chinese sounded impossible.

Even if I couldn't find Ran Ying, I was glad that my requests for an official interpreter had been turned down. Since I'd been here I'd learned that official Chinese interpreters are highly classified government employees, and tightly controlled. They probably are agents. They are debriefed either every day or at the end of every assignment to see what they've learned from their foreign guests. And the questions they are allowed to answer are very limited. If you ask a question that's off limits, you're ignored. A typical exchange with our interpreter in Tibet went like this.

"Ah, excuse me, Fang, but do you know where I could get a copy of Chairman Mao's Little Red Book?" I asked.

The Red Book is filled with Chairman Mao's philosophy and for a long time in China was like a Bible to a billion people. I figured Fang would know because I saw him more than once reading a pocket-sized edition on the bus.

The first technique is avoidance, implying "I did not hear you or I'm ignoring you. *You* decide and if you think I'm ignoring you, then maybe you will be polite and not ask the same question."

"Fang. Where can I get a Red Book?"

"What kind of book you interested in, Peter?" Fang answered.

"You know, the Red Book with Chairman Mao's quotes."

"Oh," he said, expressing joy at "finally" understanding what I was talking about, "that book. For some reason I think bookstores all out of them. You may want to check, maybe." Fang turned his face toward the window of the bus; in other words, "Leave me alone." The Chinese government of the present is trying to distance itself from Chairman Mao.

Two young Chinese women, both very beautiful, got out of a bus and began walking toward us. Their faces were rounder than I remembered Ran Ying's being. They walked leisurely, with a lot of movement from side to side. I recalled Ran Ying's stride to be longer, as if she hurried wherever she was going. These graceful, shapely young women knew exactly how to walk through humid air. Maybe the one on the right was Ran Ying and she was just relaxed being "home." Maybe the other one was the friend she mentioned that she would stay with here. Confronted with the possibility of being alone in a drastically foreign culture, my mind forgot what it knew about Ran Ying. I was confused, a bit panicky. Maybe that is Ran Ying! The young ladies walked by us.

"Ran Ying, is that you?" I said.

They stopped, turned around, and looked puzzled. Maybe Ran Ying had forgotten what I looked like. How many men with red hair, red beard, and Himalayan-reddened skin could there be in this city of over four million? One or two?

"Ran Ying . . . It's me. Peter Jenkins."

They came back toward me a few more steps. Their clothes were not stiffly pressed, but they were neater than most of the other Chinese rushing around here. They giggled and walked away toward the runway. Three pilots came by right after them. Oh. They must have been stewardesses. Wick had said that the best-looking ladies in China were from Chengdu.

I walked around the corner of the front of the airport building. There were a few buses parked in front, and a row of bicycles. My eyes scanned every Chinese person, looking for any clue that they might be Ran Ying. Everyone I looked at had on blue or white shirts and blue pants. Last time I'd seen Ran Ying she had short hair. It seemed that her face was rather thin, and more long than round. Ran Ying had said that she was planning to dress in Chinese-style clothes when we traveled because the people would be less suspicious and talk to her more.

Rounding a corner from the building to our left was a soldier from the People's Liberation Army. He looked taller than most Chinese men, about six feet. His crumpled green cap had a red star on it. There was no way of telling what his rank was, for ranks were not displayed on their uniforms. That was one of Chairman Mao's many ideas. Walking with him was a young Chinese woman in jeans and a plain white blouse. She looked pale and tired. He looked stern. I did not see a weapon.

They spotted us and walked toward Skip. Ran Ying saw me at the same time I thought I saw her.

"Pe-ter . . . !?!"

"Ran Ying!?!"

"Yes," we said. It felt so good to see someone who had been home in Tennessee recently.

I remembered that Ran Ying had worn makeup when I met her. Now she wore none. No Chinese woman I saw ever wore makeup. Just recently had women been able to wear the color red again. Only certain shades were available. The recovery from the Cultural Revolution, when Mao's tyrannical widow forced everyone to wear drab no-color clothes, was slow.

Who was this army man standing patiently beside her? I wondered. Had the government decided that I was too inquisitive, based on the reports they received from Fang and Bao, our observant interpreter and liaison officer in Tibet? Maybe they'd found out Skip and I saw that propaganda movie in Xegar. Or that I took pictures of those military-looking buildings, hidden in Tibet. Maybe this army man would accompany us everywhere we went, "helping" us ask people questions, "protecting" us so we wouldn't get lost.

"Peter, this is my friend's husband. He is our age, would very much like to make our stay in Chengdu pleasant." Ah, ha. I thought so. I'm being watched. Ran Ying said he was an officer in the army and at one time was Ping-Pong champion of all Sichuan Province. "He wants to practice his English on you. Please speak slowly." Was Tennessee-slow slow enough for him?

I reached out my hand and we shook hands. He looked me over as if his eyes were a microscope. He had an athlete's composure, or was that the calm of an espionage agent? His name was Li Jong. He said I could call him Lee.

"He shy," Ran Ying smiled, politely. "He told me to tell you that Lee was his American name. Help for you and him to be friends." The thing in China right now is to learn the English language and to get yourself an American nickname.

I didn't know exactly what to think but Ran Ying seemed to be comfortable with the guy. Ran Ying had indeed almost not gotten here. As hard as she'd tried to get a plane ticket to Chengdu from Beijing, she had not been able to, so she had to take a train. It took three days, sitting up the entire way. That class of train ride is called "hard seats." I told them some stories about Tibet and they were intrigued. The Chinese people rarely get to travel around their own country.

Now that the tensions of finding Ran Ying were over, I felt a deep sadness. Tibet was very obviously gone. The mountains were gone. The highest natural thing I could see was mounds of rice recently harvested by hand. The crisp, blue, thin air that made me feel bouncy and clean was replaced with heavy, humid air that staggered me when I first felt it. We'd left a land of rock, of white snows, of stone homes, and single turquoise earrings. Here in Sichuan Province the fields were mud for growing rice, and a white T-shirt could not stay white long because of the constant sweating and backbreaking work. The first homes I saw nearest the airport were bamboo huts with either tin or thatched roofs. It would take some time to get over missing Tibet.

Ran Ying wanted to know if I was hungry. She said, "Sichuan cooking may be best in all of China." Lee knew where all the great restaurants were, the ones that the local Chengdu people went to. "You want to go eat something?"

"Sure do." Tibetan food was something I could easily forget. Ran Ying commented about how much weight I'd lost.

# The Delicious
# Garden_____

"Yick—Shi-ma, blah, blah, blah," said the waitress who looked surprised to see me. Her black hair was pulled back, her face was sweating. It was a steam bath out in the claustrophobic back streets of Chengdu. In this narrow restaurant there was no ventilation, and of course, no air conditioning. Based on her surprised expression, I may have been the first Westerner ever to eat here.

She spoke her Chinese quickly, and with much emotion. I had no idea whether she was mad, happy, confused, or elated. Ran Ying looked at me out of the corner of her eye, kept eating her pigeon soup and said, "She say you very good with chopsticks. How you get that way, she want to know?"

"Tell her I'm a Chinese from a town next to the Russian border where the Chinese and Russians have intermarried for many centuries. I look like my Russian father," I said, feeling in a wise-guy mood. I was very happy to finally be eating the great Chinese food I'd heard so much about.

The lady continued staring at every detail of me, which was something I'd have to get used to since it happens to foreigners all over China, especially if you're alone.

"Peter! No. Maybe she think I foolish person," Ran Ying said in her high, edgy voice. She had already reverted to the Chinese way of speaking English, no wasted words to get the point across.

"All right. Tell her all Americans eat with chopsticks. Only English eat with knife and fork." She never looked up from her soup. Chinese people bend way over, their mouths right on top of the bowl they're eating from, often shoveling the rice and other food in with their chopsticks.

"Tell her I'd never been good at this till I got to China about a month ago." I was really showing off now, grabbing almost microscopic pieces of some fried pork with my "sticks."

The waitress stood there so patiently awaiting my answer. She smiled widely. Ran Ying told her I'd only been using chopsticks for a month or less, most of the time in Tibet where they didn't have much good food. She beamed with pride in her beloved China. An American using sticks so well, "not even loudly demanding fork." She acted like this was a big deal.

Her grandfather, Zhuang Zhi Qing, was an "Old Master" cook. He dealt us some unbelievable food. Old Masters are considered national treasures, and cooking in China is a national resource held in "most high" regard. The name of the restaurant, Ke Yuan, meant "Delicious Garden." The great Master, now seventy-two, had been cooking professionally for sixty years. Now for the first time in his life he was cooking at his own eating place. Outside, on the street jammed with life, was a blackboard with the menu written in green chalk. In the very front of this restaurant, the ultimate Chinese restaurant, there was a little plastic tub with some live carp in it, to entice the people in.

All the simple wooden tables around us were filled with people eating from many dishes and drinking tea. For the five years Ran Ying had been living in America she had been deeply homesick for this kind of eating and this kind of place. Everyone spoke Chinese.

Everyone had black hair. Chinese people filled the streets on bicycles, in sleeveless T-shirts, and the eternal blue pants. Householders set their pet finches out on their windowsills, for air and to sing to the passing crowds. Everyone was busy. Big city energy was everywhere. Ran Ying was in Chinese-eating heaven.

Lee, the PLA man, watched my every expression. He acted as though he expected me not to like the food. Or perhaps was he assigned to watch my every move? So far, he'd escorted us everywhere we'd gone. Maybe I was getting paranoid in all the crowd of Sichuan Province, after the isolation of Tibet. Maybe he was just curious about Americans. He seemed so very willing to please me, and very much wanted me "to have great feeling about his country," Ran Ying said. He said to Ran Ying that he couldn't understand why I wanted to come to a restaurant that all the local people patronized. We could go to a special tourist dining hall. NO, NO, I told them quite a few times before they finally believed I was not just trying to be polite.

Ran Ying was staying with Lee's mother-in-law, a high-ranking member of the Communist party. I was staying at Chengdu's only hotel for foreigners. I had wanted to stay at a hotel that the Chinese people used, but I was told that was forbidden. The guards at the entrance to my hotel at first wouldn't let Ran Ying and Lee pick me up in the morning. Ran Ying pointed out, "They have just put air conditioners in some rooms at your hotel, and there is hot water, both of which are not available at regular hotels for Chinese." And I was used to worrying about whether the motels I stayed in had morning newspapers, swimming pools, saunas, complimentary coffee, vans to pick me up at the airport . . . "Peter, I heard your hotel even serves french fries!" Ran Ying said in all seriousness.

All our food was served in thick white china bowls, plates, or platters. Lunch included six dishes. When our waitress brought out the first two dishes on oval plates, I asked Ran Ying what they were. "Peter, it's better if you want to experience this real China food, to eat it first. Later, I tell you what it is." It smelled wonderfully delicious.

Then I saw a table of four Chinese men eating something hungrily, in very thick, rough ceramic bowls that were steaming. Sticking up through the steam was a fishtail. "This restaurant famous for their whole-fish soup," Ran Ying explained. She must have noticed the expression of my eyes and figured what I was thinking. Ran

Ying was already beginning to answer my thoughts. If this was no accident, I figured we were getting off to a great start communicating.

My chopsticks tried everything on all six platters. Then there were two bowls of soup, both of which I recognized. One was my favorite and by far the most delectable I'd ever experienced. Egg-drop soup, with incredibly tasty, finely cut-up wild onions. The other was, well, something I'd never seen before. Well, I'd seen the ingredients in flight. It was whole-pigeon soup, the feet sticking up through the pigeon broth. This was "family-special" dish the Old Master wanted me to try. By now the whole street knew there was a red-faced foreigner in their eating heaven. I tried the pigeon soup ever so sensitively, which is my "Chinese" way of saying I barely tried it.

I recognized almost nothing else in the other dishes, not one like anything I'd ever seen. They all tasted fantastic. What a drastic switch from Xegar and my involuntary gagging. Cooking in Chengdu, especially using the Sichuan style, was considered to be the best Chinese cooking by some connoisseurs. So far, I loved it all, except the pigeon soup. And so far, I had no idea what I had been eating, except the pigeon.

Since there was no ice or cold drinks, the Chinese drank beer and sodas warm to hot, depending on how hot it was that day. I never thought I could crave something so insignificant as a cold Pepsi. I CRAVED one. Captain Lee ran out to a street vendor and bought twelve homemade orange-flavored Popsicles. He was feeling confident now, watching me eating faster than he was, and decided to try his English. "This"—he asked Ran Ying something I guessed how to say Popsicle—"pa-sik-L." He smiled proudly. "This pa-sik-L you try . . . afta . . . eat . . . bi-te. . . . He made a hand signal in the shape of a dish and pointed to one of the dishes. I picked up a piece of it, ate it, and took a bite of the orange Popsicle. Captain Lee was profoundly thrilled. He patted me on the back, chop, chop, chop.

Ran Ying said at one time it was not appropriate for a military man to be seen with a foreigner. She asked Lee if this was okay, and he said this was no problem and that he would say to anyone who asked that he was practicing his English. He seemed incredibly relaxed about being with me, considering that some people, especially some of his older superiors, considered it wrong. It seemed that a good excuse for Chinese who really want to get to know Americans is to say, "I'm practicing my English."

When Captain Lee heard that I would be writing about all my experiences in China, his relaxed expression changed. He and Ran Ying became involved in a super-fast conversation, in Chinese, of course. Ran Ying shook her head and said, "Peter, what I am to say very, very important. My friend like you very much. But because of all the bad things that happened during the Cultural Revolution, this young man afraid that if you use his name in book, someday, even fifteen year from now, he could be put in jail as traitor for having been with you. This kind of thing happened during Cultural Revolution. Would you please change his name if he in book?"

I looked very seriously at Captain Lee and said, "Can I change your name to Billy Bob?"

"No . . . I request . . . my name be . . . John Wayne," he retorted, catching on immediately.

(Of course, I changed his name as I promised.)

It was an interesting experience to have the Popsicle in between all these different dishes. One dish was flame-throwing hot, one was very sweet, two were remarkably tangy, and one was buttery, sort of rubbery. I was kind of afraid to find out about that one. The icy orange pops cooled me off a little. Captain Lee put his Popsicle in his beer to melt it. I didn't know how he could stand that.

Lee had a very important question to ask me. He stared at Ran Ying and me till we looked his way. He attempted a few words, stuttering, totally out of any order, and instead asked Ran Ying to ask me. "Do you really like the Chinese food or you just being polite?" He was concerned that Americans would not like their food. I told him I was not polite in Tibet, I almost starved. He thought that was funny and wanted to know how I almost starved and yet was so big. I told him so far I loved this great food and I was sure I would get bigger here in Chengdu. He smiled delightedly.

Ran Ying decided I was ready to find out what I'd been enjoying. "First we have specialty of great Master, pigeon soup. Then we had fried pig kidney. That one you like very much was red bits of fried meat with small pieces of green pepper. Then the dish that was rubbery, had buttery taste, that was pig intestine, cut up very thin." There were also crunchy, fried intestines cooked in a wok with some different vegetables like cucumber, and onion, too. Then there was red pepper and pork, which was not hot but very good. We also had some fish and cubes of winter melon. This was more like a stew and it had some sea cucumber in it.

For some reason it reminded me of the last meal we'd had in Lhasa before leaving. That special "treat" had been placed in a hollowed-out half of watermelon. Each person had to dig around with their chopsticks till they snagged something. Someone fished out the head of a rooster! Fang had become very excited upon seeing the rooster head appear and passionately rescued it from Russ's chopsticks before it hit the floor. Speaking of hitting the floor, when a Chinese bites into something he doesn't like the taste of, he just spits it out on the floor of the restaurant. Ran Ying did this several times. Including the pigeon and the soup—four dishes and three bowls of rice and six orange Popsicles, the price was eleven yuan each, or thirty-four yuan for the three of us. That was less than five dollars each.

The waitress was now very much excited. She noticed that there was little left on any of our plates. "Please come back into the kitchen with me," she pleaded with Ran Ying, pulling on her arm, gently.

Earlier, as we had strolled down the crammed street where the Delicious Garden was, Ran Ying had expressed great surprise that people were actually standing in front of their restaurants beckoning and shouting for us to come in and eat there. They were saying "Come here, come here!! We have the best food in Chengdu." When we halted a moment to discuss what we wanted, for they all had their specialties, they went wild with salesmanship. Some proclaimed their whole fish, or special noodles. The longer we lingered the more they shouted and hollered and jumped. It was nice to be wanted!

The reason Ran Ying was so surprised was that she could not remember the Chinese people being allowed to promote their business. This was considered capitalistic, a method of the enemy, which was totally unacceptable before Ran Ying had left her country for the USA. Ran Ying said it was obvious that the people were being allowed much more free enterprise.

We were led back to the Old Master. Everything he cooked with was ancient. Some of the handles on his knives were almost worn through. And they'd been sharpened so many times the blades were paper thin. There was no electric stove or gas range. Definitely no microwave. But the Master's fire and his control of it, was everything. The Master used his heat like a conductor leads twelve violins. Sometimes he steamed a food first, then deep fried. . . . Or he would know how to simmer some vegetable straight from the market, then "fry very quick" in hot oil. The Master's knowledge of his fire produced an orgy of exquisite tastes. It used to be that ancient Chinese cooking instructions said, "Cook until one bundle of wood is used up." Now coal was his fuel. He cooked on top of a primitive little clay oven that had a hole in the top of it, like the top of a volcano, glowing red/orange. He cooked much in his cherished metal wok, shaped like an inverted Chinese straw hat.

There's a real art to frying things. We watched this Old Master make us a special dish. First he put the shredded pork in the wok and then he would reach into various pots and ladle out a little chicken broth, pull out a few leeks, and at the appropriate second throw in a little pepper, sliced green onions, and other ingredients. He would flip them or stir them around. The brilliant master chef was dressed in the little sleeveless T-shirt so many of the Chinese men wear, especially in this hotter climate. When he was finished, he'd pour the result out very elegantly onto a plate. Then he would take some chicken broth and throw it into the remaining grease in his wok, and pour the chicken broth and grease into another pot where he was boiling two chickens. Every split second of his time, all his movements and all ingredients, were used super efficiently in his own special genius. I loved watching him create.

I shook the Master's hand upon leaving. I wanted to show him how much I respected him and his work, so I asked him and his family to line up in the open front of the Delicious Garden and I took their picture. I certainly didn't need a picture to remember that meal for life! On the way toward the largest open-air market in Chengdu we stopped at a specialty dessert place. We got a pastry made of two kinds of ground-up rice, soy-bean meal, sugar, sesame seed, and nuts. Ran Ying loved it, but I didn't think it was very good. It was interesting to see how quickly Captain Lee caught on that when I said something was okay, it probably meant that it didn't taste good to me. Both he and Ran Ying reacted very quickly to the subtleties of my different responses.

# 30

## *The Way the Light Shines on Jade*_____

Captain Lee headed back to work. Soon after, we passed an old man with a long stick across his back, stained by years of sweat and polished by rubbing on his shoulders. Balanced on both ends were many intricately woven baskets. Chengdu had the best baskets in China, Ran Ying said. When he was out of hearing range Ran Ying began shouting in Chinese, momentarily thinking I could understand what she said. There was no way after a few meals and some nifty stick work with the chopsticks that I could be looking Chinese. I just waited for her to realize who she was talking to and smiled. I took her speaking to me in Chinese as a compliment.

Ran Ying was slim, five feet three, and her hair was shorter than most Chinese women we saw. Her arms were long, she had a young teenager's figure, and probably weighed about 110 pounds. She seemed happy, and got happier as she closely studied my reaction to her motherland and interpreted it to be good. For the first time since I'd landed in the capital of Sichuan Province, we were not being escorted by Lee or his wife, Ling.

I have always believed that you can tell more about a person through their family life than anything else. When I'd met Ran Ying in Tennessee, she seemed almost withdrawn. Maybe she still felt insecure in America or she was unsure of how she felt about the United States. Now, on her soil, breathing Chinese air, she became increasingly thrilled with life!

"My great-grandfather had two sons and my grandfather was the younger one," she said after walking by an old, wrinkle-faced woman whose feet were stubbed and twisted. Ran Ying said the old woman's feet had been bound when she was a little girl. Then she told me about her grandmother.

"The family needed someone to help with the housework, so my great-grandfather bought a girl. He bought her for work, and for my grandfather. While she was too young to be married, she had to do housework, but when she turned eighteen, she was supposed to become the son's wife. She was sold by her father, who was very poor peasant, needed money to feed family. They were Hui people [a minority Muslim group], they couldn't marry into a rich family. That's another reason my great-grandfather bought this girl. This way she could become a lady."

"So she was your grandmother?" I asked.

"Yes . . . when my mother was seven years old, my grandmother got cancer and toward the end of life she really hurt a lot and she hated my mother. Every time she saw my mother she would try to grab her and beat her. So my mother had to run away from her every time." A bicycle drove by us with three live chickens tied to the back fender bags.

"My mother had a younger sister—two or three years younger— but she not live with the family. My grandmother send her to the countryside to live with peasant because she was not very pretty, like my mother was. They did not take her back till she was older. She grow up in countryside and nobody like her. The family send money to the peasant every year to support her till finally the family took her back. Chinese do that a lot. It's part of our culture. Girls not important like sons are. Pretty girls okay. Ugly ones could be sold, given away, even with rich family like my mother's family." I'd grabbed another homemade Popsicle, vanilla-flavored. Eating one is about the only way to cool off in the summer in central China. I was fascinated by Ran Ying's story of her family.

"My grandmother had seven children altogether. The first five died. Then my mother almost died when she was one, but she barely lived. They changed her name, she became strong. Smart. My mother was always sick. They gave her the name that meant 'Red Rays'—like in the morning sky. She was beautiful, so they gave her beautiful name. So her mother went to a fortune teller and fortune teller look at her and say, 'Everybody has five things that make up body—gold, wood, soil, water, fire.' They said my mother not have enough wood, so grandmother change her name to 'Forest,' because forest have lots of wood. And it was just like magic, she was never sick again."

"My name, Peter, means 'Rock'," I said.

"Mine means 'Light on Jade'," Ran Ying added.

September 2, 1984, would be a day to put in my top-ten eating experiences. It was right up there with Annie Winkler's Appalachian country meal of melt-in-your-mouth cornbread with fresh-churned butter served alongside canned, shredded, and home-cooked ham, roasting ears floating in butter, pickled eggs, and black-as-coal coffee; the unforgettable Cajun meal in southern Louisiana of boiled shrimp, raw oysters, fresh turtle soup and even pickled crawfish tails; the breakfast of smothered elk steak and sourdough pancakes I ate while enjoying one of Perk Vicker's views of the Rocky Mountains; the night I stopped being a vegetarian as Homer the mountain man and I devoured a feast of lamb chops we'd just cooked on a coat hanger over the sizzling coals of his dugout fireplace; salmon pulled from a fishing net out of the frigid seas of Alaska and cooked that night in the galley of the boat, while rocking in a gentle sea. It competed in its own way with an Idaho cowboy's supper at W.T. and Viola Williams's table, highlighted with one of their tender-as-bread beefsteaks. Today shot into my top ten with a bullet.

We were at Sichuan University in Ran Ying's friends' third-floor apartment. Captain Lee and his fidgety wife, Ling, rushed around the tiny apartment that was considered luxurious. In America it wouldn't meet the standards of federal welfare housing. The bathroom was barely big enough to stand up in and you went to the bathroom in a hole in the roughly finished concrete floor, then turned on a hose and "flushed" it. The walls were rugged concrete. Ran Ying relaxed and talked with Ling's deep-voiced mother. And then there was the amazing Sheng Shu Li. "My English name is Shirley" was the first thing she said. She was a teacher in the Sichuan Cooking Technical School.

Shirley's first dish was Eastern Rabbit, a specialty from her mother's hometown in east Sichuan Province. I would not have chosen the name Shirley for this surprisingly open, warmly attractive young woman. I told her she should change her English name to Raquel, as in Raquel Welch. Her husband, a nurse at the local mental institution, came home later after work.

"To make rabbit dish," Shirley said as she cooked by the open window, "you put soy sauce and sugar and 'smell material' that grows in a tree, in with ginger and wild onion." (Smell material, shaped like a star, is exactly what it sounds like. It adds a special smell to the dish.) "Then stir all of these together. Soak the rabbit for two hours. Cut it into small chunks, then put rabbit in very hot oil. Stir-fry about a minute to let the water cook out. Add dried red pepper too."

Ran Ying explained to me that one of the major reasons the Chinese always cook their food cut into small, bite-sized pieces is because fuel is so precious a thing to share with over a billion people, and food cut into pieces cooks with much less fuel. It also soaks up the special spices and sauces from many more exposed sides, and by cooking fast it retains its nutritional value.

Then Shirley made something she called Fish-Tasting Pork. She added some fungus—a fungus from a tree—it is a VERY spicy dish. When a native from the Sichuan Province tells you the food is hot, as in spicy, that means it will burn holes in your throat. "Normal" spicy melts fillings in your teeth. The people in this province eat the spiciest food in China. The red pepper used in this dish is soaked in salty water for half a year in a pot. There must be water around the cover of the pot so bacteria won't get in.

To go with the Fish-Tasting Pork and Eastern Rabbit, she whipped up something she called Cool. "It has pork," she said, "but special thing is the vegetable that grows in the fields, just like you would grow any other kind of vegetable. Grain shoot is its name."

Shirley put a splash of fresh cooking oil into her wok, which smoked slightly. She continued, "After you finish cutting grain shoot, then you get the oil hot and then pour it on the green onions. Then pour the whole thing on the grain shoot and stir into pork." Her concentration was intense.

"This dish has a cool taste. It not spicy, no pepper in it." What a wonderful combination of tastes it all was.

Then she made something called Old Man's Dish. She explained in her best English. The more relaxed she became, the better she spoke. "An old man made the basic recipe for this dish. It has cubes of pork and peanuts, leeks and ginger, pepper and garlic. This I just call spicy. It's not really hot, but definitely not cool. Nice combination between the peanuts and the pork," she said darting her hand into the wok to taste her brilliance.

I couldn't believe that after two hours she was still coming up with special dishes. She made something that Ran Ying said was Chinese dumplings and one of the most popular foods in this nation. It's called Jiaozi (pronounced "Chow-zá"). Ran Ying explained it to me and taught me how to make the dumplings. "The filling is a mixture of pork and leek, like hamburger. You roll out the little dough, whole-wheat dough, and wrap up pork and leek mix. Close it up and don't let any out." I attempted to make these Chinese dumplings with my big fingers with little success. Shirley's fingers were as nimble as a gymnast's perfect moves. She and Ran Ying and everyone joined around the table to make the dumplings and talk. They were very good boiled in hot water and then dipped in either a hot sauce or a mild kind of a soy sauce.

After more than three hours of cooking, everything was ready. She brought many dishes into their living room, as there was no such thing as wasting space on a dining room—or for that matter on a full-time table to do nothing but eat on. The "kitchen" in this apartment that anyone in China would feel privileged to live in was the size of a small walk-in closet.

They were very proud of this Sichuan feast and a bit nervous. They were still not confident that I really enjoyed, even loved, much of their food. I was not just being polite. I was an addict! They must have been feeling pretty confident because they brought out some aged eggs for their honored guest. They were black on the outside and looked like they were unearthed dinosaur eggs. Really, it's just another ingenious way the Chinese have figured out to store food. They dip fresh eggs into a mixture of lime, salt, seasonings, ash, and tea. They let it harden and store the black-coated eggs in a clay pot.

They are still "great" to eat six months later. They would have been deeply hurt if I had not eaten some of this. I was highly appreciative in my treatment of this delicacy. I took the most tiny bites.

Shirley was much more open than most Chinese and asked me many times if I could help her come to live in the United States. That was her lifetime dream, she said. She envied Ran Ying, she told me, "But I married already, so could not marry American to get to live in USA." The mother of Ling frowned openly as Shirley expressed her desire to come to America. "If you like my cooking so . . . much, maybe . . . other Americans like too. Could . . . I . . . open restaurant?"

# 31

## *The Freedom to Dance*_____

The one word that captivated all these young Chinese was "disco." They made me promise I would teach them how. Ling's mother smiled politely, and said little. Ling's father, who had died recently, had been a high-ranking diplomat to Pakistan and was considered China's foremost authority on that culture. He too had been an important member of the Party. The closer I came to finishing eating the more they spoke of learning to disco. I told him the new word for disco in America was "party."

They acted like discoing was the wildest, most forbidden thing any young Chinese person could ever imagine doing. Their excitement made me remember how I'd felt when I heard my parents discussing Elvis Presley and the horrible way he danced with the lower half of his body. Or when in ninth grade I was almost a "radical" because I wanted to let my hair touch the top of my ears. Now, long hair was boring and short hair was in. "Disco is dead," chanted hip Americans. "LONG LIVE ROCK AND ROLL!"

Disco wasn't dead here, _that_ revolution was just getting cranked up. I was being counted on to lead it! It was a thrill living so dangerously in China. The first thing my hosts did to prepare for our revolutionary activity was to pull some of the chairs out of the way, clearing a space for a dance floor. They constantly looked over at me, nervously, to see if they were following their revolutionary leader's specifications. "Is this floor space big enough for wild disco dancing?" I nodded that everything was fine.

Then they pulled out one of their most prized possessions, which was always kept covered with a beautifully handwoven tapestry. It was their double cassette deck. Owning a cassette deck in China was a major achievement. Until recently, it was impossible to get and considered a decadent waste. They treated it as if it were a brand-new Mercedes 300SL. They looked to see if I approved of their music machine. I nodded.

A woman's shrill voice sounded from the other room. Ling's mother called her out into the front stairway. Ling returned, holding her head down, her normally alert face twitching with tension. She closed the curtains. It was still daylight. I pulled out one of my trusty tapes, a recording of an old Steely Dan album. One of the songs was "Pretzel Logic," which I thought would appeal to them.

I turned it on. They were almost hyperventilating. Shirley, her husband, the captain, and Ling were revving up. Ran Ying said she disliked dancing and refused all offers. I danced a few times by myself to show them "American-way," then taught Shirley. She was the least afraid to "rock." Then the captain and Ling tried it. The only way they'd known how to dance in the past was like the dancers from _The Lawrence Welk Show_. The concept of dancing without holding on to someone was hard for them to grasp. The more we danced the more uptight they became, except Shirley. She was a natural dancer, and seemingly a natural rebel.

Ling's mother came into the room, drenching the spirit of our cultural exchange like a sudden downpour. She said something, and

Ling put on a tape of Chinese folk songs. A dancing addict could not have danced to that music. I found out later that Ling's mother thought it was fine to learn to dance like "Westerners," but what if someone reported them to the Party? What if "the times" changed? Right now China was experiencing "many freedoms" but that could change next week if reform leader Deng died.

What if there came another Cultural Revolution? During that nightmare period of Chinese history, things people had done twenty years before were printed on posters and banners and put up in front of the offender's house. I couldn't imagine it, but they certainly could. "In 1984 then Captain Lee and his wife, Ling, along with Shirley and Lu Chung, danced with 'American devil and leading capitalist' then visiting China on mission of subversion and spying." One needed to be very cautious because another Red Guard onslaught might happen. So my days as dance instructor came to an end, and so did our time in Chengdu.

Ling helped us get plane tickets as we made arrangements to leave Chengdu and begin our long journey across China toward Inner Mongolia. We would be following the old silk route that Marco Polo traveled. Some of the places I wanted to visit were closed to foreigners or required special permission from the travel authorities. Only a few cities in China, like Shanghai and Beijing, were open to visitors without official permits. To receive a permit, we had to go to a drab little office and get our visas stamped in red by a usually suspicious-looking official in a white shirt. Everything official in China needed a red stamp.

The tranquil morning Ran Ying and I left beautiful, boisterous Chengdu, Captain Lee and his Ling were there to say good-bye. I gave Lee one of my T-shirts; it had TENNESSEE across it in huge yellow letters. I gave Ling some Olympic postage stamps from America. You would have thought I had given her one thousand shares of IBM stock. They gave me a beautiful basket. We shook hands several times and bowed and smiled and nodded our heads in a display of Chinese affection.

When we stepped away from the Jinjiang, my hotel, Lee and Ling pulled Ran Ying aside and whispered something to her. She told me later that they again requested, most honorably, that I not use their names in my book I would write. They also told Ran Ying to tell me that they were sorry that they could not talk with me more freely; it was a great desire to talk openly with me. They knew it would be impossible for me to understand how they felt. They wanted Ran Ying to explain China to me since they could not. They wanted to be sure I knew that they loved China, although like any country it had its problems, which many of the young people wanted to change.

Ran Ying could talk as openly as she dared because she was safely married to an American. Ran Ying had another kind of problem— she couldn't decide whether she wanted to be a Chinese living in China or a Chinese living in America. Did she want to become an American citizen, or stay a citizen of China? Since we'd been in Chengdu she'd informed me that the main reason she had agreed to serve as my interpreter was to come back here and try to decide whether she wanted someday to return to China to live or become an American citizen who occasionally visited. She was on her own pilgrimage. Ran Ying would see more of her motherland in the weeks we would be traveling than 99 percent of the natives would in their entire lives. Chinese seldom travel. There's little time, and less money.

# The Dream of
# the Exploding House___

Ran Ying had surprised me when she had said to Captain Lee that she would never dance. Sometimes there seemed a heaviness about her spirit, as if she resented anyone acting childish and frivolous.

On our flight to the city of Xian (pronounced "Shé an") she told me a story. She was "given up," as her aunt was, not because she wasn't pretty but because Chairman Mao ordered it. When her parents were young and zealous, Chairman Mao told his people that the government came first, the family was second. Ran Ying's parents were told they must sacrifice their family for their motherland. At the time of Ran Ying's childhood, they lived, breathed, and passionately supported Mao's revolution. "He was bringing about great change," they said. They wanted to be a part of history.

"When my mother and father first were married they work as interpreters for Chinese Embassy in Denmark. I was born in Denmark," Ran Ying said. (She pronounced certain words oddly. I kidded her often about her pronunciation until she started trying to teach me how to speak Chinese. I never said another word about it after that.)

"I was eight months old, they sent me back to China. A nurse brought me back on a plane and took me to nursery. I stay there till I went to live-in kindergarten. It was one where all the kids would stay there all week and then go home on weekend. But I stayed there all the time." Ran Ying's face went coldly blank as she talked about her first few years.

"My younger brother, he not live like me. He sent to live with my mother's relatives. That was nice place to go. He stay there because he was a boy. Always remember boys more important in China, always treated better," she said matter-of-factly.

Ran Ying told me of a poem she liked by Fu Hsuan. It said:

_How sad it is to be a woman!_
_Nothing on earth is held so cheap._
_Boys stand leaning at the door_
_Like Gods fallen out of heaven._
_Their hearts brave the Four Oceans,_
_The wind and dust of a thousand miles._
_No one is glad when a girl is born:_
_By her the family sets no store._

"When my parents sent me away I was eight months old. I didn't see my mother or father till I was four. My father said when I left him at eight months old, I could already stand up and walk around. And talking, I was talking a lot—I liked to walk and was very active. Every morning I would get up at five-thirty and start talking and walk and everything. But when he saw me three years later, I was totally different—very quiet and never smiled, just blank. He was very sorry he didn't send me to his parents." A man sitting next to us on the plane seemed exasperated that he didn't know enough English to understand the story Ran Ying was telling. His ear invaded my space in this crowded plane. Ran Ying always spoke so no one could overhear her. It was a skill all Chinese worked on.

"I lived in that nursery school by myself on the weekends and holidays. There were three bad dreams I had all the time," she said. The way she pronounced "bad" sent chills through me. Bad sounded like a knife in the heart. "I remember in one there was a big, huge house and I was alone in the dark. A few kids and I were standing by a newly built house, peeking into the door and suddenly everybody ran away. They were calling and saying the house was going to explode and I tried to run but I couldn't.

"In the next dream, I dream my teacher hate me. She walk funny and I was scared of her . . . too scared to even look at her—it would be like looking at a ghost. I dreamed that she was mean and she always looked at me funny like she was going to eat me or something. I was so scared I would bend over and try to hide under the chair. The dream of her would come back and back and back." I tried to imagine sending Rebekah off and not seeing her for four years. I remembered the heart-ripping scenes at our home when I would just leave for work and feisty one-year-old Jed would grab hold of my leg and not want to let me go. And I was going to be home in eight hours.

"The other dream started when my father come visit me after not seeing me for long time. My father came back to the country first and he would take me out every Sunday—out to play and eat in a restaurant. One night I dreamed that my father came to get me and I was in a big auditorium. There were a lot of kids' beds in there and a velvet curtain separated the room where the beds were. He was holding my hand and walking through the beds toward my bed and suddenly he disappeared and I cried and cried.

"Yes, young people were supposed to think of the country first, not the family. If I talk to my father now about this, my father will say 'Yes, it was wrong.' They were young, wanted to do the right thing, Mao's thing. My mother will say, 'At the time the party said put the country first and family second and I just do what the party ask me to do.' She still not think it wrong."

I could feel my stomach tightening in anger. Every time I felt like I would get mad in China I remembered Major Rule Number 1: "Never, never lose your temper in China . . . just smile and wait like everyone else." So, I said, "I guess that's really what the Communist party wants people to do—never think or question, just do it."

Whenever I seemed to be aggravated about China, Ran Ying would jump to the motherland's defense.

She responded, "It's not only the Communist party that expects this. All through Chinese history that's what the Chinese emperor does, too. It's just something Chinese. I think that's part of Chinese culture, so for the Communists, that's convenient for them—they just pick it right up. It's not hard then for the people to obey."

And so Ran Ying spent most of the first years of her life in a type of boarding school, a continent away from her parents. Then for the next four years she lived with some relatives. "After four years with my relatives," she told me, "my parents decided that it was time for my brother and me to come back and live with them. I was eight years old.

"I would stay with them for seven years, till the Cultural Revolution would come and totally change China. Then the whole country again would have to do as Mao says."

Our airplane tires screeched on the runway as we landed in the "tourist" city of Xian, population 2.5 million. Xian is known throughout the world for the Qin tomb excavations, which are thousands of unearthed terra-cotta warriors over two thousand years old. A tour group from America got off a plane next to ours. Many had on Ohio State sweatshirts and hats. Midwesterners are normally not the brightest dressers in America but this group blinded me compared to the drab dress of the Chinese.

As I was waiting for Ran Ying, who'd gone to the ladies' room, a thin, sunken-cheeked younger man walked by and leaned against a greasy wall near me. He watched me, but not in the usual Chinese way of blunt staring. His observation was more discreet. When he determined I was probably alone, he came over and immediately began giving me some of the "must-see highlights of Xian."

"Did you know that there are seventy-five hundred life-size clay soldiers in underground site some thirty kilometers east of city? Maybe greatest archaeological site known in world." He had a hard time saying "archaeological." "In one cavern that is over seven hundred fifty feet long and more than two hundred feet wide, there are six thousand clay warriors, all about six feet tall. Each face is different, taken from army men twenty-two centuries ago." He recited it like a classroom lesson. I didn't want to ask any questions for fear of interrupting his memory.

"These most beautiful figures are in battle formation, set up with

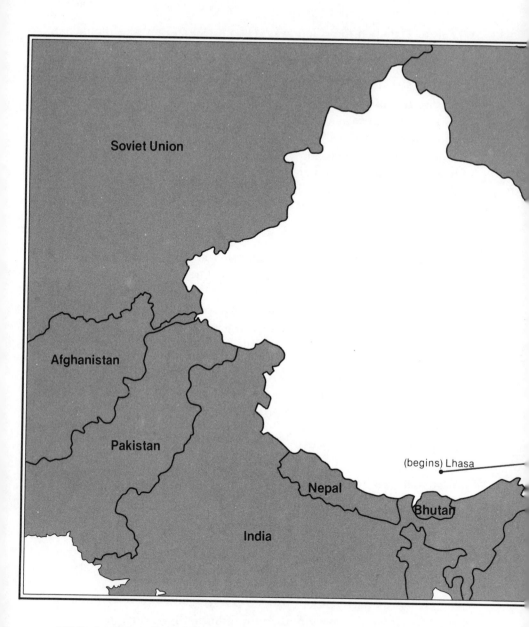

Soviet Union

Afghanistan

Pakistan

Nepal

Bhutan

India

(begins) Lhasa

While in China, I couldn't be satisfied with just seeing magnificent Tibet. So I left the climbers after establishing base camp and traveled back to central China. Once in sultry Chengdu, I met the person who would make China come alive for me, Ran Ying Porter. As we explored China, she would serve as my interpreter, but more than that, she would help me understand China's character through

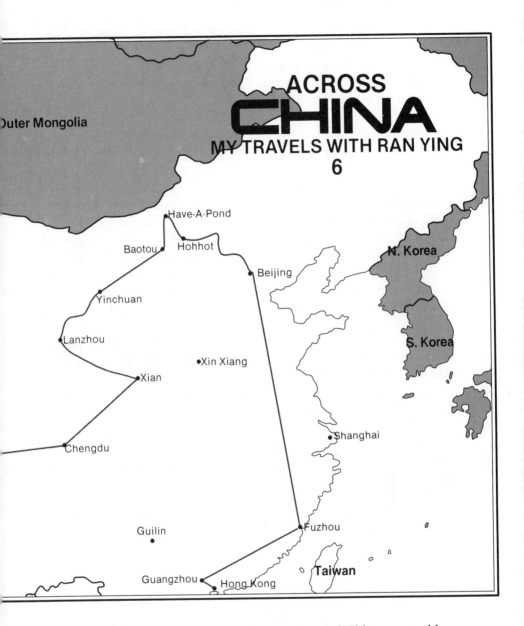

the story of her life and her people. From central China we would
backtrack along Marco Polo's historic route, angling for Inner
Mongolia. Once on the windy grasslands we were allowed to live
with a Mongolian family. From there we rode the rails to the capital
city of Beijing, and then headed for the rice paddies, water buffalo,
and palm trees of the South China Coast.

real wooden and bronze weapons and actual chariots of warmaking. There are buried near these soldiers bronze horses with gold and silver harnesses to serve their lord after his death." He went on to tell that he had spoken to many tourists from all over the world right here. He was stiffening, like he had other things on his mind. I told him I was not a typical tourist, and unfortunately I was just passing through Xian on my way to Inner Mongolia. He informed me that Inner Mongolia was a difficult place to get to, mostly off limits to foreigners since it was so close to a guarded and sensitive border area. I said I'd get there, somehow.

He pressed in a bit closer to me and was acting increasingly nervous. He said he used to be in the Chinese navy. He spoke English very well for someone who'd supposedly never spoken it except in class and to tourists. His English was at least as good as Ran Ying's.

The young man said, "I must say this." I wondered if he was about to pass some kind of state secret, he acted so intense. He was almost touching me he was so close. I stepped away. His presence made me uncomfortable.

"How do you say 'Nature cause . . . to make water'?" It was noisy, I wasn't sure I heard all he said. It had been raining, maybe he was talking about a thunderstorm.

He repeated himself after I shrugged. "Nature cause me to make water. How do Americans say this?"

Smiling, he repeated it again, "How do Americans say 'Nature cause me to make water'? I must know to practice my English." "Oh. Duh . . ." Chinese were normally so shy I wasn't even thinking that he might ask me something like this.

"We say, 'I have to go to the bathroom. Where is it?'" He bowed rapidly, bobbing like a goose, and shook my hand. Finally someone had helped him.

# Moving a
# Billion-Pound Rock_____

Ran Ying wove through the perpetual crowd toward me. "I think we
may be in trouble. The Chinese International Travel Service person
says he knew to expect us but no one ever sent him train tickets. We
will have to go to hotel where they have office and see." Ran Ying
often said that we should "see." See what? See whom? See what,
when? It was so open-ended anything was possible, and I didn't like
that. In America I was used to asking a question and getting an
answer. Why couldn't she just say "We will see if they made a mistake" or "We will see if they have our tickets" or "We will see if there

is something we can do." But instead it was always "We will see."

"It next to Little Goose Pagoda," said the ticket agent about the hotel we headed for, the Xiaoyanta. We were supposed to be leaving on the cross-country train this evening. We found the dreary little room that served as the office for the travel service. It had a few very old, very scratched wooden chairs and two musty stuffed chairs. An almost emaciated man, who nonetheless was used to wielding power, took long drags on his unfiltered cigarette. He wore gray pants seemingly stained with a week's worth of tea and ashes and a badly tailored sports jacket. To use the word "tailored" was paying it a compliment, but still he was about as "dressed-up" as anyone I'd seen in China so far.

He sat at what looked like a fifty-year-old teacher's desk. It was dusty and dirty. This tightly wound agent wanted to see my Alien's Travel Permit: #400655. The only way one can travel in China to cities on the restricted list is with one of these. On the back it said:

## POINTS OF ATTENTION

1. It is required that this Travel Permit be produced at Foreigner's Checkposts for inspection while traveling in China.
2. Wherever stopping overnight, the bearer is required to report for registration at local public security organs within 24 hours after arrival and have it cancelled on leaving.
3. Having served its purpose this Travel Permit should be submitted to local public security organs.

He looked it over. On the inside was my name in Chinese, "Nationality," "Passport Number," "Accompanied by," and "Places to Travel." The agent saw that I had the official red stamp and the listings of the restricted places we would be going to when we left here. Lanzhou. Yinchuan. Bautou. After seemingly photographing it with his mind, he slid it back to me. I passed, I guessed.

I would probably still be living in Xian today if Ran Ying had not spoken such excellent Chinese and known how to make her way through this system. After the ticket agent made us wait for a few hours he decided he could talk with us. When we told him that we were supposed to have train tickets to Lanzhou waiting somewhere in this city, he said he would see what he could find out. He waited for another half hour and then made a call to somewhere. Ran Ying said he called the train station.

"They say there are no tickets waiting there for any foreigners. They say they look everywhere. There is train leaving after midnight; they say maybe you get tickets if you go down there. If not could be a long time before we get you out of here," Ran Ying reported.

He then went into the same rap that the young man back at the airport did about all that there was to do in Xian. We told him we wanted to get to Inner Mongolia. He said he had always wanted to see that area, too, but it was hard to get to. I was beginning to get frustrated with China!

We had to hassle around and get an old man to drive us down to the train station for the outrageous price of thirty yuan. He knew we needed him. The only thing I could compare the train station to was every movie I'd ever seen about India. There were thousands of Chinese people everywhere, lying on the ground and sleeping on their baggage. One middle-aged peasant lay sprawled out, snoring, while hundreds of people per hour stepped over him. Little children cried from the stress of being surrounded by strangers.

The ticket windows had a special sign for foreigners but no one would answer our knocking. As usual when people saw me I became their evening sideshow. A large crowd gathered around us. Finally someone opened the shade and said they were closed. I told Ran Ying to tell them they couldn't be closed, we were lost. A blank-faced man said they couldn't help us. We told them they must. They told us to come around the back of the building. Once there we banged on the door for a good while. No one would answer. After repeated banging, when even Ran Ying wanted to give up, the metal door creaked open.

Some younger person, holding her head down, pointed to an older woman. She never looked up from what she was doing as Ran Ying told her of our dilemma. I got the feeling we could tell her a hundred small children had just been machine-gunned outside and she would not change her expression. It was mean, even hateful. I guessed it could have been caused from working in this madhouse all the time. Outside everyone was shouting and shoving and pushing and lying all over everything. She was in charge of all tickets. Ran Ying told her that back in Chengdu we had been told our tickets would be waiting for us here. She said she knew nothing of us. Her sullen eyes kept looking at some pages of figures.

I was about to start yelling for effect, even though no one would have any idea what I was saying, when Ran Ying read my mind and told me, sternly, to say nothing. We were about to use Chinese Negotiating Rule Number 4. "If you're getting nowhere, just stand next to the person long enough, and you'll drive them into doing something." They will almost never tell you to leave, or scream at you. That would be violating Rule Number 1: "Never get mad in public." She was trying to ignore us long enough so we'd go away. And I would have if Ran Ying had not known what to do. We would stand right there till she got some tickets. What could they do, throw me in jail? Of course not. The tension in "her" office became more and more intense as all her subordinates became silent, waiting for the end of our showdown. Maybe this iron-faced, stiff-bodied wench had never been stood up to by foreigners before.

Ran Ying asked the same questions over and over: "Why aren't our tickets here? . . . How do we get tickets? . . . We know. Someone in this office gave our good tickets in a 'soft-sleeper car' to friends. . . . Who would like to know that? . . . Why can't we get tickets, where are they?"

We asked these questions maybe twenty-five times before someone other than iron-face said, 'You have to wait three days, maybe a week. This most busy time of year."

The woman looked at a man standing by a huge schedule board and nodded. Ran Ying asked the questions for about another five minutes and then the man said, "We have some tickets available for this night. Hard-sleeper only. Take them now or leave. Don't come back." He was talking about the night train, which left at ten that night. That changed our whole plan. We would not get to see the great terra-cotta soldiers. We would have to leave in an hour. Thank God we'd brought all our stuff with us.

From Xian to Lanzhou, which would be a sixteen-hour train ride along the Wei River valley, through the heart of China, would cost me thirty-eight yuan (about $15.20). Ran Ying's ticket cost twenty yuan (about $8.00). I thought it was strange that in a Communist country where everything is supposed to be equal (no upper class, no lower class), they charged foreigners close to double and sometimes triple for everything from food to plane tickets to lacquer ware. After we were out of the office and back among the whirlpool of people, the man who sold us the tickets came up to us. He explained what had happened to our good tickets. The travel agent back at the hotel with the stained gray pants, in the office with the dusty light bulbs, had already come down and picked up our two tickets claiming he was getting them for us. Of course, he said to us that he'd not heard about us or our tickets. He must have sold them to somebody else. Ran Ying said it was a classic maneuver—nobody's answerable for anything, so who cares? In China, once you have a job it's almost impossible to get fired, no matter what you do. "Sort of like the people who work in your post office," Ran Ying mentioned casually. The travel agent probably sold our tickets to somebody else and made a little profit.

I'd never been on a train overnight before. The aisles were narrow, and everyone seemed to be loaded down with bags. Legs, bags, bodies, and excited conversation filled our train. Sticking out of the bags were all kinds of fresh vegetables, threadbare blankets, everything but live eels and loose chickens. Ran Ying said that for 99 percent of the Chinese people, going somewhere on a train was their biggest thrill. The thrill was not where they were going but what was happening on the way. She said part of the excitement was that no one asked anyone else's name so there were many free-flowing conversations. I was the only foreigner on the train of many cars.

Some cars were for sitting up; they were called "hard seats." A few cars had compartments with four "relatively" spacious bunks, with clean sheets, and a door. That was what we were to have had before our tickets to the "soft sleeper" were sold to someone else. They were usually reserved for foreigners or overseas Chinese. Then there were "hard sleepers," which were cars of compartments with no doors; they were open to the hallway. Each compartment had six bunks, with barely enough room to lift up our knees.

The floor was yellowed with age, clean but dull, and faded by hundreds of moppings with nothing but cold water. Hot water cost money and so did floor-cleaning detergent. On the legs of the lower bunks were the strands of many mops. We squeezed our way through what seemed like the whole train; not all of it was air conditioned. I was sweating, lugging all three of my overstuffed packs, and trying hard not to knock over too many people while cramming myself and all of my stuff through the aisles. When we got to our hard sleeper, four bunks were already taken.

On the bottom was a sick-looking man who seemed to be about sixty. He opened a small bottle and shook a couple of odd things that looked like herbs into the palm of his hand. Ran Ying said he was taking "traditional Chinese medicine." The man had the look of a person in the last stages of cancer. Just as Ran Ying said, no one asked anyone's name. One man was an oil worker from the oil fields up north, close to the Russian border. On the top bunk across from me was the son of an army officer. He was in the navy, and said fewer than ten words. His father said it all. The army man was short, feisty, aggressive, and loud. He appeared to be in his mid-fifties, and I called him "the little general."

Before the little general took over our hard sleeper, the oil-field worker made polite conversation about the Olympics. What a great job the Chinese women did in volleyball. Who did I think would win the election for president of the United States, Reagan or Mondale? They all wanted Mondale, saying that "Democrats were closer to Communists than Republicans." The short, stubby general was squirming on his bunk, just across from Ran Ying.

"Chinese soldiers are very brave; they are the bravest soldiers in the whole world!" blurted out the little general. "They can fight much longer than American soldiers. Chinese soldier can stay on battlefield for two, three years. American soldier fight a little bit for six months go home to his mother."

Ran Ying didn't really want to translate, but I made her tell me what he was saying. I thought maybe the guy was trying to get a reaction out of me. I just lay there, expressionless.

His voice was an Oriental growl as he kept on talking. He found out that Ran Ying had married an American and was just visiting. He was obviously bothered that she spoke such perfect Chinese, which meant that she had grown up in China and yet still left for America. He acted hostile toward me.

He began to quiz Ran Ying, saying,

"Why is Chinese system so much better than the American system? Why is it that in America there are a lot of social problems? Why is it in America rich people are very rich and poor people are very poor?" (He had the delivery of a drill sergeant.) "Why do Americans try to take over other countries, but Chinese don't? Why do so many people starve in America? Why does America band together with Russia against China? Why is that in China everybody is equal, they don't have prejudice against each other like in America? In America there is racial discrimination toward black people."

You could see the red Chinese flag with its yellow stars going up in his eyes as he spoke.

He carried on as if he couldn't stop. He said, "Chinese people are much more brave and diligent and smart—very, very much smarter than in America, that's why China is better."

At this point I wanted to say in the same tone of voice he used, if that was true, why was China so incredibly backward in technology? Where was the tractor? Had he ever heard of Tibet? I just lay there. Everyone else in our hard sleeper was obviously uncomfortable but dared not interrupt his speech.

He kept asking Ran Ying which country she liked best. What difference did it make to him? He already knew. He must have asked her ten times, finally resorting to yelling at her. I thought he might grab her and push her up against the wall. If he tried that I was planning some counterattack. I wouldn't have been surprised if I'd had the help of everyone but his son. His son acted like he'd heard this ten thousand times and knew to just keep quiet.

Finally, Ran Ying told him that no one country is better than the other, just different from each other. He didn't like it and got really offended.

Now he was getting out of control, like a sobbing child, saying anything that came to his mind. The little general asked Ran Ying, "DO . . . Americans . . . DO THEY STILL CALL CHINESE 'Asian patients!'"

"What's he talking about, Ran Ying?" The little general was almost hyperventilating.

"Has anyone ever said to you when you were a kid, 'Now eat all your food because there are people starving in China?'" Ran Ying asked me.

"Yes, my mother used to say that sometimes."

"Well, some visiting Chinese in America overheard someone say this many years ago and came back to China and told people of this. It was picked up by the government and made into bad propaganda against the United States. They took the part about eating all your food and people starving in China, as though American people wanted to eat all their food so that starving Chinese would not get any of it. Chinese added to it and say that Americans think all Chinese thin, starving, so sick and weak they are patients in hospital. They especially use this propaganda in the army. Isn't that crazy?" Ran Ying said, glancing over toward the general, who was turning red in the face.

Ran Ying explained to the general that Americans did not say that anymore. She didn't bother to explain that they had never meant it the way he thought they had, because she knew that would start another argument. We later learned that the little general's job was that of professional propagandist for the People's Liberation Army. Ran Ying said that for every so many men in the army, there was a propaganda person.

I heard some loud snoring. The oil-rig worker had taken all he could, I guessed. The sick old man was sleeping, too, restlessly, and sweating.

In these hard sleepers, they give you one grubby sheet, two brown wool blankets, and a kind of a beanbag-type pillow. Of course, there's no such thing as nonsmoking and smoking, so everyone was lighting cigarettes, smoking, and blowing smoke all over me. I kept thinking I should feel like I was locked in a prison, but it occurred to me that the Chinese were always crowded, crammed into everything from buses to beds, that they felt comfortable in here, and their relaxed way affected me too.

After a few hours, the people who had come from other cars to hear the little general's lecture had gone. His son was sleeping. Only Ran Ying and he and I were still up. He became slightly less RED-neck. He actually was wearing down, and he became a bit reflective.

"I join the army when I seventeen, fight Chiang Kai-shek. Live most of my life in southern China. Later transferred to Chen Jong and now whole family live in Chen Jong. I soon get ready to retire, let young people run country. Soon the government set up resort area where a lot of retired army leaders will spend the rest of their lives." Both Ran Ying and I were worn down like we'd been stood up against a wall and screamed at all night.

The little general climbed up and looked to see if his son was still asleep, as if he didn't want his son to hear what he was about to say. The son was safely sleeping, so the general began, "China is much better now and the policies are much more open since Mao die. People can do a lot of things very freely." As if he remembered we were passing through a poor, badly eroded part of China, he explained, "But in this area, it's still very poor and people live very hard lives. China is still a poor country," he admitted even though it was pitch-dark out and we couldn't see. Ran Ying interpreted that with an edge of surprise in her voice that she tried to cover.

But he countered, "China will get richer all the time; just wait until the twenty-first century. China is really going to be changing and will become very rich and advanced, much more than America."

Before he went off to sleep, and he was one of these people who lay their heads on their pillows and snore, he said, "There's no doubt that the judging at the Olympics for men's gymnastics was rigged." (The American men gymnasts had won the team competition, surprising the Chinese.) He said, "The Chinese gymnasts deserved to win every gold and silver medal, but Americans bribed all judges.

"What do you think about that?" he asked, piercingly. Ran Ying turned her back on him. There was no one left awake except me, and I couldn't argue with him. I looked at him as if to say, "Well, there's not much left you can say to me, is there?" That made him mad.

In moments, he was snoring loud enough to keep me awake. The beautiful perpetual click of the train wheels on the tracks was so soothing. The train, wailing across China as fast as any Chinese train could go, finally put me to sleep. I felt so far from home.

# 34

## *Lao Li in Shades*————

The interior of the Russian-made cargo plane was lined with military-green canvas across its ceiling and down its sides. Had I mistakenly been put on a Chinese army paratrooper plane? I was halfway expecting to be given a parachute and told to jump down to Inner Mongolia. There were two rows of seats running along the sides of the plane and they held some very nervous passengers, especially Ran Ying. The center of our C.A.A.C. plane was filled with cargo, and our uniformed stewardess had to reach through the boxes to give out some candy. The rest of the time she stood in the front of the plane and seemed to wonder what she was doing here, a "stewardess" for cargo and a few people. We had just flown over the Mu Us Desert.

Our pilot lunged the plane toward the ground as if he'd dozed off or overflown the landing strip. We slammed down on its old wheels and almost bounced off the runway before the plane came to a pounding stop. "Welcome to Baotou [pronounced "Boẃ-toe"], Inner Mongolia," Ran Ying translated for me.

A dry wind blew down the runway that had many cracks in it. The airport looked like an isolated military outpost and we were led into the airport's one-room headquarters. Three bored soldiers stared at us. Dirt was piled in the corners as though the room had been hurriedly swept out just in time for the arrival of our plane. A faded picture of the Chinese flag was the only thing on the walls that caught my attention, and the furniture would not have brought a dollar per piece at a garage sale back in America. And Baotou was supposed to be a major Inner Mongolian city? But who cared. I WAS finally here, in the lands of the man who once ruled the world, Genghis Khan. His Mongol people still lived north of here, up on the plateau, in the places where these arid winds blew from. Where did the Mongol's herds of tireless horses run as swift as the winds of a storm?

We waited. I was not in the mood to be forgotten, again, or have someone sell our hotel reservations to someone else. A shiny black car whizzed up. A couple of Chinese officials got in and were gone. Another car came, waited, picked up no one and was gone. Then a tan car came with two men in the front seat. A tall, wiry Chinese man jumped out. He had on dark sunglasses, pointed black shoes, white socks, black straight-leg pants, and a dark polyester sports coat. His thick black hair was cut flat on top. He had a natural flair.

He came right up to me, threw out his long arm and said, "So nice to make your acquaintance. We must rush, we'll be late to finest restaurant in all of Mongolia." He had energy and he had verve. I'd not met a Chinese yet who came on this strong. Who was this man and what was he up to? His driver stayed in the car, as this man in shades carefully lifted all our gear into the trunk. The car, an '80s-model Chinese car from Shanghai, was shaped like a 1950s-model Ford.

He found out Ran Ying spoke perfect Chinese and that she was functioning as my interpreter on this journey, but he refused to speak anything but English. He spoke fast and fluently. I was told to call him Lao Li ("Low," pronounced like "now," "lee").

Lao Li was very concerned that we would not make it to this "most incredible restaurant in all of Mongolia, maybe one of greatest in China." The driver turned off a fairly smooth highway into an old section of town, where the roads were like the surface of the moon. We could not go faster than 15 mph for all the carts, burros, bikes, and bouncing of the car. The homes on this road were made of mud, and clouds of fine red dirt blew in our faces.

We dropped off a curb into a mud-walled alley barely wide enough for our car. Lao Li made us feel that we were the only foreigners he'd ever met, and that he'd waited for this moment since his birth. He hung his angular and bony shoulder over the seat and kept his eyes on me. He let it slip that he'd brought some businessmen to this same place yesterday. They were Australians. If we'd met another car they or we would have had to back up for a long way. I got the feeling that Lao Li was powerful locally, and got his way. Many of the peasants on the street recognized the car and waved in homage. Everyone seemed to salute. The driver stopped and I was surprised to find there was a huge pond in front of us, almost the size of a small lake. Men in rustic boats threw long nets into its silty water. On its banks, surrounded by more mud homes, was a rough-looking mud building with no door. The eating place was surrounded by bare dirt, which was hardened by many people having walked on it. There were many bikes parked outside. Lao Li said the restaurant was not run by Mongolians, but Chinese. It looked more like the world's most primitive Mexican cantina. THIS was the great restaurant Lao Li had been bragging about? He hadn't stopped selling its super dishes since we'd met him.

He'd told us the place was run by a commune of about two thousand people. This commune raised just one thing. "Only since Chinese allowed to be freer in business has this restaurant opened," Lao Li explained. We walked in and my red beard hushed the crowd that before had been head down into their food. There seemed to be close to one hundred people in one room that was no more than twenty feet across. There was no ventilation except for a couple of grease-coated windows. Everyone was smoking, drinking, eating, talking loud, or slinging their fingers around at each other, playing what I later learned was a popular Chinese drinking game. The space between the tables was wide enough for the thin thighs of the

Chinese, not my thick ones. Lao Li had reserved a table in the far corner. I could not tell from the plates what the specialty of the house was. It certainly didn't look like the same thing. The food was variously red, purple, tan, yellow, and dark brown. There was nothing that looked like vegetables and there were a few bowls of mostly uneaten rice around. Lao Li announced proudly, after his hour long buildup, that they served nothing, that's right, nothing, but CARP.

As soon as we'd entered this place that Lao Li was so wild about, the leader of the commune came out from the kitchen. When the shabby door swung open I heard the sounds of steaming, crackling, dicing, sizzling, and chopping. The commune leader treated our guide like he was mayor, or something much more than a travel agent. Lao Li made a sweeping motion over our little round table, like a magician would, and the commune leader disappeared back to the kitchen. There were no menus. The charismatic Lao Li, always hoping to impress, proudly announced what would be served.

"There will be 'sweet and sour' carp. Then will come the wonderful 'garlic carp,' followed closely by carp soup! That sound good to you, my foreign friend?"

"Yes . . . Yes," I said with no enthusiasm. Carp . . . I raised the little orange fish as a kid. Carp, the fish that lived in the most stagnant duck ponds back home subsisting on . . . Carp . . . Uggh. I remembered the food in Tibet. Quickly, I wondered how far up Everest the guys were.

"Then they'll bring to you fried carp, red-cooked carp, spicy carp, and maybe they'll have some boiled carp, too." This guy was the Crazed Chinese Gourmet. If there had been cooking shows on TV he would have had one. He could make fried yak ears sound exquisite.

And so, the long line of carp began. Carp in bowls. Carp on a dish. Carp eaten with your hands, carp picked apart with chopsticks, carp that melted in your mouth. Melted in my mouth! All of it but boiled carp was fantastic. Delicious. The Chinese amazed me with how they could take one thing, like carp, and make it taste a thousand different ways. They fried small carp at the perfect temperature so that you could eat bones and all, crispy as perfection itself. The commune's cooks used huge carp for what they called "red-cooked carp," which was cut in sections and cooked in soy sauce, sugar, and lots of garlic. Something about Lao Li made me joyful. His laughter split through the noise of the many carp connoisseurs. He made me laugh. It was a rare thing between us. I felt like I'd known him all my life and immediately we could share the secrets that best men friends can share. Not only was I finally in Mongolia, even if I was eating carp at a Chinese commune and not mutton on the plains, but I'd made a new friend, on the other side of the earth.

Next to us were four young men. They were red in the face, which Ran Ying had told me meant they were drinking liquor. "Chinese always turn red when they drink liquor," she said. I'd been amazed at how much the Chinese drank. They drank beer and alcohol a lot. The rowdy guys were almost knocking their table over in their out-of-control conversation. The largest man next to me spilled a glass of beer when someone seemed to tell him that I was here. They were drinking beer and a clear liquor and got louder all the time. They flung their arms around and shouted at each other. I didn't want to stare in case they might want to pick a fight or something. I was slightly outnumbered. Usually, I didn't think about it, but sometimes I felt as though it was a billion to one.

The drinkers' boisterous, semi-slurred talking was louder than everyone else combined. They were throwing their fists at each other, as if they were playing some kind of finger game. I asked Ran Ying to explain what, if anything, they were doing, but Lao Li answered before she could. He explained it was a drinking game where you threw out one of your five fingers at the same time the other person did and someone won. The loser took a drink. He said the big guy behind me was losing more than winning.

"Go ahead, my friend Peter," the show-off Lao Li said so that many would hear. "Let us play. Count one, two, three"—he moved his closed fist—"now put out a finger."

I frowned at him as the restaurant listened. "Come on, my brave, adventurous American friend, this is a Chinese custom. Now try it just once."

I shook my fist three times and put out my pinky. Lao Li put out his thumb. I won. That was the only time when a lower finger beat an upper one. Lao Li pretended to take a drink and rolled his eyes at the wild ones next to us. Suddenly, there was a strong hand pulling me backward. It was the loudest, biggest Chinese guy behind me. He began shaking his closed fist. He wanted to play the drinking game with me. I shook my head. His face was very red and sweaty.

Lao Li, the instigator, chimed in, "Peter, this is great honor that this young, impressionable Chinese person wants to share with you time-honored Chinese custom. . . . Please go ahead." The rest of the restaurant was waiting to see what I'd do, as well.

We started to play. Of the first six times, I lost five and had to drink a shot of _mao tai,_ clear Chinese liquor with the punch of Tennessee moonshine. These guys had been playing this game already for over an hour. Then I began to get the idea and I started to win more than lose. The poor, impressionable young man had to begin holding himself up. He put his arm around me, the way many drunken instant friends will do, and insisted on playing. He kept saying that I was too good at this, that I must have grown up playing it in America. The whole restaurant was laughing and living it up now.

Finally, after we'd played for about an hour, the young man's friends insisted that he stop. They carried him out of the restaurant, after he'd shaken my hand many times and told me he would soon be to visit in America, and how much he hoped I loved my visit to China. He had ridden his bicycle here but there was no way now that he'd be riding it anywhere. How he stood up, I never knew. Lao Li was very proud of himself and my abilities. I don't think Ran Ying liked the rowdy atmosphere much. Lao Li informed us that he would take us to our hotel in Baotou and he'd be back this evening to my room to discuss our plans in Inner Mongolia. I told him I wanted to go deep into the grasslands away from this city. He said nothing.

I had hoped for a bath, but there were not enough foreigners staying in the hotel so they would not turn on the hot water. At about 7:30 P.M., Lao Li showed up at my room. He rushed to turn on the TV as intensely as if there were a news special on about World War III. He sat down and was instantly engrossed. The program was by far the most popular TV show in China, although it was really a Japanese show, dubbed in Chinese. It was so popular that the Chinese "actors" that do the dubbing are heroes all over China.

The story line goes like this. The main character is a college-age Japanese girl who's dying of cancer. She's so sweet and pretty in a wholesome way and always doing something for someone else. She's also illegitimate but doesn't know it. Her Japanese mother is a French citizen and in this episode has come home to see her dying daughter, who has been adopted by her brother, a doctor. The cancer-stricken heroine thinks her mother is her aunt. Almost every scene is melodramatic. It's the Orient's answer to *Dallas,* and all of China that can watch TV, which is an increasing number, comes to a screeching halt when it's on. Lao Li acted offended when he had to interpret.

The first scene is taking place at an ethnic restaurant. The girl, Shen Zu, a name in China more popular than J.R., is with her boyfriend, who is actually her brother. Neither one knows. No, Lao Li explains, her boyfriend is only her half brother. Her boyfriend's father is also her father!?!?!

The boyfriend's mother is a very mean and selfish woman, kind of like Mrs. Olsen on *Little House on the Prairie.* The dying heroine claims she wants to be a doctor, even though everyone knows that soon she'll be dead. She wants to be a doctor to find a cure for cancer. They pile it on so thick I find it funny, but when I laugh Lao Li is deeply hurt. This is serious drama. Since this is a series, she gets better and worse, better and worse. Tonight she happens to be worse. I never thought she'd live through the episode. After fifteen minutes I didn't need an interpreter anymore, which made Lao Li happy. The sound track, made by many bad violin players, told the story. The show ended with the girl in intensive care in a hospital, her life-support system beeping slowly. Would she be alive next week? Lao Li would surely find out. Hopefully I'd be far away, with some Mongolian descendants of Genghis Khan, where there was no TV.

# From Bad Families ____

"OK," Lao Li said quickly, "what you want to do in Inner Mongolia before you leave?" Was he hinting that we should leave soon? I could tell he was used to pushing the conventional "foreigner" in the direction he wanted them to go with the right amount of dazzle, rushing around, and intimidation. I didn't feel like a foreigner anymore.

"I want to leave this city and live with a Mongolian family. Maybe find some family migrating across the plains, moving toward their winter range." I could already feel the slightest whisper of fall coming from the direction of the great white north, Russia.

"Very interesting, Peter, but may I speak openly with you? This is quite impossible. Those kind of Mongolian people are totally off limits to foreigners," Lao Li was sad to report. Having learned the Chinese techniques of negotiation, I figured this was my first hurdle. If I accepted his excuse, it would make his job less of a hassle. The Chinese dislike having to come right out and say "No."

"Come on, Lao Li, carp is not Mongolian. I have yet to even see a Mongolian!" I explained that I'd come halfway around the world to experience Mongolia, and Baotou was not enough of Inner Mongolia for me.

Lao Li said we could see a group of singers and dancers. Some of them were "real" Mongolians. I told him that wouldn't do. He told me of a temple we could visit. No way, Lao Li.

"All right, Peter. We leave right now. We go to my superior's apartment. See if we can receive special permission for me to take you to where Mongolians live. . . . I will take it upon myself to get you there. We will not give up!"

We drove through the still streets of the city till we got to an apartment building. Lao Li yelled from the street for someone. In a few moments a woman, his boss, stuck her head out of the fourth-floor window. They spoke a few fast sentences. She came down and shook my hand. He told her what I wanted, making it sound dramatic in Chinese. She asked some brief questions, he answered, and then he began patting her on the back and smiling as big as the moon over Mongolia.

"We can go! Be ready at eight A.M.," Lao Li said excitedly.

He made special arrangements for a canvas-topped jeep that was rugged enough to travel over the primitive dirt and sand roads of the upper plateau of Inner Mongolia. "Sometimes the sand gets so deep on these narrow roads, we may have to travel overland," said our driver to Ran Ying.

In China, since almost no one has his own vehicle, everyone has to rely on "the drivers." Although these drivers are low on the job-status ladder, they are treated like princes. If a driver in your "unit" does not like you, he can make things very difficult; therefore, the drivers are catered to. The driver made many excuses to me about how rough our trip would be. I told him nothing on these wild plains could compare to Tibet. We were quickly out of Baotou and climbing onto a plateau, the beginnings of the Mongolians' land.

We saw an ox and a man plowing a long field in the moist morning sunshine. This reminded Lao Li of his years spent living on a commune during the Cultural Revolution. Both he and Ran Ying had been raised in Beijing (your basic Chinese city slickers). Both had been sent to the countryside, as had all nonpeasants during the Cultural Revolution, to learn the meaning of work from China's peasants. Lao Li had been sent to a commune in Inner Mongolia near here. He had not been back since the Cultural Revolution had ended.

As we bounced down some sandy roads that cut across the empty plateau, Lao Li remembered his tale of love blighted because of a "bad family."

"My first girlfriend, my first love—we met at the commune. We fell in love and we got along very well. We were to get married so I wrote my beloved family telling them about this girl. The girl was from a family called a 'bad' family—her grandfather used to be rich." (When Chinese said someone was from a 'bad' family, they meant either a formerly rich family or an intellectual family. A good family was a family of peasants, factory workers, or army people.)

Lao Li said his father wrote back and said, "We are from worker's family—we are pure and good. Please don't marry girl from a bad family, because later if there is a political movement, our whole family is going to be in trouble. Also you will never be able to do anything better—like be chosen to be a leader."

"When the letter got to my hut at the commune, I was in the fields cutting wheat," Lao Li kept on. "But my girlfriend was there and she opened it. We loved each other, and always opened each other's mail. She read it. She saw what it meant and got very upset and said, 'Ok, let's forget it.'

"I assured her that it didn't matter what my father said. I loved her and still wanted to marry her. But she said I would not get over that letter and she would not marry me. She insisted on our breaking up, so we broke up and soon after that she met a boy from a family like hers," Lao Li said.

"One day a few years later I would make father happy and marry woman from good family. She's given me two sons and look how I am rising within the travel service. I would not have, had I married my first love." In spite of what Lao Li said, there was no doubt in my mind he still loved the young woman from the bad family.

Heading into the middle of Inner Mongolia was like driving on one-lane dirt roads through the middle of Wyoming. The land was mostly overgrazed wild grasses, parched golden brown from little rain. The ground was wavy, and every twenty miles or so, there was a place where the dirt could be farmed. Where farming was done, there would be a Chinese commune, never very big. Still I saw no signs of Mongolians. Real Mongolians never farmed. "Breaking the ground" and farming held them to one place and made them prisoners to the land. Then they would not be able to ride in whatever directions the winds blew. "It is still much jeep travel to heart of Mongo lands," Lao Li said. "Mongo" was the way they shortened Mongolian in English.

He seemed to have the Cultural Revolution on his mind, as did most Chinese who had lived through it. Although it ended in 1976, the Chinese were only now beginning to talk openly about it. Being in China so soon after that revolution was like traveling through the South a few years after the Civil War. It affected China at least that much. Lao Li and Ran Ying were grateful to have someone to talk to about their experiences.

"No one in America has idea what I went through and so it very hard to find anyone to share experience with," Ran Ying said to both of us. The Cultural Revolution consumed a total of nine years of her life, "like many worms eat apple."

Lao Li wanted to know if Ran Ying had been in the Red Guard. "In the very beginning of the Cultural Revolution we did not join; my family was considered a bad family," Ran Ying answered. "You had to be from good family to join the Red Guard then. Both my parents were intellectuals [which meant they'd gone to college], and they came from families that before Communists took over China had owned their own business. It was said they were from rich families, but they really were not. One family only own a restaurant and the other a lumber store," she said.

"Being from a family of intellectuals that also used to own their own business was the 'baddest'-combination family in China. The worst thing was to have been from a rich family, and the next worst thing was to be from an intellectual family." Ran Ying and her parents were punished by being put into this bad-family category when they had nothing to do with the "riches" earned by her grandparents. Ran Ying's tone showed how absurd she thought this was.

"My brother and I, we just stayed home when the Red Guard and the Cultural Revolution start. All schools in China closed for a year and a half. We just played in our courtyard, afraid to go into streets," Ran Ying told us, more serious than usual. Even Lao Li had not cracked a joke since they'd begun talking of the Cultural Revolution. Normally he couldn't go five minutes without twisting some word or phrase into a joke.

"Actually it was three courtyards that my family and about five other families lived around. Every family in these courtyards worked for the Foreign Ministry. There was one courtyard after another—you go in one and go to the end of it and there is a little door that leads you to another courtyard. Our houses were built around these courtyards. They were very beautiful, peaceful. I lived in the first courtyard. There were three big trees in there—they had big leaves, their bark was a gray-white, and they grew fast. We also had one pear tree and two wild-cherry trees. In spring they were full of white flowers that made courtyard smell delicate and sweet. The whole courtyard was made of stone, big square stones," she said.

"Every family had bathroom and every bathroom had bathtub. Toilets were like Western toilet—and that was very unusual in China. When my cousins would come to visit I would take them to the bathroom and they would say—'What is that, where do you go bathroom?' They were used to traditional Chinese hole in floor." The way Ran Ying spoke of these courtyards, they must have been very nice. It was a rare moment when she spoke of a pleasant memory.

"One boy in the courtyard was a member of the Red Guard. His name meant 'Red Flag.' He was the only one in our courtyard from a good family; all his past relatives had been poor peasants. He was eighteen, about five years older than me. He was a big, strong-looking boy." Never had Lao Li sat so still and been so quiet, especially when Ran Ying spoke, as he seemed to always be competing with her, trying to be my favorite interpreter.

"All the kids in my courtyard knew this boy was not very smart, but he was so much older we all respected him and were afraid of him. His parents were diplomats, pretty high up, both in their late thirties—joined Chairman Mao's army. His parents name all kids revolution names. His brother named 'Red Star.' His sister name mean 'Red Light.' Chairman Mao always was compared to sunshine, the beauty of sunset." Lao Li proudly mentioned that two of his uncles also had been members of Mao's army. His father had been too young, he was sorry to say.

"This boy became very active. Actually he started a Red Guard organization and got all his friends from good families to join. They went out and started to beat on people, kill people, and get into people's homes to search for bad things," she said with a detached coldness. "The boys' Red Guard activities started in the early summer of 1966. I was thirteen," Ran Ying said as if these "activities" were as common as Boy Scout troops in America.

Bad things were anything that had to do with the "four olds": "old ideas, old culture, old customs, and old habits." The old things were now bad things, although they had served China for five thousand years. To get rid of these four olds, Red Guards tore silk clothes off people as they stood on the streets, kicked in their doors, and destroyed antique vases and masterpieces of lacquer ware. Books were burned. They even bulldozed almost every graveyard in China because "graveyards were an old custom" that took up too much valuable land!

"Every night we'd be outside in the courtyard, all the kids playing, and we would wait for him to come back to tell us what had happened that day. I remember the story of the old widow woman. She lived not far from us. It had been found out that she had been rich before 1949 [the year the Communists took over]. It was known that in her house she had a lot of antique vases from Ming dynasty, a big antique sofa, a soft chair, jewelry, some leather-bound books. She even wore some silk clothes." Ran Ying sounded as though she wished she could wear silk.

"So that day they went in that old lady's house and took everything they wanted and smashed the rest—took it all away from her. Then they cut half her hair very short and shaved the other half. This group of Red Guards were all high school students. With her hair cut and shaved, when she walked out, everyone would know she was from a very bad family or she used to do very bad things. About ten or fifteen boys did this to her. They tell the old lady's maid to go home and told her she shouldn't serve this 'capitalist dog' anymore. They gave this maid some of old lady's things.

"During the liberation [1949], the government just told people, 'We hope you can give up your wealth to help the country,' but a lot of people didn't do it. My father's family was very stupid and they gave everything—they only saved two vases and they still have those. From either Qing or Ming dynasty—very old. Many families, even though they gave a lot, they still had much left, and I think this old lady was kind of that way. It was almost twenty years later and this lady was being punished for keeping some family heirlooms. Now you see why Chinese people afraid to do things like dance because twenty years later they can be in bad trouble." Lao Li came alive when he heard the word dance.

"When did you dance?" he wanted to know.

"Oh, never mind, Lao Li," Ran Ying answered before I could, as if she didn't really trust him.

Ran Ying kept on. "Every night for over a week that summer this boy would come home to our courtyard and tell us story about what they do to old lady that day. They make the old lady sweep the floor and clean the boys' shoes, make her lick them. They make her wash their clothes. Make her get on the floor and pretend to be a dog. They spit on the ground and ask old lady to clean it up. They make her say things like 'I am from a capitalist family and I drink a lot of people's blood.' 'I pay workers very little so that I could get rich.'

"They did this every day to the old lady—I don't think they beat her, they don't beat women—they only beat men," Ran Ying said. Even the driver, who'd certainly overheard hundreds of conversations, was exceptionally quiet. He even drove quietly.

"Finally the old lady couldn't endure any more, so she commit suicide. She hung herself after they shave her head second time. We were afraid to go out, but he and his Red Guards would have things to do like that every day. Then come home late in afternoon and tell us about them," she said.

Mao had asked millions of the young people of China from the "good" families to cleanse his nation of noncommunist elements that he felt were beginning to infect China. He chose the young of China to do the cleansing because they were his "revolutionary successors" and also because "youths are impulsive and ignorant of history and easily persuaded."

Lao Li repeated his question. "Ran Ying, were you ever in the Red Guards?" Surely after that story and the fact that she was from a bad family, she couldn't have been.

"Yes," she said. "I was about fifteen at the time I joined the Red Guard. It was after Chairman Mao said, 'Stop beating up on people and let's unite—everybody can be a revolutionary, not just people from good families.'

"When I joined the Red Guards, there was nothing to do in school—so we all joined because we were bored. School had started back, but there were no teachers—every day we went to school and

we read Chairman Mao's works. The children just organized themselves, and we would take Mao's Red Book and read it. We'd recite
the book from memory and talk about how we could carry on Chairman Mao's revolution.

"We used to say same things over and over, like:

"'Chairman Mao say, "A revolution is not a dinner party, or writing
an essay, or painting a picture, or doing embroidery; it cannot be so
refined, so temperate, kind, courteous, and restrained. A revolution
is an insurrection, an act of mighty violence."'

"'Chairman Mao say, "We should support whatever the enemy op-
poses and oppose whatever the enemy supports!"'

"'Chairman Mao say, "Revolutions and revolutionary wars are inevitable in class society and without them, it is impossible to have any
leap in social development and to overthrow the ruling classes."'

"'Chairman Mao say, "Every Communist must grasp this truth:
Political power grows out of the barrel of a gun."'

"We shouted these things for months on end, and that was all our
day consisted of all day long. No math, no science, no physical-exer-
cise class, nothing."

Ran Ying added, "Farmers even got so wrapped up in propaganda that millions of Chinese people starved. Farmers would say,
'We would rather have communist weeds than capitalist seedlings.'"
I couldn't understand how she could relate this insanity and make it
sound so normal.

"Eight of us girls joined the Red Guards together—it was after all
the killing had stopped, mostly. We liked to sing and we were all
very outgoing and all good friends. We said, 'Why don't we get into
a team and we try spreading Chairman Mao's thought to other people.' We went out on the streets and to railway stations and sang and
danced. Actually we just wanted to have a good time, I think," Ran
Ying said. She spoke fondly of this period as if she were recalling
being a cheerleader for the local varsity football team. Because of
the Cultural Revolution, Ran Ying never went to high school.

"Since your parents were highly educated people, did they ever
say that they were worried that you weren't getting an education?" I
asked, wondering how a country could call off all education for a
couple of years.

# FROM TIBET TO CHENGDU

The monastery of Gyangtze stands solemnly facing a crossroads used since the beginning of time for traders and travelers. The Dalai Lama turned south here on his escape, heading to the Chumbi Valley and India. We headed west.

PETER JENKINS

A Tibetan horse and burro rest in Xegar after their journey.

A Himalayan wind blows just right for kite flying.

JIM WICKWIRE

A large herd of yaks make their way from summer grazing in mountain meadows to their home villages in the lower valleys for winter.

Here a yakker carries some of his own equipment: blankets, clothes, and feed for the yaks.

Alice, a heroic yak

This yakker, who was also a medicine man, taught us to dance. However, he would not rock and roll.

PETER JENKINS

Right before we got to base camp, we stopped at the Rongbuk Monastery, elevation 16,500 feet, where we met some nuns who offered us tea.

PETER JENKINS

Beautiful prayer-stones at Rongbuk Monastery, with Everest in the background

JIM WICKWIRE

Chris Kerrebrock, the inspiration and instigator of the 1982 China/Everest expedition

JIM WICKWIRE

Marty Hoey, a great friend of our team

Goat slaughter in preparation for barbecue at base camp

Tibetan dancing, lesson number 3. The medicine man is third from the left.

Some of the yakkers see their pictures for the first time.

沙锅鱼
·shaguoyu

An Old Master chef
and his family
gather in front of
the Delicious
Garden Restaurant
in Chengdu. What
incredible food we
ate here!

A spice merchant in Chengdu market, Sichuan Province

Two Chinese friends hold
hands, a common sight.

晚婚晚 优生

All over China there are billboards explaining that little girl babies are just as important as
boy babies.

"No—they were crazy themselves—crazy about joining in the revolution—they were very active in the Cultural Revolution—stupid," she said with a growl.

"After a time, this part of the revolution came to an end," Ran Ying said, tensely, "and Chairman Mao decided all city people, young and old, needed to go live on the land, learn from peasants. That's when I went to live in a village by the Russian border. Stayed there for eight years.

"You know, I forgot since I lived in America what it's really like in China." Ran Ying sounded as though she were seeing something more clearly. "I had to come back here and feel it and remember. I only remember the good things when I'm gone." The way Ran Ying pronounced the word "remember" almost always made me laugh, but I couldn't—not after the horrifying things I'd been hearing. I was still shocked about the Cultural Revolution. In America she missed "very badly" Chinese music, food, newspapers, the language, the maze. Now she was reliving it all, not just as my interpreter but trying to make one of the most difficult decisions of her young life. Did she want to become an American citizen?

Lao Li was very still and completely silent. Surely he wanted to share his stories, but he would not say anything. Maybe he would have opened up if the driver had not been there. We turned down a white-sand road, as narrow as an oxcart. Lao Li said this was where we would see many Mongos.

# *Like Sand in a Storm*_____

"Here we have come to most haunting home space of special Mongolian people," Lao Li said, sounding more like a car salesman than a historian. To get to this place, we'd driven down roads that looked like wagon trails. Then we'd hit a stretch of paved road, which was ending here. We pulled our jeep into a lonesome village. The village was stark and isolated in the vast openness of the land, a land that dwarfed everything but the great sky that lay across it.

Lao Li said we should "go right away, talk with unit leader" of the Travel Service office here. What was a Travel Service person doing out here? No matter where I went the Chinese were trying and succeeding in controlling and watching over everything. Putting this office so far out was like putting an American travel agent's office at the front entrance of a Navajo Indian reservation a hundred miles from nothing but a bunch of cactus. The Chinese probably used this location as a front so that they could watch the Mongolian people whom they feared.

The Travel Service man's name was Muran (pronounced Moor-Ann). Muran immediately seemed to dislike Lao Li. His face was longer than those of most Chinese, his eyes rounder, his hair had some curl. He proudly stated he was Manchurian and did we know that Manchurians were the northern Chinese who had conquered the Mongolians after Genghis Khan's reign. He did not say that they were cruel rulers turning most Mongolians into serfs and slaves. Ran Ying said later that Lao Li was trying to tell him what to do and this was Muran's turf! Besides, Lao Li was suggesting that Muran break the rules by introducing us to some real Mongolians.

Muran told—more like ordered—Lao Li to go back to Baotou "right now. . . . I am quite capable of taking care of these foreigners," Muran said in a tone of voice that was meant to feel like sand in the winds of a storm. The two men had a momentary stare-down until Lao Li came to his senses, remembering, "This is China. What I am doing?" Maybe in the past few days some of my American independence had rubbed off on him.

He'd made Muran so mad I doubted we'd experience anything here but a Chinese stone wall. Muran told us we could stay here, in Mongo-style tents, called yurts, tonight. He said nothing more. When I asked Ran Ying to press him for more information, he stood up before she could say anything, as if he'd understood what I'd said. He demanded sternly, "Give me your passports, travel permits, and some money to pay for tents." His voice was slow and paced, but cut a mean slash. He said "please" only as an afterthought, as if he'd remembered what it said in his Chinese government training manual about speaking to foreigners.

We were so far out I'm sure he didn't worry too much about the eyes and ears of the government in this isolated outpost. More than likely he just didn't care. There was no place to hide in China, the land of a billion eyes and a trillion secrets. As we handed him the documents, I knew we were in trouble, since our travel permits had not been stamped for this place called Wu Lan Tu Ge Su Mu (pronunciation, Wu Lan Tu Ge Su Mu). The only place we were "legal" for was Baotou. I doubted Lao Li would escape his anger. Muran obviously was *the* Chinese ruler on this chunk of high prairie, and the locals seemed afraid of him. He looked out the window at dust blowing and said he would have to make some calls to his superiors about us. We needed the RED STAMP to go any further. He said he was disappointed with Ran Ying for leading me here, that she should have known better. She could have told him that Lao Li insisted we come, but she didn't.

"Come back in the morning," Muran ordered.

The next morning we met with Muran again. I guessed he was in his mid-thirties. He kept a cigarette lit, always. He spoke very slowly, letting the smoke puff around his face and never looked at me. He either stared out the window or looked toward the bathroom door. Ran Ying explained to him what we wanted to do. Muran said he could not give us back our passports or travel permits yet; he was still checking on us. He demanded more money for our two yurts and meals. He reminded us that no foreigners were allowed past here into the grasslands. We said we knew, we were very sorry. We asked him what there was to do here while we waited. He smiled slyly and said, "Nothing."

On our way out, toward the end of his shadowy hallway, Muran called for Ran Ying and me to come back. He told us that tomorrow there would be a great celebration here. Mongos would be coming on their horses, walking, riding in commune trucks, on bicycles, however they could, because there would be a festival to celebrate the rebuilding of their temple. It had been viciously destroyed during the Cultural Revolution and had sat crumbling for almost twenty years, till now, he said. The temple was a few doors down, surrounded by a courtyard that was padlocked. He mumbled that his wife was a Mongo and she would be here. He lived here at work and she lived in her home village. He said that many of his best friends would be at the festival, then squinted his eyes again, looked out the window, and turned back to stone.

"See you in morning," he said after I gave him a pack of some of China's best cigarettes. Maybe he liked us! His voice had a dot of warmth. I told Ran Ying that I would come back every morning to Muran's ill-lit "room of power" till he either kicked us off the grasslands or gave us permission to meet some Mongolians out where the winds blew away from his control. Strangely, the longer he made me wait and the more he tested my patience, the more patient I became.

Ran Ying said she'd been missing her children and Ed really badly the past few days. She wanted to go back to her tent, write some letters and think. At breakfast she'd wanted to talk of America, not Mongolia. She missed shopping. She'd forgotten till returning to China how easy it was to do everything . . . "back home," she let slip—"I mean in Tennessee." When we got back to America, she said, she was determined to get her driver's license. She still had not decided whether she would become an American citizen, though.

Earlier, as the golden sunlight brightened our Mongolian morning tea, she'd mentioned that she and Ed had discovered a brand of inexpensive disposable diapers that were as good as Pampers. In fact, to get them at Fred's, a department store near their home, you had to be there the day the shipment came in because they sold out fast. They were the kind with the ugly purple wrapper. In China most babies ran around with a hole in the back of their pants. There was never a need for diapers here.

Her homesickness overwhelmed her. This day I could not get that quick, intelligent smile out of her. Other than missing her husband and their sons, I think she missed the freedom, the comforts, her bright-colored summer clothes, her refrigerator and shower. Everything that wasn't China. The things that we'd found to be China—the irrational delays, the perpetual suspicions, the smothering controls, and the primitive conditions—embarrassed her, but she dared not express that before me. Showing her country to someone like me, who was seeing it for the first time, filled with a thousand questions, made it all look different to her, it seemed. We were seeing parts of China that native Chinese would never see in ten lifetimes. The Chinese almost never get out in their country and just travel. I had the feeling she was seeing her motherland, her people, and "their" government in a way she never had before.

# 37

## *Their Souls Are Like the Wind*_____

I decided to take off walking. We were on an island of man-made things, all dreary except for the temple, surrounded by the wind, the sky, and the grass. There was a boarding school for the Mongolian children, a post office, Muran's office, a circle of yurts for the tourists, a general store, and a single phone line. I could walk in any direction a wild horse could run and seemingly walk for months without encountering a city, especially if I went north toward Russia. I headed toward Russia.

I still had not met any real Mongolians, although I'd seen a few lone horsemen, far off, riding with the wind, going somewhere far away. There was nothing but the occasional, solitary home and corral in our view. Eight hundred years ago, I would have seen the ancestors of these Mongolian people riding with autumn winds at their backs, breaking their camps, moving to new pasturelands. The winds spoke to the Mongolians, giving them much information. After it blew warm for many, many days, it would blow cool for one day, maybe two, then warm again for five days. This meant that fall would come to the grasslands in one more full moon.

The wind has nothing to hold it back here on the great plateau of the Mongolians. The Mongolians could ride like the wind here. They sang with the wind and loved the wind. They felt the wind sting their faces with sand. It calmed them when the wind was puffy and warm, made them "want to take a long nap after eating much lamb." They watched it blow from every direction. Sometimes the wind had snow in it, sometimes dust. "In spring it lifted the magic things [pollen] from the flowers of the prairie and blew them to other plants that make them grow," said a Mongolian father to his son. "Sometimes wind carried rain cloud away from home village, sometimes it carried rain cloud to home village. If it carried rain away from home village, that could be good. Then it rained on pasture, made grass for horned cattle." Bad winds moved searing fires that blackened the land, but that could be good for their land since it burned up weed seeds and made the grass grow back stronger. Like the wind, Mongolians must move on. They believe their souls live in their blood. Their souls are like the wind and the wind demands freedom.

Everywhere the grasslands are open so that your eyes get lonely for something to see. No wonder the Mongolians felt that they could ride with their Genghis Khan to the ends of the "great, wide-open world." They wanted to ride till they could ride no farther.

I imagined hearing the twenty thousand hoofbeats of a tribe's five thousand horses moving toward their winter grounds. Around A.D. 1200, the nomadic Mongolian tribes were surrounded by many foes. They had to move quickly across the grasslands. Those were dangerous times, so their scouts rode first, fanning out as they went. These Mongolian scouts had the keenest eyes in their tribe, eyes that caught movement on the grassland as easily as a prairie falcon saw a field mouse. They sought campsites. They tasted the well water and searched for cool springs. If information came to them that a warring tribe lay in ambush, they concentrated on the flat horizon for the tiny silhouettes of the enemy.

I'd heard that many Mongolians still lived like this today, traveling with the seasons and the winds and the grass. They could not go to war, although some probably wished they could. Would I ever know these people? Were we in another Chinese maze of diversion, pointing us away from the Mongolians, or would we get what we'd come so far to find this time, too?

The grass was bitten down very close and my feet kicked up some dust. There was need of rain. I walked a mile or so, since it was impossible for me to judge distance with nothing to judge it by—no tree to look back at, no pile of prayer-stones ahead. The land was not tabletop flat; it had curves like a sheet on a clothesline in a full, humid breeze. The hard, gritty ground dropped off into an empty stream bed. In front of me was a charred place where someone had stopped for the night and made a fire of cow chips. There were many sheep droppings circling it on the bare dusty earth. I kneeled down to listen to the wind blow over me.

By walking over their grasslands, I could "see" the Mongolians and understand their spirit. It was no wonder they chose to live free from the bonds of fences, why they did not want to be planted in the soil like a farmer. They must move, travel long distances. Their faces needed to look across long open spaces. They did not want buildings and things human in their eyes' way. The awesome stillness of the Mongolian plains and plateaus soothed me and spoke of a people who were like the wind and its thousand moods. I was thrilled by this freedom, being away from the sweaty Chinese crowds.

A swirling Mongolian breeze full of warming sun and the dry, sweet smells of grasses cleaned away the confusion my Chinese "captors" had created for me. I got back to my yurt, which was covered with felt, and lay on my sleeping bag. Maybe I should have felt as invisible and unimportant as a hair from a horse's tail in a field of grass. But I didn't. I felt power from the quiet. I felt alone, but not lonely. It was the power of freedom. No wonder the Mongolians felt they could take over the world.

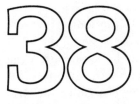

# Black Leather Vests___

Our fourth morning meeting with moodless Muran began with my offering him the usual cigarette. The brand I had was from Beijing and considered the best in China. The way he smoked it, I would think that smoking that "fine" cigarette was one of his greatest pleasures. He still expressed no liking for us, but did seem to be getting used to our unchanging desires. Is there a family of Mongolians we can go live with . . . et cetera . . . et cetera. . . ? He mentioned that today would be one of the most important days in the last twenty years for the Mongos around here. There would be much celebrating. He hoped we would attend. As we left his room he said, "Be ready right after breakfast in the morning. I will be taking you somewhere."

"Should we pack all our things?" Ran Ying asked, reading my mind.

"Yes," he said frigidly, stepping into his bathroom. He seemed to enjoy the power he had over us. We had waited and now he had made a decision. We were either being taken back to the train station or he'd arranged something for us.

I stood at the edge of Wu Lan Tu Ge Su Mu, which I'd nicknamed The Village, and looked to see if anyone was headed this way. We were at the "hottest spot" this side of Outer Mongolia. The winds blew dry from the south and were coming out of the west a wet-cool. If I had not been accustomed now to looking at these open lands, they would have looked the same as any other day. Void of movement, begging for life. But when I focused my eyes, almost bobbing my head as a hawk does to focus better, I could see specks of traveling Mongolians coming from every direction. To the southwest there were five figures on horses. The winds, too, carried the faint sounds of their coming. A truck came straight out of the west, with some people walking a few miles back of it. From the south came folks on a tractor pulling a cart full of people. A closer look down the dry-dirt street in front of the temple gates showed quite a few horses tied to hitching posts.

It was September 11, 1984. The stout padlocks had been removed. Everyone had gathered in the courtyard! Powerful young Mongolian men stripped above the waist except for a tight, very heavy-looking black leather vest, leaped into the air, their arms arched like wings. Two at a time they hopped and leaped toward the front steps of the temple, where the Living Buddha sat with visiting dignitaries. The wrestlers would hold their arms like wings, bow before the restored temple, turn toward each other, square off, and begin their wrestling. They were imitating ferocious eagles as they leaped toward each other, but they wrestled like quick-muscled panthers. Men of any age over seventeen, and from every weight and height, were allowed to take part. A 220-pound, twenty-one-year-old wrestled a thirty-five-year-old combatant weighing only 155.

All the people circled around and formed the wrestlers' ring in the pale dirt of the temple courtyard. This courtyard had not seen such great Mongolian spirit for twenty years. The men wrestled standing up, most of the time grasping each other's leather vest powerfully with both hands. Some wore regular pants; others wore baggy, flowing cotton pants with Mongolian symbols sewed onto them. They would shift their strength from one arm to the other trying to catch the opponent off balance, just as a bad horse shifts and stumbles trying to catch his rider off balance to throw him. These men had extraordinary balance, much of it developed from riding horses bareback since the age of five.

Next they were grunting, now spinning each other. If one did not touch the ground and lose, they would often come to a standoff, neither one moving. Each was trying to sense a shift in the other's power. If a Mongolian was both powerful and skilled he might react instinctively to such a shift one hundredth of a second before his foe tried his move. Then he'd often throw him to the earth first. There were two teams from different places in the grassland. They kept wrestling one another till there were four winners. After the morning's round they took a break for lunch and had the final wrestle-off. The men's power was brutish, yet tremendously controlled.

The four young men left were of different sizes. One weighed about 215, another about 180, one about 160, and the fourth about 150. The guy that weighed 150 was five feet seven, had greasy hair and a few adolescent pimples. He had to take on the 215-pound guy "built stout like bull." Their meeting was remarkable, lasting over fifteen minutes. Finally the small one got thrown and rolled up against a freshly planted tree. It wasn't a lack of strength, but he was matched in quickness by the man sixty-five pounds heavier. The Mongolian crowd was very silent and cheered only after both men finished this exceedingly long match.

The winner had a wide, flat face, which expressed the invincible spirit of these people of Genghis Khan. The four best wrestlers were lifted atop four black horses and led in front of the Living Buddha. The wide-faced winner received a multicolored wool blanket woven by a master Mongolian weaver. The second-best wrestler won a smaller blanket, colored the green of spring grass. The other two wrestlers won tapestry fabric embroidered with gold thread. They got off their shiny black horses, bowed to their brilliantly painted and restored temple, and leaped like eagles back into the crowds.

Next came dancing Mongolians dressed as deer and spirits, some looking like white-faced death. They jumped and weaved around, taking on the spirits of the life they represented. Then the people lined up to enter the temple, to be touched and blessed by the Living Buddha. We were not allowed inside. While I stood on the stone steps of the two-story building of worship, Muran walked by and acted as if he'd never seen us before. Surely I stood out at this celebration, being the only white-faced human here!

After much happiness and blessing, the men from varying places on the grasslands who were known to have the fastest horses lined up under a Chinese flag. Their great horse race began. They would race many miles to a place where there were storm clouds building. The Mongolians talked quietly to each other about who was gaining on whom, how their favorite horse was running, and a lot more, although my eyes could barely see anyone or anything. At best I could identify the dark shape of a horse. Their eyes could write books about what they saw miles beyond mine.

As we left the great celebration there was some sort of commotion behind us in the large crowd that was now leaving. We were headed toward the post office to mail the climbers a postcard from Mongolia. I had promised I would, and we might not get another chance if Muran was taking us away in the morning. I glanced back to a lone rider passing by the crowd. He looked like the man who'd won the race. His horse reared up on its two hind legs and came down on someone. The man who'd been pawed and kicked went crazy and instantly four men restrained him. He began yelling out what Ran Ying said were horrible Chinese cursings. He yelled to the rider, "You will never have a son. . . . Your family name will stop! . . . You're not even man enough to father a boy baby." Ran Ying would not interpret the really horrible curses.

At that, the drunken rider galloped back into the crowd and began whipping the swearing man with his reins. He whipped wildly, hitting the people holding back the curser. The tightly packed crowd ran in every direction just far enough away to watch. The man on the ground tried jumping up, attempting to pull the rider down, screaming more insults like a crazy person.

The rider was red-faced and occasionally he seemed to lose his balance on the horse. Someone who knew the rider grabbed his reins; people said it was his brother. Then the wild rider started whipping his own brother, making hand signals that meant something more than "Let go." Ran Ying said the hand signals must have been in Mongolian.

The guy on the ground kept on getting away from the people holding him back, and again charged the rowdy Mongolian on his black horse. The crowd was delighted. Ran Ying then said the man who'd been stepped on said something about the horseman's mother. With the comment about his mother the riding-while-intoxicated Mongolian galloped back into the crowd, knocking down a few people and a couple of bicycles. He then reached down like a trick rider and grabbed the man by his hair. He probably could have held on if he hadn't been so drunk. He looped back around the crowd and galloped down the middle of the dirt road. He escaped in a cloud of dust and rode toward his home village. A worker at the post office said it was lucky that the horseman had not brought his knife or gun with him. She said this man was quick to use his knife when he was drunk, but that Muran had ordered that none should bring knives or guns to the temple celebration. "Some men go crazy," she said, "when they drink whiskey."

## 39

## *"Sleep on Kang"*——

Muran had told the truth. He had a jeep ready to take us somewhere. Ran Ying asked where we were going. He smiled. Was that a
wicked smile or was he just playing with us? The first thing I noticed
was that there was no driver for the jeep. Muran started off fast and
went in the direction opposite to Baotou, headed toward Russia.

As he drove up onto a higher level of the plateau we were circled
now by nothing but the grasslands. There were no trees, no bushes,
not even tall grasses. No grass would have risen higher than my
ankles. The great sky was a dome over us with see-through clouds

wispy as an old Mongolian's beard. These clouds meant no rain, Muran said.

Why was Muran so tight with his information? Were we going somewhere never to be heard from again? He began talking to Ran Ying in Chinese and she listened longer than usual without interpreting it to me. Finally she said, "We are going to his friend's village. . . . His friends were at the celebration. One of their horses won the race." Ran Ying did not seem happy about this. Could she be doubting him, too?

The road was a sandy, lumpy trail that had two tire ruts and grass growing in the middle of it. Since Muran spoke "a tiny bit" of English, and maybe more than that, I was afraid to mention my fears to Ran Ying. He also had a pistol with him. Maybe that was for a wolf if he saw one.

Sometimes, like right now, I surprised myself. Maybe I was too bold. After all, I had more than myself to think of. What of my children's future? . . . What was I doing going with this man? Was I stupid for trusting my instincts about people? Over the years, both on the walk across America and since, I'd gone places with many strangers. Surely China had its share of crazy people and this man was purposely hard to understand and belligerent. Maybe I wanted this Mongolian experience so badly I'd thrown all caution to the winds. Where was anybody?

Way far away I saw many dots on the grasslands. Muran said it was one of his friend's herds of horses, and he went on to talk about the importance of Mongolian horses. He told us that if a horseman gets caught in a blizzard covering these easy-rolling hills, it becomes impossible for him to find his way home. There are no landmarks. So he gets off his horse, in snow often thigh-deep, and the horse leads him back home. If there's a whiteout, then he just holds onto the horse's tail. After an hour more of bouncing and driving, a man on an Appaloosa horse trotted by. The horseman acted as if he wasn't lonely and as if he was coming from somewhere.

The road ambled over land that reminded me of the open water of the Gulf of Mexico. Like the gulf, this land rolled smoothly. But often the gulf's movement created smooth low places that were always lower than they looked. That's how this Mongolian land was. It looked flat from far away, but it had many low places and high places. We came off one large, high place on the plateau and below us was a sunken bowl maybe five miles round. In it was a settlement called Baiyinnar (pronounced "buy-yin-nar"). "Probably reason they settle here is because they have a pond," Muran said with a rare smile. In Mongolian, Baiyinnar means "Have-a-Pond."

"This place, no foreigner ever see before," Muran said. "My friends and their ancient blood live on this grassland for long times. . . . Were first family to settle here. They very close. They let you stay with them. Is this what you wanted?" he said turning toward me and looking triumphant as he stopped and we over-looked the valley.

"Yes, this is perfect," I answered. It looked like a gathering of ten or fifteen tepees.

Muran stopped on the road where we could see the whole settle-ment and explained it to us. "There are six or seven families that live here." In the middle of a cluster of four tan-colored homes was where his friends, the Xiaos, lived. (Xiao is pronounced "Shá-how.") He said the homes were made from soft mud bricks. The homes were dwarfed by the grasslands, looking as small as a postage stamp on the side of a battleship. In the middle of the valley was a rectan-gular-shaped field of grass much greener and deeper than the rest. It was about a mile long. Muran said this was a pasture fenced off with stones. "Keep cattle and horses here in winter," he said. A small hill to the east was where the Mongolian people went every spring, on May 17, to ask for the blessing of much rain. There was a dry creek bed that had water in it only after big rains. A single line of scraggly poles, strung with wire, ran through Have-a-Pond. They'd had electricity here for over two years.

We pulled up to their place. There were a couple of hitchin' posts out front. It reminded me of a stagecoach stop, except that a black iron gate led into a courtyard. Only the wife of the family was home. Her two sons stayed at school all week in Muran's village, and her husband was away. Muran said that he'd driven here a few days ago and asked them if they would take us in. They said they would give him their answer at the celebration. Muran stood with his arm around Mrs. Xiao and told us this family was his favorite on the grasslands.

He left us immediately, as if he were nervous about staying too long. Muran said he'd see us later, he just didn't say when. He drove off. We stood in the middle of a glaring Mongolian day with Mrs. Xiao and a few clucking chickens. She said her cat killed one

This open-air market is where the citizens of Chengdu can buy the freshest food: red chilies, aged eggs, bean curd, hot and spicy preserved vegetables, carp, young green beans, eels, and live chickens.

A Chengdu eel merchant is happy to sell me "many, delicate, flavorful baby eels."

Four generations of a Chinese family at their home on the Inner Mongolian Plateau near the village of Bayan Obo. Although no one in this village had ever seen a non-Chinese before, the young teacher at the upper right knew that Jesse Jackson was running for president of the USA.

Chinese villagers' first view, ever, of a "white-faced" man

Rice field just harvested by hand in Sichuan Province. Almost all farm work in China—planting, cultivating, plowing—is done by a peasant's hand.

A guard in Beijing observes us with suspicion.

Mongolian holy men, wrestlers, dancers, and local people came to celebrate the reopening of their sacred temple, destroyed during the Cultural Revolution. Some came from as far away as "two days' horse ride" to this village of Wu Lan Tu Ge Su Mu. (overleaf)

Thunderstorms come to Baiyinnar, the Mongolian village where we lived. Baiyinnar means "Have-a-Pond."

Ran Ying, in traditional Mongolian dress, with our Mongolian mother, Chaganda Xaio, which means "Fair Girl." We called her "Mongo Mama."

I stand with a neighbor shepherd boy on the left and Mongo Mama's second youngest son, Wu Ri Gen, which means "Wise Man," on the right.

A Mongolian horseman be-
fore a race across the plains.

Mongo Mama's herd of "running-free" horses come to a rock well for daily watering by
her sons.

A man rows across the bay as the sun sets over the coastal city of Fuzhou, four hundred miles south of Shanghai.

Performers move gracefully to traditional Mongolian dances in Bautao.

A traditional sailing ship heads out of the port of Fuzhou toward the East China Sea. *(overleaf)*

yesterday. There were only five left. The wind was still, as if it hadn't made its mind up about what it would do today. Suddenly, this open space was crowded. Mrs. Xiao was having two strange people move in.

There was no other vehicle in town. There was no way out except by walking or borrowing a horse. Our hostess said to bring our stuff inside. Mrs. Xiao spoke Mongolian usually but did very well conversing with Ran Ying in Chinese. I would sleep in the east end of the house, which was their winter quarters, and Ran Ying would stay inside with her. When we got to my austere room Ran Ying said, "Oh," in a squeaky voice, "you will be sleeping on kang" (pronounced "kong"). Was there a gorilla I didn't see?

The kang is a type of bed for winter, used throughout the cold parts of China. It gets so frigid on the plains of Inner Mongolia and northern China that there are few ways to keep warm. There is no such thing as central heat and air conditioning, and no insulation in the homes. Mongolian houses of mud never have windows in the north wall but they still offer little shelter from winter's brutal cold beyond a windbreak. That's where the kang comes in. It is a brick bed built about two and a half feet off the ground, usually taking up one end of a room. It's something like an elevated brick patio, but much more—it's a life-saving bed. Usually quilts are spread beneath and above people sleeping on the kang. The mother, father, children, grandparents sleep on it. Sometimes guests, perhaps lost in a winter storm, may sleep there too, along with everybody else.

What makes the kang so interesting is that it is heated. The cooking stove in Mongolia is a brick box where coal or wood or dung is burned. It has a hole in the top where the wok fits. This is built right next to the kang and all the smoke flows through the kang before leaving the house. Instead of the hot smoke rising, it heats the top of the kang and keeps the people cozy-warm. It would certainly not get cold enough to have to heat it for the whole family, and the guests(!), while we were here. Nah, the winds were not talking of fall yet.

Our Mongolian hostess said to Ran Ying "Mongolian people seldom meet strangers, so when they do, they would be very kind. They will receive you happily and you can do anything as you like. You can have dinner with the host, they don't mind about this. During the night you can stay on the same kang with them, too. But if they have daughter they put a belt between daughter and guest and father checks belt in morning to see if it's still straight." Mrs. Xiao chuckled softly and said that her daughter was grown and working away from here. "No need for belt."

Mrs. Xiao had short but thick black hair and appeared to be in her late forties, or perhaps early fifties. She spoke so softly that over her voice you could hear the sheep walking outside. Her body was thick with power and behind her black-rimmed glasses was a shrewd, subtle intelligence. Her first name meant "white girl." She was an energetic but slow-moving woman, only because there was no reason to move fast. She smoked a lot, often a very powerful, thin cigarillo and sometimes an occasional cigar. She also rolled her own cigarettes.

It was so profoundly quiet here in Have-a-Pond. Even quieter than at Chomolungma. There were no falling rocks, just herds of running-free horses coming in to the well for water. The sounds of this wildly open Mongolian land had no stone cliffs to bounce off. The sounds just got caught by the wind and carried away. Mongolians spoke as quietly as a whisper.

Now that we were here I couldn't stop asking our new Mongo Mama questions. I felt immediately at home and welcomed by her as if I'd been gone for ten years with a great Mongolian army and had just returned. I wanted to know how many families lived in this village?

"Seven. She knows all their names," Ran Ying interpreted. She said them all, beautiful Mongolian names that sounded like a song. Her voice was as soothing as a small brook dripping over moss-covered stones. "Her husband's father grew up here. Their house was built in '55 and they've always lived in Have-a-Pond. The old house was too old, so they tore it down and built another. Her husband's people were the first to settle here. Until 1950, just their family lived here; then other families started moving in. Used to be grass soft, knee-deep. Now too many people.

"Most of the families have moved here just recently. Next door they have six daughters and one son. None of the kids are married. There are ten people in that family, plus an old grandmother. Usually not have such a large family, but they just wanted a son. They kept trying, but have six daughters first." She added that after this family had four daughters they named their next daughters boy's names hoping to confuse the gods that were jinxing their chance to have a boy. Ran Ying explained, "If you named a girl a boy's name there was always the chance that the gods who decided whether you had a boy or girl would, if they were in a hurry, get confused and send you a boy by mistake. Seventh child, they got boy."

As Ran Ying pointed out beyond the courtyard she said, "The people by the well are a young couple with small children. They live at head of valley. His parents found him a wife—he already knew her and planned to get married, but his parents bought furniture for the house and rushed it. It hard for man to find a woman on grasslands. But not as hard as when many Mongo men became Buddhist priests."

She was referring to the time on the grasslands before the Chinese took over, when from almost every Mongo family one son became a priest. "During that time if a woman was bad and 'be with' the wrong Mongo man [an already married one], then their priest would punish this woman and make her marry a whip," Mongo Mama said.

"There is family on hill. That's Osa Dai's living place. He's the little boy who takes care of our sheep, waters our horses. There are five brothers and sisters altogether. His mother died four years ago. One day she was milking baby cows and their horse went crazy. She tried to protect the cows, but horse kill her. The youngest child was three years old, a little girl." I heard something rubbing on the outside walls of the house, and Mongo Mama said it sounded like camels. Sure enough, it was a free-roaming herd of double-humped camels that happened to be passing by.

Mrs. Xiao continued her story. "Many people ask boy's father why doesn't he get married again so there will be someone to take care of the children. He would rather take care of them all by himself. In China there is a reputation for stepmothers as being very mean, very bad. That is true usually. So he say he doesn't want to get married again so the stepmother will treat his kids badly." She rolled and lit another cigarette. "Osa Dai had to quit school, help father take care of younger brothers and sisters, and cattle and horses. He herd cattle on his bicycle," she said smiling. "He does not like horses much.

"Then family with six daughters, one son, live a hundred yards away. Very close. They used to live near where you stayed last few days, but it was hard to get grass so they move out here. Mongo Mama pointed out a window toward some smoke coming out of a home far down the dry creek bed. The only windows faced south, into the courtyard.

"She say," Ran Ying interpreted, "that grandfather, grandmother, mother and father and kids live over there because it's far away from other people and the grass will be higher and easier to raise cattle. They live a couple of miles from here, up on a hill, kind of behind little knoll. Snow sometime blow, cover their house there. Not naturally protected like here in our small valley.

"The people build their houses here not too close to each other. Because every family has sheep and cattle and they need to scatter around. Not live too close together so they will have places to put cattle and sheep. Old couple next door, in seventies, eighties. Work hard, still. Everyone works till they die on grasslands."

# 40

## *A Terrible Energy*————

"Can you tell me a story about Genghis Khan?" I asked Mrs. Xiao. Mongo-Mama had no story to tell. "When I was growing up there were many stories about him and our people were very proud. But now I have forgotten them." She would say no more. We tried, but all she would do was go to her bed and, reaching under it, way under the mattress, pull out a couple of time-worn pictures. They were black-and-white photos of a painting of Genghis Khan. But for some reason she would or could not talk of him. Don't tell me the Chinese will not let their Mongolians talk of their former great

Khan, who lived over seven hundred years ago. He was the only Mongolian to have ever really conquered them, and the Chinese still fear the Mongolians.

Ran Ying said that she and Mongo Mama would now begin to prepare supper. Mongo Mama said I could go to the well and fetch water, as if I knew exactly how to do that from all my experience in America. She said there was a weathered stick about five feet long with two dented metal buckets tied to either end in the courtyard. I should go off toward the village well and make three trips till I filled up the large ceramic storage container.

To stomp out my frustration about Mongo Mama not being able to talk about Genghis Khan, I kicked the ground. I was getting tired of all the controls and oppression of things I never even considered controllable or oppressable. I felt rising up in me a stronger desire to search back to the beginnings of my tribe that once roamed the lands of Europe and the seas of the world.

If only the winds could tell me the stories of the Mongolian people who'd lived here before. I remembered my favorite stories from the many books I'd read about Mongolians and their history. To spark their nights while on the trail of conquest, warriors sat by a fire. They were known as great singers, and all their songs told a story. The light from the flames would light their deep-bronze, wide, and wild faces. The warriors sang songs about the heroic deeds of the past Khans and sad songs of a wailing loneliness that comes over a man moving across the steppes. They sang with strong, high voices that could slice through the cutting winds and carry into the night. Many wolves heard their night songs. Mongolian voices could not be timid on this endless land of grass.

I thought of the greatest nomad of them all, of Genghis Khan, who pushed his kingdom as far as his wild Mongolian ponies could carry him and his warriors. Since I was a child I had been fascinated by the legends of this world-conquering leader. I could hardly believe I was standing on the same ground as he did, listening to the same wind whistling across the steppes. Genghis Khan once conquered China. To the Chinese this must have seemed like yesterday even though it happened eight hundred years ago. I was sure that's why Mrs. Xiao wouldn't talk about him. But even the Chinese couldn't silence the wind, so I listened for a while till I thought I could hear the drumming of hoofbeats and the songs of ancient riders singing of a hero unlike any the world had ever known. Then I went to the well to carry back the water, Mongolian style.

I would never have thought that just carrying water a few hundred yards across open prairie could be so tiring. It took three trips to fill the container to the top. Although a million Chinese may run around balancing poles and buckets filled with water as if they are light and easy to carry, they aren't. I spilled half the water out the first few times and the stick cut into my shoulders. Thank God for water that comes out of a faucet. During my last sloshing trip back to Mongo Mama's place, I heard a sound. I stopped but the great energy of silence and the slight slurp of the water in the buckets made it impossible to locate the foreign sound. Back in the house Mongo Mama probably heard something too, and five minutes later her husband, a stern, intensely proud and private man, rode in on his quiet motorcycle. It was red.

He walked into his house, said nothing, sat down on their bed, which was in the main living room, and looked at me. I smiled in his direction. He nodded, without expression. I couldn't say anything, so I went over to my pack and got out a picture of my horse, Shocker. He's black, a stallion, and big compared to this man's horses I'd seen. He looked at it with a horse expert's eyes and handed it back. I could hear Ran Ying and Mongo Mama talking in the cooking room, which had to be entered by walking out into the courtyard. I studied the room we were in, the one they stayed in during the spring, summer, and part of the fall. They usually moved into the cooking room with the kang in September and lived in that tiny room for three months.

The main room had a very worn, soft brick floor. Their twin-sized bed was in the corner, covered with a beautiful Chinese carpet with dragons in the middle and blue trim. A small desk was next to their bed with their family pictures under a piece of glass. There was a plastic blow-up cat on top of a clothes dresser, which Mongo Mama told us they got the one time they went on a trip. Muran took them to Beijing. Mongo Mama disliked the noise and the great number of people in Beijing.

The mysterious Mongo Papa (whose name, Tu Meng Ge Xi, I never learned to pronounce) stood up and walked into the courtyard to breathe. I guessed he couldn't get enough of this pure air. He soaked in the hugeness of his land. In the corner of the courtyard was a storehouse built of mud mixed with straw. There they hung their saddles, dried their meat, stashed some crude wooden tools, and cured some sheepskins. Mongo Mama kept some pumpkins and pumpkin seeds in there, and also stored large amounts of flour. The chickens had a nesting box outside it. The roof was straw.

After dinner, some sweet Chinese wine, and the mighty calming effects of the Mongolian moonlight, we got shy Mongo Papa to talk to us. It wasn't easy. Ran Ying explained that in China there's a saying that fits Mongo Papa. "They say man like him has gold mouth. Everything he says is rich like gold." I felt as though I was before a wise man who was summoned to answer my many questions. I taped this special conversation and what follows is what he said, translated as usual by Ran Ying.

*Have you always used those wooden saddles like they use now?*
"Yes, we like the wooden saddles. We don't like the leather because you can paint the wood or put silver on it, and it is comfortable when you sit on it, too."
*Where did your grandfather and great-grandfather live?*
"My father was born here so my grandfather was here, but before that I don't know."
*Has the grassland changed much since you were a boy?*
"When I was a boy the grass was very high and now not so high. Now there are too many cattle and a lot of people. Also when I was small there was only one family here. Also all around here there are people who grow food. Their cattle come here to eat grass too."
["People who grow food" are the Chinese who are gradually creeping farther and farther into the Mongolian lands and taking over.]
*Are the cattle skinnier than they used to be?*
"Yes, smaller."
*How did you get to school?*
"I lived at school, like sons do now, and rode a horse when came home. I was eight when I learned to ride far away by myself."
*How old were you when you first learned how to catch a horse with one of those nooses?* [Mongolians have to catch their horses in the wide-open spaces, since they let them run free. They don't lasso them like American cowboys, but carry on their horses a long pole with a rope noose on the end, which they maneuver around the neck of the horse they want to catch, while riding full speed. It takes a real

strong Mongolian rider to do such a thing as catch one of their horses with a pole and rope.]

"I was sixteen when started to go out with horses and at that time we had big pack of horses, over two hundred. Three or four people took care of them together, so they had to change their riding horse every day, so they have to catch a horse every day. I start catching horse then." [Muran had told me that in his prime Mongo Papa was considered the best rider in Inner Mongolia, and that's competing with a people who at one time were considered the best riders in the world.]

_Do you remember when the wolves used to be here?_

"Used to be the grass was very high so the wolves could hide. Every night when I was working with horses, one person would have to stay outside with the horses so the wolves wouldn't come and eat the horses. There were also a lot of wild sheep, yellowish sheep. Wolves would eat sheep, sometimes people. Later when the grass was low, wolves all went away."

_Do you know of any wolves ever eating anyone, lately?_

"It was in the food-growers' [Chinese] area. Sometimes the wolf came and took the baby away."

_How big were the wolves and did you use to shoot them?_

"The wolves are scared of people and all night the person watching the two hundred horses would have to walk around and around. We had not gun at the time, just had thing used to catch a horse. If we saw a wolf, we just started hollering."

_Were the wolves big enough to pull down a big horse or just a baby horse?_

"They try to eat the baby ones, but sometimes they catch the big ones."

_Did you see a wolf on the grassland and maybe try to run it down on your horse and catch it?_

"Usually horses could catch it. Especially if the wolf caught the horse and started to eat it, then we just let him eat, and when he get real full, we start to chase him. Could not run fast. If we catch it, we use the skin to make a beautiful coat."

_Could just one wolf catch a horse? Would it take more than one?_

"Just one."

# "Visible from Moon"___

We drank some hot tea and Mongo Papa said he wanted to watch some TV. Mongo Mama said he should talk to us some more since he would be going somewhere and would stay gone for some time.

"Has there ever been a winter that you were just stranded inside?" I asked.

"One winter it was three feet deep. People can still go out, and cattle too, but when they go out, they have to ride on the horses. Horses can still walk but nothing else. Airplane came over and sent food for the people. The snow was so deep they had to take the cattle somewhere else to feed. They could eat nothing here."

Despite all the questions I asked Mongo Papa, he volunteered only the following, which he said in the same seemingly emotionless voice. "Most young people have left. They don't like to be cattle or sheep people; they like to work in cities. They are mostly high school graduates; they don't want to stay home and do farm work. When I was small the grass was very, very good; we never cut grass for the winter to feed the cattle, but we have to now, and every time it snows it will cover all the grass. Used to, you just let the cattle out and you didn't have to take care of them, but when the first snow comes, the cattle will come back all by themselves. They know they won't have anything to eat anymore."

He stood up and went to where their black-and-white TV was and began watching a movie. Mongo Mama cuddled up next to him and this embarrassed him a bit at first. Ran Ying said later he was the kind of man who talked only to Mongo Mama, the rest of the time he kept quiet. She put a quilt over them as it was cool in Inner Mongolia tonight. The movie was about some war. It was not a documentary, but a drama. At first I wasn't watching it but looking out the window at the slow-moving silhouettes of a herd of horses. Mongo Mama, whom I was sitting next to, laughed nervously. My first thought was maybe Mongo Papa had said something to her, but then Ran Ying giggled; she was very uptight.

I asked her what was wrong. She said, nothing. I asked again and she said the movie on TV is stupid. I wanted to know why. She said it was one of only three movies that the Chinese were allowed to watch during the Cultural Revolution. That meant they were limited to the same three movies for ten years. It was a movie about the Korean War. I asked Ran Ying to share with me what was going on and at first she wouldn't. She said it would embarrass our Mongolian family. They watched our conversation very carefully to look for my reaction.

Ran Ying finally gave in and explained a scene that was on at that moment. A young Chinese soldier stood alone on top of a hill in Korea. All the trees had been stripped of their leaves by bombs, and the ground was smoking from the intensity of the battle. Ran Ying said the soldier had stayed behind to protect his retreating comrades. Down at the bottom of the hill a large group of soldiers was advancing toward the young Chinese. The tension in the room was building rapidly. Mongo Mama and Mongo Papa seemed to be embarrassed.

"Ran Ying. What's happening now!"

"I cannot say. It is very stupid," she kept on.

"Come on. Tell me," I demanded.

"Well, this young Chinese soldier is about to kill all of those soldiers coming up the hill at him." Practically all of China had this film memorized.

"What?!?" I said, confused.

"Yes, all those soldiers coming up hill are Americans. He kills them all, over two hundred by himself. First he shoots them, yelling things like 'Long Live the Revolution.' Then he runs out of bullets and kills many with rocks and sticks," she reported. Mongo Papa got up to turn it off.

I spoke up. "Tell him it's OK. I would like to watch what happens next. Tell him I know this is propaganda and it is not true, anyway. I think it's funny." I was furious.

"Now," Ran Ying said, "there are only twenty American soldiers left. He has been out of hand grenades and bullets for a long time. Bullets are zinging by the Chinese hero on all sides. He kills the remaining Americans with a few punches, a few more rocks, and finally, he stands up on the sandbagged wall and screams. The last couple of American soldiers drop dead of sheer fright!" On each American helmet, all played by Chinese actors with slightly round eyes, is a skull and crossbones.

Mongo Papa said something. Ran Ying interpreted. "Peter, he says he knows that Americans are not this way. They are a brave people. Good warriors." I thanked him for saying that and went to my kang and went to bed, but not to sleep.

By now I was somewhat used to China's silly propaganda and I quickly forgot about the TV movie. But I couldn't get my imagination to turn off about Mongo Papa's family. I wondered what part of the grasslands his relatives rode when Genghis Khan was their king, when the grass was deep. Where did they live when the wolves ate horses because there were no Chinese babies to eat. When the Great Khan ruled, there were no Chinese on the grasslands; they stayed on the south side of the Great Wall, which they'd built to keep these horsemen out. Wasn't it fantastic that the only man-made object visible from the moon, the Great Wall of China, was built to keep the feared Mongolians from taking over China? There was no doubt in my mind that Mongo Papa's people had fought with the great Khan. Even now, in his fourth or fifth decade, he looked as if he could ride across Russia. I wondered if his people took part in one of the greatest battles the Mongolians ever fought.

\*   \*   \*

It happened in the thirteenth century, the battle against the Shah and his four hundred thousand fighting men. If Shah Mohammed's spies had not produced the following report, the Shah probably would have been bolder in his assaults on the Mongols. He was told: Genghis Khan's army is as numerous as ants and locusts. His warriors are as brave as lions, so that none of the fatigues or hardships of war can injure them. They know neither ease nor rest, neither flight nor withdrawal. Whithersoever they go, they carry everything they need with them. They satisfy their hunger with dried meat and sour milk, disregarding the instructions as to what is allowed or what is forbidden, but eating the flesh of no matter what animal, even dogs and swine. These horses need neither straw nor wheat, being content to scrape through the snow with their hoofs and eat the underlying grass, or to paw the earth and munch roots and vegetables. When the Mongols effect a conquest, they leave nothing alive, either large or small, and they even rip up the bellies of the women with child. No mountain or river can arrest their progress. They cross every ravine and swim their horses over the rivers, themselves holding on to the mane or the tail.

It was the autumn of 1218 when Genghis Khan told his huge army that they should assemble next spring after they had spent the winter in their home yurts. When the snows melted he would lead his troops through a main mountain pass that had been used from time immemorial by nomad tribes of the Central Asian plateau. He knew that before he could reach the Shah's land he would have to cross a wasteland that was almost waterless and foodless. Over that desert he would have to transport an army of a quarter of a million men and more than a million horses, who must nourish themselves as best they could—for there was no other route. The whole of the eastern border of the Shah's realm was protected by impassable mountains ranging to over 20,000 feet.

The Mongols proved their ability to endure inhuman suffering when Genghis Khan's son Juji (jew-G) crossed the Pamir Mountains to battle the Shah. In midwinter, they began a brutal ride into the unknown. The army of some thirty thousand men entered the gap between two mountain ranges. They rode through snow four feet deep and the cold was so frigid it threatened to freeze the horses' legs. Snowstorms cut them down as they struggled across 13,000-foot passes between mountains over 20,000 feet high. They wrapped the legs of their horses in yak hides, while they hunkered down covered in double-sheepskin coats. To warm themselves, they opened the veins of their horses, drank the hot blood, and then closed the wounds. Their route was littered with the skeletons of horses. Only the skeletons, for the riders ate every bit of the dead horse before it froze. Every mile along their incredible route were frozen corpses of men.

Then, after unspeakable hardships and privations, there opened before the Mongols a lovely green valley, a land of vineyards and silk culture, of wheat and stud farms, no less celebrated for its goldsmiths' art than for its glassblowers. Here the spring was already in full bloom.

But as soon as they had descended into this oasis, as soon as their advance guard appeared in the villages and began to drive off cattle, Mohammed arrived with his army to destroy the Mongols, weakened by their incredible journey over the mountains. When he caught sight of the skin-clad nomads on their little rough-haired ponies, men without iron shields, the ruler almost felt compassion for them. But he didn't, and what transpired was a battle of terrible bloodshed. However, it was not the first or the last time that Genghis Khan's Mongols would loose their terrible energy on a land and a people. Right before I went to sleep that night I listened for sounds out on the quiet grasslands. A light breeze whispered through the window and the sound of a blowing feather would be the loudest sound I'd hear till I began dreaming.

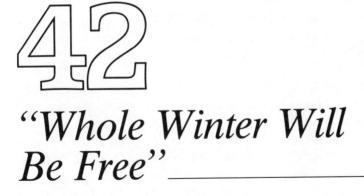

# "Whole Winter Will Be Free"

We'd just finished our breakfast. The breakfast was a typical herdman's breakfast of millet, which you put in hot milk and tea. First you put the tea in and then you put the milk in, then you put sugar in, and then you put the millet in. If you want to, you put in little fried cookies too. Then we had moon cakes with red dots on them.

Mongo Mama said she needed to go to the store. There was a small general store on the other side of the stone-walled pasture. The store had been here for ten years and it was run by a couple of

Chinese girls. They're the ones, Mongo Mama said, with the white donkey that rode by yesterday. It was about a mile walk over there. I felt so close already to Mongo Mama. I was getting to the point where I could basically understand what they talked about in Chinese.

In the store was a poster. It had big red Chinese writing on it and was very harsh-looking. I asked Ran Ying what it was. "In China," she said, "if there is a serious criminal convicted, they put up posters in all public places like stores, commune centers, schools, and offices. The poster was about a young man, twenty-one years old. He'd raped a high school girl who was fourteen and he tried to rape her again, but she wouldn't let him. He was a Han from the province southwest of Mongolia. He was a worker in this county. They put the guy in jail and in jail he slashed his roommate's head with a can, so they sentenced him to death. This was done in County Court.

"For it to go to a national court, you would have to rape lots of little girls or kill a lot of people," she continued. "Lately a lot of criminals being killed in China, like in each province in past two weeks, they would kill twenty to thirty by firing squad. In China, people don't say anything about death penalty. They like it. People who rape just make Chinese really mad; they don't have any sympathy for them.

"In China it's always death penalty if anyone rape kids. Usually if a person tries to do it, he doesn't do it just once, he will go on, and on, it's really dangerous, so if this kind of person gets caught, they shot. People just hate this thing in China, especially if it involves little girls because they are not supposed to know anything about sex until they get married."

Mongo Mama bought some fruit and some yellow fabric, a very "wild" color. On our way back home from the store I asked Mongo Mama what she did during each season. She started talking about February. "We begin to get busy then because that is when the sheep and cattle have their babies and people will have to help so no cattle and sheep will be left alone to have baby. That's in February and March. In May we will start to cut the wool. Usually we go out with the sheep and cut it right there on the grasslands and bring the wool back. In June we give injections and wash the sheep and cattle so they won't get diseased. That's a busy time for Mongolian people. After they protect cattle and sheep this way by injections and washing, usually the whole summer will be free. They will go out with just the sheep; they don't go out with the cattle. Women will stay home doing nothing." Mongo Mama seemed to be glad when summer came.

"It's not until early September that we start to cut grass for winter." (They cut all their hay, "grass," with a small knife, by hand. We cut some with Mongo Mama while we were there.) "Cutting grass usually lasts about a month. From mid-September to mid-or late October, or not even that long, is the breeding season. After that the whole winter will be free. In winter all we have to do is feed cattle when it is real bad snow. Oh," Mongo Mama remembered, "at the end of September we move from this part of the house into the cooking area where the kang is and we stay there about ninety days," she said, finishing her year on the grasslands.

For many days we led a blissful life in Have-a-Pond, Inner Mongolia. Mongo Mama and Ran Ying really liked each other very much. I had not seen Ran Ying this happy since we'd met in China. Mongo Mama was a mother to the earth, she was the type of woman who would take in all people to her. Ran Ying acted very joyful around her and seemed to appreciate the simple days and nights of gathering water, sweeping the brick floor, collecting the eggs, cooking one major meal a day, listening for what the wind would do during the day, and walking over the grasslands.

When Mongo Mama's young sons arrived home on their bicycles from school, she said something to them in Mongolian so Ran Ying couldn't understand. When Ran Ying asked where they were going, Mongo Mama said, "Oh, they just go out to play." We did not see them again till another darkness was moving in on the village of Have-a-Pond.

Right before full darkness a big, almost square man burst through the front door and in his arms was a roasted sheep, dripping juices. He slammed it down on the bare wood eating table. He went back outside. A lone headlight caught my eyes. It was coming toward the courtyard and pulled into the mud horse barn by the front metal gate. It was Mongo Papa; we hadn't seen him for a couple of days. Up toward the top of the hill overlooking our village the sky was still deep purple. Coming through the sky were four headlights, bouncing madly. My eyes followed them till they skidded to a halt out front. The headlights remained on to light up the front of our house like a policeman's spotlight. Some days we had not seen any motorized vehicles through Have-a-Pond. Other days one, at the most two.

Low voices of men could be heard coming toward us. The first man through the door I recognized as one of the four champion wrestlers from the celebration. His stare focused on me was as strong as a headlock. Another larger man dressed in blue cotton came in and kissed Mongo Mama on the cheek. It was her eldest son. He lived in a town south of here and was chief jeep driver there. A beautiful woman in Mongolian costume was escorted in by a young man with thick wavy black hair and artist's eyes. They were famous around here as traditional singers and dancers who performed down at Muran's village.

Mongo Mama opened a dresser drawer, cradled a beautiful white piece of silk in her hands, opened it, and brought out a handful of knives. She put them around the cooked sheep that was dripping onto their brick floor. She motioned for me to sit down at the table, saying to Ran Ying that I should sit at the back of the sheep by the best meat. I was given a knife with an aged, finely cracked bone handle, yellowed by many feasts. Everyone sat down then and began cutting into the meat. I hesitated for a moment until I realized there would be no plates or napkins. I cut off a chunk of sheep's leg. It dripped onto my beard and tasted as good as anything I'd ever eaten. I occasionally imagined my mother telling me to remember my manners. When Mongolians eat they slurp a lot.

The door popped open again and my eyes saw only a slim silhouette. It was . . . Muran. His arms were filled with bottles of beer, Chinese wine, and clear liquor, called by some "liquid razor blades." Muran came right over to me, patted me on the back, and began opening up enough bottles to fill the open spaces on the table that were not taken by the sheep, bones, and knives. Huddled around our sheep feast were Mongo Mama and Papa, their eldest son and their two youngest ones, the wrestler, the young singing couple, Ran Ying, me, and Muran. Oh, and there was also Muran's "brother." Well, he really wasn't his brother but he said he called him that, for he was his dearest friend. Brother was sickly thin, his arms not much thicker than sheep bones. His cheeks and eyes were sunken, his hair uncombed. His eyes sort of floated in his head. He was definitely not a Mongolian.

Muran never sat still; he walked around the table, patting everyone on the back, pausing to see how Brother was doing with his drinking. He kept all the empty bottles removed and assisted me in getting the best cuts of this special sheep, which the others seemed to be leaving for my knife. Muran was a totally different man. Something had changed his manner toward us. Maybe he now trusted us and accepted that I truly loved the "primitive" conditions of the grasslands. Maybe Muran could tell that the spirit of the Mongolians and their skies and grasslands had become part of mine. Whatever, he was rocking with his dearest friends and me. Periodically people went out onto the grasslands, for that was the Mongolian "bathroom."

The short "princess" stood, about fifteen minutes into our eating of the sheep, and began to sing. She said that based on the years of birth of the people there, "We have two dragons here. We have two horses here . . . so I will sing a festival song." Never had I heard a voice like hers. It covered the room, pierced through the mud walls, and headed straight out across the open land. It was shrill yet hauntingly melodic, cutting my lonesome heart in half. I had no idea what the words were. The Mongolian words had the gentle sounds of a baby cooing. Surrounded by the massive skies and soul-stretching lands, the Mongolians had to learn to sing over and through the wind. I was enchanted.

Then the young, handsome man next to her stood and danced a dance of a returning hero. Next the wrestler stood and sang a "crying" song about a young boy and girl lost on the plains with their sheep and rescued by a she-wolf. Mongo Mama's eldest son did not want to sing; he was shy like Mongo Papa, so he and Mongo Mama danced, arm in arm. Mongo Papa, the truly shy man, had slipped away, without drinking anything, with his two young sons. Someone said he had recently quit drinking. They were watching a kung-fu movie on TV.

Mongo Mama's place here on the southern edge of Have-a-Pond was moving into a level of excitement reserved for Mongolian weddings and extra-special occasions. Muran put his arm on my shoulder and said, "A toast to our new friend, 'The Rock.'" Everyone drank down a whole bottle of beer. Muran had asked Ran Ying and found out my name, Peter, meant "Rock." They wanted me to sing, and Muran walked to each of them and whispered something. They began chanting something in Mongolian. It sounded like two words. Was there some really weird Mongolian custom they wanted me to try? No, Ran Ying said, "they all want you to sing 'Jingle Bells.' They know this song from English lessons on TV, one of the most popular shows in China now." I sang "Jingle Bells" and they all knew some of it. Hopefully the Russians didn't hear any of it. They might have thought the Mongolians now had American military advisers. Then Ran Ying sang "My Motherland."

After the Mongolian princess tried to teach me to dance like a Mongolian, and Muran danced with Ran Ying, the wrestler walked up to me and put his hard hands on my shoulders. His name meant "Brave." He had watched me all evening and had decided that I was a big guy and that I needed to learn to wrestle Mongolian-style. He took my arm and began pulling me outside. I shook my head, tried to keep from being yanked around, and was pulled outside anyway. We stood under a ceiling of stars and black sky, but we had no black leather vests to wear. He grabbed the top of my pants and stood there until I grabbed his. Then he tensed the muscles in his arms and showed me some of his power. But he did not move. He was waiting for me to make the first move. I shifted one of my legs and could tell I was at least as strong as "the brave one," but in the time it takes to wink I was on the ground. Well, he didn't let me hit the ground—he held me up, sort of. They all clapped; even Mongo Papa came out to watch this. They were proud that I was learning their way of wrestling.

Everyone but the wrestlers and I went back inside. We stayed out there long enough for me to wrestle with all of them. The whole idea in their style of wrestling is that you don't usually use your brute strength; you have to use finesse and technique. We shook hands, bowed to each other, and went back to the lights and music. The wind brought a cold chill from the northeast tonight.

There were many, many toasts after every song. Toasts to Mongolia, the grasslands, new friends, a great party. Pale Brother had been staring at me all night. Now he was standing in front of me holding out his arms in my direction! Muran said, "Brother says that if you are my friend, you are Brother's friend, too. Brother wants to dance with you, Rock." All over China it is very common for men to dance with men. I didn't want to but Muran harassed me till I did. I had to oblige and be a good guest, Ran Ying chimed in. I'd never seen Ran Ying so loose. "In China it is real important to be respectful of other people's ways," I was telling myself, so there I was dancing arm and arm with Brother. We couldn't decide who should lead. I felt highly(!) self-conscious, but at least I was twelve thousand miles from anyone who knew me. Ran Ying tried to take a picture. I stopped dancing. This was one custom I would not plan to bring back to America.

Muran said he'd be back in the morning to take us to the train. Everyone except Mongo Mama and her family (including Ran Ying and me) disappeared into the night as they'd come. I felt as if a Mongolian thunderstorm was raging inside my head when my Mongo Mama woke me up and said Muran was here, it was time to leave. Where was my aspirin? was my first thought. Before I could sit up she handed me a bag of millet, a green apple, and a little silk pouch. She touched me on the arm, the closest she'd ever been to me, and walked out. The first sounds I heard were of bones cracking. This morning there was some leftover lamb, mostly bones, and Mongo Mama's young boys had been the first ones up so that they could crack the bones and get the marrow out. They offered me a few bones. I passed. Mongo Papa was already gone.

I opened the silk pouch and inside was a cast-metal round thing. I turned it around to see the face of Genghis Khan. We left quickly; Muran was in a hurry as usual. He looked unusually pale on this, our last morning on the Mongolian Steppes. I had gotten my chance in Inner Mongolia, but now I didn't know how to say good-bye to Mongo Mama. Ran Ying hugged her for both of us.

Before Muran's jeep was out of sight of Have-a-Pond, Muran said he wanted to tell us something probably no Mongolian ever would. It went something like this: "Round the campfires, from generation to generation, there has been handed down a great dream. When the most 'lasting' things on earth, the Empire in the North and the Empire in the South, fall in ruins, and the White Tsar in Russia and the Son of Heaven in China have vanished—then will there arise a new Genghis Khan, to create a new Mongolian Empire worldwide."

# 43

## *A Soft Pillow*_____

I loved the sounds of the squeaking of the metal springs as our train slipped through the cool Inner Mongolian air. I loved the clicking noise of the shiny metal wheels as they hit the places where the tracks came together. The conductor blew the wonderful whistle frequently, now that we'd passed out of the city of Huhehot the place where we'd boarded. The traveling sounds of the whistle made little peasant children stop and watch. I wondered if they yearned to follow the train to the end of its tracks. I loved the way the whistle changed its tone when we entered a stone tunnel. I couldn't have felt any better. I lay under my down sleeping bag, snuggly warm and stretched out on my narrow top bunk feeling the chilled, foggy-damp air rush around my face. The window was open. I'm not sure I'd ever slept better than on that train headed for the capital of China, my head on a clean, soft pillow.

Below me, on the lower bunk, a lady was getting very sick to her stomach. Ran Ying said that many Chinese get motion sickness like this on the train because Chinese almost never move fast, no faster than a bicycle can take them. Right before we entered another very dark tunnel, another gush of colder air entered our window and a momentary sorrow held me. I missed the winds of Mongo Mama's world already. Just last night we'd thrown our voices to the winds, cut roasted sheep on a wooden table, wrestled under a black Mongolian sky, and I'd danced with a Mongolian 'princess.' But the sadness didn't last. I was on the last leg of my journey across China, and it would not be long before I'd be crossing the ocean headed for home. I was like a Tennessee horse close to the barn. I couldn't see it yet, but my head slung around, my nostrils flared, my expression intensified, I could feel the barn coming around the next corner.

The old lady in blue on the bottom bunk said something to Ran Ying. Her face was deeply lined, "like a most wise person's should be." Her hair was not yet totally white; she was eighty-four. Ran Ying said to me, "Peter, she thinks you're an old man, like over seventy."

"Tell her I'm two years older than you are, that's a young thirty-three." This was not the first time someone in China thought I was an old man, because in China anyone with a beard is considered old. A few kids had been calling me "Grandfather."

When Ran Ying told the old lady how old I was, she stood up. She was slightly less than five feet tall and one of her eyes was swollen shut. She made embarrassed sounds and motioned for me to come down off my top bunk. She patted a spot on her bunk as if she wanted me to sit next to her. I did. She poured me some tea and reached in her little wrinkled paper bag and pulled out some tasty cookies. We sat there together eating cookies and drinking tea. All the soft sleepers had pots of tea in them, kept refreshed by attendants. There were four of us and four bunks in our compartment. Ran Ying in one top bunk, me in the other, the old lady in the bunk under me, and an old Chinese man below Ran Ying.

I felt that the old lady was waiting for the right moment to say something, but the old man was talking with Ran Ying, asking why she wore blue jeans. She told him she lived in America. He asked if I was her husband; she pulled out the pictures of Ed and their boys. After finishing my tea I began to stand up, but the old lady put her hand on my leg, for I was to stay there. She was used to being obeyed.

She said a few words in Chinese, say maybe four words, and there came over our compartment a hush, an almost reverent awe. Ran Ying told me the old lady had been on the Long March. Mention in China that you made the Long March and you're an instant hero, wherever you are, whomever you're with. In the land of one billion one hundred twenty-five million people, there are only a few thousand who can make this statement. Even the sometimes cynical Ran Ying was awed.

The Long March was just that . . . a long march from the bottom of China to the top of it. It was a march of hundreds of thousands of Communists, in which four out of every five died. The Communists in the south of China had been fighting Chiang Kai-shek when they heard that the Japanese had landed in the north and were planning to take over China. Mao and his people decided that they would march from one end of China to the other and go to war with the Japanese.

"My whole family was murdered by Chiang Kai-shek army when I young girl," Ran Ying translated what the sweet old lady said, "so I join the Red Army. During the march everyone had to carry four big guns shells, plus personal things. One night we walked to top of mountain pass. Many people die walking up pass. We had to sleep in a Buddhist temple that bomb had blown off roof. Bandits had used it as a hiding place. All we had was one sheet each, so two girls and I, we huddled together. We put two sheets over us. Much snow that night. Next morning woke up warm, covered with two feet of snow. When we went to wake up the others sleeping in there with us, everyone we touched was frozen to death, sitting up." Some of the brave Long Marchers made it to the front of the war and the fledgling Communists had worked miracles for their image in China. They were beloved for going to the rescue of a nation under attack.

The eighty-four-year-old Chinese hero dropped off into a secure-person's sleep and didn't wake up again until we pulled into the large train station in Beijing. We hauled our bags off the train onto a concrete passageway. Two of Ran Ying's bags were falling apart and so we took some time to tie them back together and then talked about what we should do first. We needed to go see her parents who had moved into a new apartment, and also get some tickets for our next destination, Fuzhou (Foo-joe). We got a cab, a brand-new Japanese car, and went to the Travel Service office. The man behind the counter first said we would have to wait four days. Then he looked something up and said, "Or, you maybe would prefer to leave in the morning." If we waited four days here we'd have to fly directly to Hong Kong, and fly home. Then we'd miss the coastal city of Fuzhou, considered by many the home of the finest artists and craftsmen working in China today. After Tibet, Mount Everest, Chengdu, and Inner Mongolia, even Beijing felt too touristy, too easy, too Western. They'd just opened some Western hotels here, like the Hilton, that had discos and Philippine bands playing "Top 40" American dance tunes. We would leave for Fuzhou, four hundred miles south of Shanghai, in the morning. In that case, Ran Ying said, we must go over to her parents' home this evening after they got home from work. She called her mother and told her to expect us.

The first thing I saw that looked only part Chinese in their apartment was a family picture. It was a group shot of Ed, Ran Ying, and their triplets, proudly displayed next to her father's most prized possessions, three full bookcases. Her parents had recently moved to this ground-floor apartment in an area of Beijing where there were many new high-rise apartment buildings going up. Most of the new buildings were for employees of certain departments of the government. All the people who lived in this building were from The Chinese Academy of Social Sciences. The building next to it might be filled with people who worked for the Travel Service.

Ran Ying's parents acted as though they'd seen her yesterday. There were no hugs, no kisses, just "Hello, good to see you." Ran Ying hadn't been back to China for four years. She hadn't seen her mother for two years, since she'd visited them in America. It had been only a year since she'd seen her father. He traveled especially often for a Chinese, since he was in charge of the Western European section of the Academy of Social Sciences. The academy was a kind of Chinese think tank that passed on information and intelligence to government leaders. He was about the same height as his daughter, about five two, and weighed about the same as Ran Ying, 110 pounds. He wore glasses, had a very narrow face, and his hair was a bit ruffled, like a "mad scientist." He had the look of a man who'd smoked many packs of cigarettes, inhaling all of them long and hard. Ran Ying said he'd recently quit smoking when he became very ill. He did not look physically strong, yet his mind was as quick as a striking cobra. He spoke English at least as well as his only daughter.

Her mother, who was under five feet tall, came out from the standing-room-only kitchen as we came in. Her face was rounder than her daughter's or husband's and she had the energy of a doer, a worker, a woman who plunged headlong into things. Ran Ying and her father were more the thinker types. Her mother was an editor at *The China Daily*, China's largest English-language newspaper. It was widely distributed throughout the world and considered by most to be a propaganda sheet. Even Ran Ying told me that.

Her father, Ran Ying, and I sat down, and we began telling stories about our trip across China. He was amazed that we had been given permission to live with the Mongolians and he was very curious about Tibet and Chomolungma. It was almost impossible for any native Chinese to get to Tibet unless they were assigned there. I apologized for wearing cutoff blue-jean shorts, but I'd done no laundry since we'd been in Mongolia and we'd just gotten to Beijing. Even though I'd lost twenty-five pounds since I'd left America, I still felt like a giant next to most Chinese people. And I felt that I looked like a Mongolian horseman who had just ridden across the heart of Asia in the dust of ten thousand other horsemen. My beard had grown wild, my face was weathered by Tibet and Inner Mongolia, and my clothes were dirty. There was no such thing as a Laundromat that I'd seen and Chinese laundries were more common in America.

Ran Ying began to talk rapid fire in Chinese, then realized I was sitting there and switched back in midsentence to English. ". . . What's she doing now, where she living?"

"She's a nurse at a mental hospital, at outskirts of city," her father answered. He was talking about one of the young girls Ran Ying had lived with when she lived as a peasant for eight years near the Russian border. That time she was away from her family because of another of Chairman Mao's nationwide decrees: "that all Chinese who were not peasants needed to be purified and live and work as peasants, learning from the peasants and building up the country." This period of Ran Ying's life was during the ten-year Cultural Revolution.

"My girl friend went crazy, one time. She was one of four classmates of mine who went with me to the countryside to do Chairman Mao's will, to work and learn from peasants," Ran Ying said matter-of-factly.

"What happened?" I asked, so used to expressing my curiosity with her all the time.

"When I was in countryside eight years, the first year we lived in tent, about seventy young people. Usually this girlfriend didn't talk very much but this certain day she talked to anybody—boy or girl—anybody. I started to wonder how come she talk so much. Then she started to talk all through the night and wouldn't let anybody sleep, then she talked during the day and if you paid no attention to her, she would cry." Ran Ying's father asked her if the way she was speaking English was the best she could do. She said that it wasn't, that she had just got in the habit of speaking that way with me.

"What would she talk about?" I asked. Ran Ying's mother finally came in and sat down in a chair in front of the couch. I noticed for the first time a _People_ magazine on a small table. I wanted to hug it! Ran Ying said Ed sent them every once in a while.

"She would talk about her family, and she had never talked to anybody about her family. Right before the Communist takeover, her father, who was college graduate, was working in Taiwan in a bank. After the take-over he took the whole family back to mainland China. But during the Cultural Revolution everybody says, 'Who knows what you did in Taiwan—we couldn't go over there and find out, we would never know whether you are a spy or not,' so he was sent to the countryside and worked—actually he was a very, very proper person who would never say anything against anybody and was not active in politics or anything.

"She was a very proper Chinese girl, never say anything harsh, very active in political movement and supportive of the party. She was hard worker, too. Something inside her quit and she didn't sleep for a whole week and another friend and I took care of her—every night, if my friend slept, I would talk to this girl and we would take turns—during the day we had to take care of her," she told us.

Ran Ying's parents had also seen many people go insane during the Cultural Revolution. They were sent to the countryside as well, to the south of China. Ran Ying's mother picked tea leaves and her father took care of pigs. In their group were all high-ranking government officials. In fact, there was one former ambassador to a European nation there, and his primary job was to take care of two pigs. China even called all her ambassadors home to work in the countryside, to learn from the peasants.

"I'm glad she's better now because we were afraid she would never get better. During the day, she wouldn't eat, wash her face, take care of herself or anything—we had to tell her, 'Now you change your coat, now I'll fix your hair, now you eat.' We had to tell her everything and she became very, very suspicious—anybody that came in the room to say something, she would say 'This person came in to see me because she heard that I went crazy.'

"She wouldn't eat at all. The leaders, who were all peasants, thought, 'She is really funny'—we got really mad at a lot of people because they said that she pretend to be crazy so she could go back to Beijing to live and we tried to tell them she was really crazy, no one could pretend like that. Finally, they gave her injections to go to sleep and she still wouldn't go to sleep. They didn't have doctor. We trick her to go get the injections because she wouldn't go.

"Then the peasants said she go crazy because of a weasel. It can become a spirit and get into you, and make you do things. This one peasant man told us girls this, but we wouldn't believe it. He told us of this neighbor who had this young girl about sixteen or seventeen and every evening at the same time—about seven or eight o'clock— she would start being crazy and singing and dancing in a very weird way, talking, just make no sense. It went on for a while and nobody knew what happened.

"Finally, every day at the same time the girl went crazy someone notice there was a weasel sitting outside their window doing exactly the same thing the girl was, making noise. They said that was the way to make her do that. Finally they drove the weasel away and the girl became normal." Ran Ying's mother shook her head as if this was a ridiculous idea.

"My friend got so she couldn't recognize anybody except the other girl and me. Everybody that came in, she would curse them and try to throw them out. She just cry and talk. The leaders decide she was really crazy and send her home. Other girlfriend took her home to Beijing by train, three days and two nights on the train. When she got home, she didn't know her brother, she couldn't recognize her mother, father, anybody. She probably just couldn't take it—a lot of people couldn't take that—those harsh living conditions trying to be like peasant after growing up in city their whole life, staying gone so long." Ran Ying lived this way from the age of fifteen to twenty-three.

"You remember," she said to her father, "when you used to send me letters when I was in countryside about how you used to watch the fish in that small pond. And that the big fish would always eat the smaller fish. That the strong fish would kill and eat the weak fish. Those letters helped me survive."

When Ran Ying got on the train as a fifteen-year-old in Beijing headed for the countryside, she weighed 110 pounds. After eight years of peasant work, she weighed 150 pounds of compact muscle. It was the job of her group to take a piece of wasteland and make it grow wheat. She had to dig ditches all day long in frozen ground, dig water wells by hand. She related, "I could carry hundred-pound sacks of grain myself and cut wheat from sunrise till far past sunset for weeks. We built our own threshing ground." All this and still live through winters on the China/Russian border. Maybe this brutal life was easier for Ran Ying than for some of the other Chinese kids who'd spent most of the time growing up with their families. Since she'd spent the first eight years of her life without her mother and father, maybe she was prepared for the eight years on the Russian border.

Although most young Chinese would not have talked of the Cultural Revolution as openly in front of a foreigner and their parents, Ran Ying seemed to be unrestrained. She turned and spoke to me. "The last time I was in Beijing, four years ago, people I knew that had my experience during the Cultural Revolution didn't like to talk about it. They want to forget it—I don't want to forget it—I want to remember it because it taught me a lot. It made me much more mature and I can take a lot of things now I couldn't if that hadn't made me so strong."

After dinner we talked of the "incredible" changes in China now, since Ran Ying had been in America. The incredible changes all had to do with material things, which the Cultural Revolution was to have cleansed the people from desiring. Her parents said that the rage in China now is for color televisions and motorcycles. Her folks walked us out onto the street where we would catch the bus. We stood in the dry air of a fall night in Beijing and they said their good-byes from a distance. After we got on the bus, I remembered a saying Ran Ying had told me that was very popular during the Cultural Revolution. "I would rather have Communist weeds than capitalist seedlings." Now they seemed to want the seedlings.

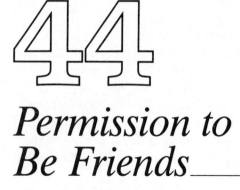

# 44

## *Permission to Be Friends*_____

Our C.A.A.C. plane was full. The stewardess brought around a cart full of giveaways. There were key rings with pictures of pandas on them, paper fans and snack boxes. I remembered they'd given us the same kind of boxes when we'd been en route to Lhasa from Chengdu. I had gotten quite excited noticing the box was made out of cardboard, the same kind of cardboard as the snack boxes on airplanes back in America. I opened the box and looked inside. It was the same thing they'd put inside the boxes on the way to Lhasa, and we'd called that "Yak in a Box." Skip named one of the packets of candy "Sugar-coated Camel Toenails." I'd named some of the gumdrops "Aged Panda. . . ." Never mind. I gave my box to the man next to me. He treasured it.

I pulled out some postcards from my camera bag. There were a few of the Great Wall, some of a Mongolian horse jumping through a ring of fire, a couple of brass Buddhas, and one or two of traditional Chinese paintings. I chose one of the paintings for my needs. I had an idea. The climbers had now been away from America, as I had, for many, many weeks. I'm sure the time often felt like months. There at Everest it may have been like years. They'd been living in the Death Zone on Chomolungma, hopefully making great progress toward the summit. Surely they could use some diversion. Maybe we could send them a postcard with some ridiculous message. They'd said that mail from home and friends was very important to their state of mind, their sense of mission, and condition of humor. It was doubtful, even if everything had gone perfectly on the mountain, that they could have reached the summit yet. But they could be close. It was also possible that something tragic could have happened by now.

Ran Ying said she would help. She wrote, in Chinese, a postcard to the guys that went something like this:

Dear Most Enchanting American Mountain Men,

We are a club of most adventurous Chinese women who yearn to be highly skilled climbers of world-class mountains. We write to you hoping that after your most incredible conquest of the "Goddess Mother of the World" you will come to our hometown and teach us your techniques. Especially we would like to learn of your exceptional knot-tying skills. Our mountains are quite unique and present a high degree of difficulty to climb, even though they are not as tall as Mount Everest.
    Please be careful.

_Your excited admirers,_
The Beijing Girls Mountaineering Club

Throughout the creation of this message, which we knew would be translated by their interpreter, if it ever got there, every Chinese person within view of our postcard tried to read what Ran Ying was writing. We included a P.S. that said:

This postcard is not true. It is being sent to you from Peter Jenkins and Ran Ying Porter, flying at about 30,000 feet over China. Here's hoping that you guys are nearing the 30,000-foot level. Hope to hear the good news soon.

Ran Ying was glad to be leaving Beijing even though she would like to have introduced me to a few of her and Ed's friends. She asked if I would like to hear about how she and Ed had met. That was one story I had not heard yet. Before I could say anything, she began to tell me.

"After eight years some people my family know helped to arrange for me to leave the countryside. My parents, they came back from countryside, too. Soon after I come back the government announce that young people could take an entrance exam and that small amount will be allowed into college. Chairman Mao had canceled school when I was in sixth grade, so I completely miss high school. In China little more than five percent get to go to college, and here I had been from intellectual family, but spend past eight years living peasant life. My mother and father push me very hard, help me to study. I don't think I would pass." Anyone who spoke a few words of English was listening to what Ran Ying was saying.

"But I pass, somehow, then admitted to the English department of Xinxiang Teachers' College. Ed saw me, said he liked that I did not wear pigtails like other girls. [Not wearing pigtails was considered daring then.] Ed was English teacher at college. Even when we could not wear any colorful clothes I was always very neat. Ed said he liked that. We first meet, talk about what is better, socialism or capitalism." She seemed to be getting more and more ready to get back to her family.

"We had to keep our friendship very secret. When boy and girl seen together in China, then everyone assumes you will be married soon. It is very bad to go on dates with many people. This considered antisocial behavior. Can even affect your whole life if this fact of many dates with many members of opposite sex end up in your file," Ran Ying explained, knowing I would make my usual comments about how outrageous some of the things they did in China were. Every person in China has a file that contains anything questionable or "bad" they ever did, which follows them everywhere they go for life.

"Also, many Chinese think, 'Why be with foreigner? There are already many Chinese men to go around,'" she said. "Ed very sensitive to Chinese way. He felt we should talk to Communist party representative because they must give their permission for us to be friends." She went on to say that every department and every dorm had a Communist party member who 'represented' them, who must clear anything out of the ordinary. This was also true of every group of people in China. Everyone in their neighborhood, and at their factory, had their Communist 'rep' who watched them, making sure they lived like "good" Communists.

"Our favorite meeting place was by a small circular garden, always under cover of darkness," Ran Ying said. "At other times, we would meet on a small back lane just within the college grounds and make our way to the sports field and then to the volleyball court. Walled in, these places seemed dark enough. After few months we decide it would be good to be married. But to get permission, we must meet with the Communist party secretary of the foreign-languages department, also a party member. They inform us that because I was interested in a foreigner we had to have permission to be 'friends.' Of course this was stupid because we already friends. They would have to discuss it with higher leaders." An unusually beautiful stewardess came by with a plastic tray serving tea. I took a cup. Ran Ying wasn't interested.

"It was silly, but strange how word soon spread throughout college and before long people in other cities and provinces had heard the news. 'A foreigner and a Chinese girl are going to marry.' People took sides on the issue. Some said it was disgraceful. The vice–party secretary of our department told some students, 'Chinese are Chinese and foreigners are foreigners and we should not lose our national pride.' This reaction made me mad," Ran Ying reported.

"Believe it or not, some leaders at the college criticize me for being seen with Ed in public 'because you have not even been given permission to be friends yet.' Because we were constantly reminded that we were not yet 'friends,' we change our plan about getting married in America, and decide to be married in China. Again we must talk with leaders. We ask them to be married in China. Our department leaders took our request to the college Party Committee, the highest Communist power in the college. They said . . . yes." I must have been really getting used to China now because Ran Ying's story of her "romance" sounded normal. Normal! What was happening to me!

"Their 'yes' had to be sent to two other offices, one being the Office of Foreign Affairs. It was 1980. They gave permission, so we got married. On September twenty-sixth, we walked into the Red Flag District Marriage Registration Office of our city where we signed our names to the two marriage certificates, stating that we would support each other, practice family planning, and uphold China's socialist principles."

# 45

## *On Stalin Street*_____

The steamy sidewalks of the port of Fuzhou were attacked with bodies. Sweaty bodies. Hot people. We walked along Wusi Road asking different people who looked as if they might know, "At what production center do they make the most outstanding lacquer ware?"

I was now used to being surrounded by thousands of Chinese all the time. But when I turned my head slightly to the right to wipe away some sweat with my T-shirt, my head just about hit the cheek of another person walking that close to us. Close was a part of

China, but this close was at the very least nosy. I whispered to Ran Ying to begin walking as fast as she could, to see if indeed that man was following us. He looked about forty-five. We really poured on the speed; Ran Ying could walk surprisingly fast for someone so small. I said if he kept following us, which he did, when we got up a good speed I was going to count to three and at three, STOP. We'd see what he'd do then.

He was surely following us, and obviously trying to listen to our conversation. "All right—one, two, three." WE STOPPED! Right in front of a parked line of about one hundred mostly rusted bicycles. Our tail crashed into us, never apologized nor said one word, but tucked his head down and was gone. If I'd been followed before, maybe I'd not noticed it. But come to think of it, we had always been in a place where we were really isolated. In this swarming city of over a million and a half, even I could get lost in the crowds.

In Fuzhou it seemed someone was following us all the time. Ran Ying said that many times Chinese people follow "suspicious"-looking people on their own initiative, for the good of the country. In my hotel room there was someone in the next room pulling wires inside the wall, near where my phone was connected to the wall. Not just once, but every night. The closer I got to leaving, the more I wondered what the Chinese would do to me if they felt I had found out too much or seen something I shouldn't have. Would they introduce some kind of poison gas into the ventilation system while I slept? If they wanted to get rid of me, maybe it would be better to do it after I'd left China, say in Hong Kong. There it could be made to look as if I'd been robbed.

By now I'd become used to people staring at me as if I was a display at a newly opened museum. If I stopped, a crowd would always gather and inspect the buttons on my shirt, the hair on my face, the color of my eyes, and so on. Lately, just to turn the tables on people who acted as if I was a slide under a microscope, I started staring back. I would get about a foot from the starer's body and look him over. After that they seemed to understand how it felt to be stared at. This kind of reaction from the Chinese didn't happen just to me; it happens to almost everyone who goes to China. Especially if you're traveling alone and in a city or village where they're unaccustomed to seeing foreigners.

Never having been even slightly paranoid before, I figured all this was my reaction to having been watched and controlled so tightly since coming to China. Now there was less than a week to go and I felt a bit of the revolutionary rising up in me. I told Ran Ying we would go to the Travel Service office on Stalin Street this afternoon and see if we could get permission to travel by boat to a coastal fishing village. We'd wait to find out about the lacquer ware till we got back. She said OK, but she gave me a look that added "When are you going to realize that we can't always be going places that are off limits?" I was sick of having to worry about every minor place I went, trying to figure out if it was off limits. I felt as if China was a giant domineering parent that stood over me night and day, shouting out orders.

The palm trees shaded this portion of Stalin Street a bit, but the shade in south China offers almost no relief. The city smelled like a blending of fresh fish and not so fresh fish. Down side streets there were markets where anyone could buy crabs and shrimp, mussels and seaweed. The more fresh seafood we saw, the stronger my desire became to see the Chinese coast. Fuzhou not only felt like New Orleans but its older sections looked like it, except older. The homes were painted in bright colors, a trait of humid tropical cities in many places. Since the year 200 B.C., Fuzhou has been a port city, a city of narrow winding streets. The people looked a little different here— they were a little shorter than the Chinese I'd seen so far in the north, and their skin was much smoother.

A carnival atmosphere ruled the streets. Again I heard a sound, a different sound coming up from behind us. It was a kind of chirping sound. Behind us was a man with a stick over his shoulder, from which hung many little straw baskets, each one with a cricket in it. Parents bought them for their children to play with, to have as pets. It reminded Ran Ying that her father used to buy her little pet crickets when he came to see her at her nursery school, and the cricket would always die after two days.

We slowed down and stopped at the curb for a white-gloved traffic director. Our trusty tail closed in. We had been playing games with him, slowing down to a pace that was as slow as a hundred-year-old peasant's, then speeding up to a near run. Then without the slightest head movement we'd duck into an alley or doorway, stop suddenly, and wait for him to come face to face with us. He seemed to be following orders and stuck with us regardless of the hassles we gave him. Ran Ying was getting a kick out of our games. She also pointed out, however, that a common Chinese trick is to make something, like our tracker, very obvious, while all the time depending on a discreet observer for the information gathering. She said that she wouldn't be surprised if this person eventually disappeared so that we'd relax and really do whatever "bad" things we had in our "plotting" minds.

Up ahead there was a large crowd of people circling something. Inside the circle were two middle-aged men with many scars on their tan bodies. They had pants on and that's all. The smaller one had a large metal ball in his hand and was holding it up to the attentive crowd for their inspection. It was a big metal ball. He'd swallow it and then make it come back up his throat and out his mouth. The idea, Ran Ying explained, was to show that he had magical powers so that he could better sell his traditional Chinese medicine. Then one of them pulled out some of this black, sticky medicine. He had it rolled into a small ball, the way you can roll some types of glue (like rubber cement), without its sticking to your hands.

Many times traditional medicines will be so messy they will get all over everything. "BUT," these men shouted, "you could wear this magic mixture all day long for up to three days. . . . Wear it all day long, even wear it to work. This will not get your clothes dirty" was their claim. They swallowed a couple of metal swords, juggled some really large metal balls, and sold a small amount of their medicine. A few people threw a few small coins to them for their entertaining performance.

Ran Ying remembered that when she was a young girl, you could see this all over China. "Then some of these kind of people would even have poisonous snakes and snake medicine. They put snakes on themselves and the poisonous snake would bite them and then they use medicine. That kind of thing was banned during the Cultural Revolution, but now it is coming back." She was surprised by this, I could tell. China was changing faster than even she thought was possible.

"Before liberation," she mentioned, "this was very common. Also, people travel from city to city doing gymnastics and contortions with their bodies. Sometimes, in order to have really good person who can bend their body, they would get a young orphan when they small child and put them inside pretty big clay pot, let them grow in there. Feed them but not let them out. Then their body grows all twisted. Had a hole for them to go to bathroom. When the kid became the age of stop growing, they have very strange-shaped body from growing inside of clay pot. Then they start to teach the kid to do all kinds of terrible movements with their body. Chairman Mao outlawed this."

Halfway down Stalin Street was the Travel Service office. We would see if we could get permission to go from Fuzhou to the ocean. I was really getting tired of going to the Travel Service offices and asking permission to do the most simple things. Sometimes I felt as if I was in a clay pot, lost in a maze of illusion, lies, and rules. The man in charge here was unusually young and obviously very ambitious. He was neat, tidy, clean, and answered all our questions like a tape recorder with new batteries. As always he tried the usual tourist rap: "Would you not enjoy our lovely park, West Lake Park, dotted with peony bushes of violet and red and most graceful willow trees? Or you may wish to see the Twin Pagodas. One was built in A.D. 904. . . ." Ran Ying knew exactly what I was thinking now. I did not even have to say anything.

# 46

## *Ancient Sailing Ships*___

Tired of being stopped and restricted and controlled, we left the office, saying "Thank you so much, we would enjoy normal tourist activities." So far everything we'd wanted to do, after the proper checking of our documents and probably pertinent phone calls, had been allowed. I told Ran Ying that it was time to try something daring. In the morning we would either get on a bus or hire a cab and go as far down toward the coast as we could get. I was beginning to wonder if my good fortune traveling in China was my own special combination of persistence and blessing, or if the Chinese were just making it look that way.

Was there a reason I was being "allowed" to experience Inner

Mongolia, etc? Could it be possible that they'd created the illusion of many restrictions, but they'd secretly decided that they would allow me to see places in their nation so that I'd write about them? We could test them and see how far into restricted territory we could get. Did Ran Ying think we might get kicked out of the country for this, I asked her? She seemed momentarily confused and didn't have an answer. Then she said, "I don't know."

I looked around for the man who had been following us and he was gone, for now. On the streets at this time of the year were solitary merchants selling apples and pears and oranges. The superb thing about their fruit was that it was picked ripe and was sweet as heaven. Not like in the USA where most fruit had to be picked hard and green so that it wouldn't spoil while being transported. This delightful fruit was carried in on a farmer's back or possibly in a small cart behind a bicycle. There were also fresh pineapple and bananas. Our high-tech experience of the day came when we walked by a small, Japanese-made refrigerator on the sidewalk, which was plugged into an extension cord inside someone's street-side home. Inside were banana-flavored, homemade Popsicles. They were the only cool thing for miles.

The next morning in the "Venice of China," Ran Ying checked around and found out that we could take a cab about halfway to the ocean. Standing in the shade of a huge flowering bush, someone told her that if we got the "right" cab driver, we might get down as far as Mawei—meaning "horse's tail"—a little place where they repaired ships. He said there was a seamen's hotel there that maybe took foreigners. The cab driver took us there. He was the first Chinese we'd met who took a tip since tipping is not allowed in China. He asked us what we were doing here and Ran Ying never answered.

Mawei village is on a big bay, maybe twenty kilometers south of Fuzhou, down a narrow little road with rice paddies on each side. It so happened that no ships were in, so we were able to get rooms. At first the manager at the seamen's hotel acted obnoxious and mean and asked us all kinds of questions. He looked at and studied our passports over and over again. The manager was trying to grow a beard and had about five or six hairs on his face. It didn't look as if there was a fishing village anywhere close, so we went for a walk through the sounds of a lot of banging of metal, a typical shipyard. The countryside was very rocky and hilly, not flat the way a lot of the land near an ocean is.

We walked down into what looked like the old part of town. We talked to a lady who sold hot sodas. She had her soda cart set up right there at the bus stop, a long-distance bus stop where people tie their chickens and their ducks and their bamboo buckets and everything else all over the bus. Ran Ying asked her how we could get to the nearest fishing village. She pointed down toward the lower docks and said there was a boat that left every morning that ferried people to this place.

It went down the river, she said, and we could find out about its schedule by going down into this old part of town. We went down to the boat dock and found out the boat left the next morning at seven A.M. So we got tickets for eighty fen, which is less than twenty cents each, for a boat ride that would last about three hours. At seven we found out the boat to Guanto would not leave till nine, so we waited. While we waited, people came down and did their laundry by hand in the dirty river water. They also were cutting up chickens and ducks and cleaning out assorted poultry intestines.

Elegant old sailing ships, three of them, with tattered sails, slipped through the water on their way to sea. I pulled out my camera and began taking pictures. First I used my telephoto lens; then I put my wide angle on. A young man who'd been watching us walked up next to Ran Ying and became obnoxious and started shouting at me. I ignored him as the people around here seemed much more aggressive than any we'd met yet. He started saying to Ran Ying, "Why are you taking pictures of the old China? Tell him I command him to stop taking pictures. This is not the modern China. Take pictures of the modernized China." He pointed toward a metal ship that had some rusty sides. A lot of Chinese, Ran Ying explained to me, are very sensitive to the fact that they live in an underdeveloped country and they are proud of the fact that they are modernizing. We tried to tell him that I wanted to take the pictures because I thought it was beautiful, not because we wanted to show Chinese backwardness or anything. I told Ran Ying to tell him that in America many people like to take pictures of old barns. He would not listen.

Our ferryboat chugged into the dock, riding low in the silver-colored water. The paint had all peeled off. This ferry is the only transportation for a lot of these river people. Some of the fishing villages have no roads connecting them to anywhere. We sat down on a bench. The other people waiting to board had an unbelievable combination of stuff with them: There were baskets full of ducks, buckets full of crabs, chickens in cloth bags, fresh-caught shrimp, and fish on stringers. Their groceries were stuffed into two buckets that they carried with a split piece of large bamboo that curled up on either end. In these buckets were sugar beets, turnips, and greens. Many of the smaller boats that passed were powered by a single oar. They had to be very careful of the large cargo ships that plunged by them.

The land on either side of this ever-widening bay reminded me of pictures I'd seen of Greece. The hillsides are rocky and very barren and right on the water is where all the people live. The fishing village was five stops down the river. The river was very brown and very muddy and there were all kinds of different boats. Sitting next to us was this real old woman who had sores all over her legs; her legs were all scarred up. She was barefoot and put her feet all over the seat in front of us. The guy behind me, barefooted, was putting his bare feet all over our seat.

Now that we were on the ferry I figured there was no way anyone could get us. So far we'd made it. The long narrow ferry eased up to another dock, and the captain put the engine into reverse to fight the strong current somewhat. We assumed and had been told that this place could be off limits. I felt a strong current of fear come over me and thought maybe we shouldn't get off, just turn around and go back. Maybe we could get in really bad trouble for this. No, what if we had some spectacular adventure here?

The streets in the village were very, very narrow—about eight feet wide, hardly wide enough for any vehicle to pass. The village was built right on the water and hanging over it. The houses were built mostly of brick. All the villagers ran around in sandals and T-shirts and shorts. People had ducks and chickens in open bamboo baskets outside their doors. Dogs and little kids and pigs and chickens and white ducks wandered in and out of people's homes. Rice paddies filled in what little flat land there was before the bare rock mountains began. When the peasants were not using their water buffalo, the slick black animals crawled into canals and all you could see were their curved horns, nostrils, and eyes. Even on the hillsides people grew pumpkins, squash, and anything else that would live to be eaten.

There were a few big, exceptionally old trees, with vines hanging from them, growing in the midst of all this and every little shop had something different going on. In some, people were "working bamboo," in others whole families were weaving fishing nets by hand. As we walked, knowing not where we went, the occasional stink of sewage blew by us mixed with the warm breezes blowing off the ocean. Most people had these little holy signs over their doors, a symbol of good luck or something. They put these up because fishing season was coming up in a month. I wished we could stay for it. But who knew? Maybe we'd be here, waiting, in jail.

I was the first foreigner that many of these people had ever seen, and immediately we were the head of a parade of young people following behind us, following our every move. Ran Ying said that we should ask someone where the Communist leaders of the village were and we should tell them we were here. We were led by this young boy on a bicycle, who offered to carry one of my bags to the leader's office. So we went to the commune leaders, a couple of hundred yards away from where our ferry docked, through a series of humid alleys. We were taken into this very white, three-story building. There were a couple of pictures of Chairman Mao on the stark walls. The only leader-type anyone could find walked in, saw us, asked Ran Ying something, and started making calls all over on a real old-timey phone, the kind you crank. He started jabbering in Chinese, actually in a southern Chinese dialect, so neither Ran Ying nor I could understand what he said.

Eventually two leaders showed up and they talked to us and asked for our passports. The man with the black-rimmed, seemingly inch-thick glasses was the secretary of the commune. They asked what we were doing here and if we had documents, if we had Travel Service papers. We told them that we had heard a lot about this small fishing village and we really wanted to see it so we came down on a boat and we were happy to be here. It was most beautiful, I had Ran Ying tell them. They nervously looked at our passports for the fiftieth time and asked us if we'd had lunch. We said no. They said we were welcome to come with them to lunch at the only restaurant in the little village, an eating place just for the leaders.

# 47

## *A Dish of Crab*———————

Everyone in this little fishing village walks everywhere. I enjoyed stopping to watch Chinese woodworkers planing old wood. Fragrant smells from the old wood resurrected from old ships drifted out their workshop doors. It smelled a lot like cedar. The restaurant was a place to walk by. No sign said its name, if it had one, and even once inside we had to walk through the kitchen and the cooks and then go up some slanted stairs to a little eating area. There was a little homemade table with a seat about as wide as a two by four around the thing, a hexagon in shape, painted blue with red seats.

Another picture of Chairman Mao stood out from the light-blue walls. Ran Ying said you could tell this was a backward place because there were still pictures of Mao. In most big places they'd been taken down, his Red Books thrown away or hidden till another movement started.

First they gave us a hot moist towel and a basin, which was nice because it was so humid and sweaty. Looking out from the second floor I could see old clay roofs and ancient southern Chinese houses. The young girl brought us some Chinese cabbage. It was dark green, kind of like spinach, and they'd cooked it in a sweet sauce. It was very good. Then also, as an appetizer, she set some cold sliced pork before us. Then up the moaning stairs came this incredible dish of boiled shrimp in the shell with a brown sweet sauce with onion and garlic and sliced bamboo shoots that was out of this world. I would just pick up the shrimp and suck the sauce out of them and then peel them like a normal boiled shrimp and eat them. They were as good as the best shrimp I'd ever tasted in New Orleans and I didn't think that was possible.

Then they brought out a dish of crab. It was cut up into pieces, quartered, then cooked scrambled with egg, onion, and different flavorings. The crab wasn't too juicy, or too watery, it was just perfect, wonderfully spiced. A refreshing strong breeze blew in through a small window onto my face.

Next, they brought us four different soups. There was an eel soup, which was a clear broth with pieces of a silvery moray eel. This is a favorite of the Chinese and was one of the last soups they brought out because they often bring out the best last. The eel has a white meat and many very fine bones. It is sliced in half and then cut in pieces and put in this soup with some kind of a vegetable. Maybe bamboo shoots were included with it. Another kind of soup had pork dumplings. We were getting tremendously full. Then there came up the stairs another fish soup and another soup with pork and turnips. The latter was good and had a spicy, different kind of taste, a little bit tangy. By now I was so smooth with my sticks I felt as though I could perform surgery with them. I sort of did with the fish soup, which had big chunks of white fish in it. I picked it out of the soup, peeled the skin off, and dipped it in all the different shrimp sauces.

Then a cook brought us another plate, this time of fried seafood and pork liver. Also he was very excited to present us with his specialty, duck stomach. This was the part of the meal when I didn't ask what I was eating anymore. I'd never eaten anything here that I'd ever wanted to spit out. Ran Ying and I sat feeling as full as a large-stomached Buddha. At the other table were all the leaders of the little village and some visitors from somewhere. They seemed to be having a great time as they were all getting tremendously red in the face, and having toast after toast after toast. When the leaders didn't want to drink anymore, they put their hands over their cups. One of the visitors was having trouble seeing and so would pour the beer over their hands. Sea breezes coming through the window right behind me were my dessert.

Then I saw this giant plate of noodles being delivered to the other table and I thought, "Uh-oh. Please. No. Not for us." A few minutes later, here came this incredible plate of fresh hot noodles cooked with Chinese clams and diced onion, little vegetables, little chunks of pork; this was excellent even as full as I was. It was cooked in some sort of buttery grease. If the leader had asked me right then to choose my last meal, this would be it.

The leaders of the village, who seemed to be very pleasant and very happy at this moment, said that they were going to allow us to stay. I told them that I would love to meet a master Chinese ship-builder because they still build wooden boats by hand. Maybe they could find someone who fished from a sailboat to take us out to the ocean. Also we would love to come back the next day and learn how the chef cooked these amazing seafood dishes.

They said, "Why don't you take the afternoon and look around the village and walk around and explore?" So we did that.

First we went to this really run-down hotel with bars on the windows and mosquito nets only over the beds of the higher-priced rooms. They said a room was less than four dollars a night. Where the sailors stayed there were four beds to a room—metal beds with woven cane mats on them. The bathrooms were a hole and a hose and that was it. They were kind of embarrassed, but I said no problem, and Ran Ying said the same. I felt victorious. We came here without permission and the local leaders had made up their own minds and given us permission. Good for them! They seemed like progressive thinking men.

So we went exploring around the village. It was low tide. Thirty children followed us as we wandered around for three hours, watching working people far off in white shirts in dark-green rice fields.

When we got back after taking some pictures of some boatbuilders, the teenage girl who ran the little store at the hotel for sailors said the secretary wanted us to call him. Ran Ying said he started by talking real slow, kind of embarrassed, and said, "Our leaders . . . uh . . . talked to the Provincial Foreign Affairs Office . . . uh . . . uhhhh . . . and they said that . . . you didn't have permission to come here. . . . This place is not open to foreigners so you cannot stay. . . . You have to leave this evening. . . . If there are no buses running back to Fuzhou, the commune leaders will try to arrange a car for you."

He was very apologetic and said that they didn't know anything like this would happen. Of course we were very nice about it and said that if we could not stay, we would just leave, we didn't want to cause any trouble. We asked around and there was no bus back to Fuzhou. Everyone in the village seemed to be running back and forth trying to find us a car. First they were going to put us on a motorcycle with one of those little carts on the back, because all the buses had stopped running. They said they were afraid to let us spend the night. We truly must to leave immediately. The Chinese never get aggravated, but if they tell you to leave immediately, that's what they mean—they don't mean tomorrow morning.

About two hours later, they found a girl who'd grown up in this village but had somehow left fourteen years ago and moved to Hong Kong. There she owned a restaurant and had apparently become very successful. She had a child who, I guess, had become very spoiled by growing up in Hong Kong with their wealth. Her thirteen-year-old refused to come back to this little funky fishing village because they had to walk everywhere. For that reason the lady bought her village a minivan to use. They put her name on it. Every time she comes to visit, she gets picked up in the minivan and has it to drive her thirteen-year-old around in. The people of this fishing village had no chance of getting to Hong Kong, and they seemed almost to worship her for her jeans and black T-shirt, and her stories of "unbelievable" freedoms and wealth. She drove us back to Fuzhou and told us much about Hong Kong, which is where we would be going, FAST.

# 48

# *Counting Backwards*___

As we got to the outskirts of the city, I began to think that maybe this lady could be someone other than who she claimed. My imagination started working the way a Chinese imagination would. Had she been given instructions to take us to jail, or take us to be searched, or questioned, or take us to the public-security bureau? Would someone try to take all my cameras, film, and tapes away? The fewer hours I had left in China, the more I wanted to get out of here. I would not feel secure till I put my body on free ground. Was it possible that the seemingly innocent things we saw in the fishing village were some sort of top-secret installation? Could the pictures I took there be of something top secret? Maybe a hidden sub base in the rock cliffs next to the village was detailed in one of my pictures. Since all my film was slide film, would they ruin and destroy it all to get rid of anything I might have taken that was classified? Hopefully she would just drop us off at our hotel and leave. She did.

When I got to my room I walked around it looking for anything suspicious. I didn't see anything. I picked up the phone and asked for an overseas operator. I was shocked when one called back in less than ten minutes. It was getting near the end of September.

"Yes, I'd like to make a collect call," I said.

She put it right through. The phone at home was ringing and Rebekah answered, as usual. The Chinese operator could not speak English real well and especially could not understand a five-year-old with a southern accent. I broke through and told Rebekah to say yes to the collect call. She did.

"Daddy, are you still on Mount Everest?" she asked. Her voice was like a cure for an incurable disease. It transformed me.

"No, honey, I'm in China."

"Guess what I learned to do this week? I've learned how to count backwards." She spoke better English than anyone I'd talked to in weeks. "Daddy, I can count backwards from ten. Listen, ten, nine, eight . . ." Till she got to one. "The reason I learned how to count backwards is so that I can count the days till you get home to me."

"That's very smart, sweety." I breathed deep to keep my voice from cracking.

The usual Chinese phone-tapping person cut in on the line. I wondered if they thought that this could be ingenious new American technique to pass spy codes using small children. He or she listened longer than usual.

She proceeded to inform me of all the things that were going on in the family. Every night Mommy was reading her TWO stories. Jed had learned how to climb up on the top of the sofa and jump off. Sometimes he hit right on his head and didn't even cry. She said that Mommy was getting really big and the only way she could get to sleep was on her side.

She said, "Daddy, I went to the doctor with Mommy. We could hear the baby's heart beat! . . . Since you're not here I went with her." Rebekah told me that she had started school again and she really liked it and that she was getting smarter every day.

"Dad," she said, sounding very serious, "don't get me too many presents, just get me really good things." I told her that I would.

I told her I'd call back later that night when Mommy was home. Later I talked with Barbara and she was feeling too full, too big, very uncomfortable and missing me. Her due date was about twenty days away. We both got kind of sad, just wanting the days to hurry up and pass. We talked for about an hour. When I hung up, I could hear Jed. It sounded like he was jumping off the top of the sofa. Barbara wanted to know if I'd gotten her anything? Like mother, like daughter. (I got Barbara a very beautiful lacquer-ware screen that had taken over a year to complete. They would ship it to America. Rebekah got a stone carving of a Chinese beauty, lying on a lily pad, with a beautiful bird perched next to her watching.)

Flying over China at night there's no way you'd think that below was more than one fifth of the world's population. The land looks almost blacked out, like they're expecting bombers to fly over. But they're not. There is just not an abundance of electric lights. Our plane banked to the right and there below was one of the most stimulating views my world had ever known. There were black silhouettes of mountains and in between them, like the space between two spread-out fingers, was water. Rising into the sky were amazingly tall buildings sparkling with lights. Their insides were lit with the white of neon and their outsides shimmered in the yellow heat of spotlights. In the magnetic harbor were boats with lights strung between their masts, reflected in the glossy surface of the water. As we lost altitude I could see cars driving free on rain-slick roads lit by mercury-vapor lights that gave off an eerie orange glow. Those cars were owned by individuals! It was as if the plane had flown through a curtain of time and we'd come from the early 1900s to the year 2010. Below us I could see the most beautiful city I'd ever seen. Hong Kong. Down there I could go anywhere I wanted, anytime I wanted.

It was raining this evening and raindrops streaked across the window of our jet and blurred the beautiful white lights of the buildings and blue lights of the slickly modern runway into a light show. We touched down. A monstrous weight leaped off my chest. I was free again. I would not be detained. They did not take my film. Red China was back there, over the mountains, surrounded by the darkened countryside. Never before had the big city lights thrilled me.

Right after we got our luggage inside the squeaky-clean, high-tech airport filled with stainless steel and efficiency, we hailed a cab for downtown. In Hong Kong they spoke a different type of Chinese and we could not make the driver understand where he MUST take us first. Ran Ying tried talking with him, he just shook his head and drove in the direction of most of the tall buildings. The sounds of the rain splashing under the car's tires was invigorating. She spoke more; he just shook his head more.

"Ran Ying, maybe he understands some English. Let me try to speak with him," I suggested. I said one word in English. He shook his head some more. Was he playing dumb the way a New York City cabby can with someone from Iowa in his car? I said the word slowly. Then fast. Next medium speed. He skidded around a sharp curve getting us onto a four-lane and something lit up inside his head.

"Ma . . . Da . . . Na's." He shook his head excitedly like he'd just discovered the atom. "Ye . . . Ye . . . Ye . . ." he said. I guessed that meant "Yes, yes, yes." He sped up. I kept saying the word. It became a chant: "McDonald's . . . McDonald's . . . McDonald's." Since Tibet, through Inner Mongolia and down to southern China, I'd promised myself that when I got to freedom—I almost felt that I was being paroled from prison—the first thing I would do was go and get a couple of hamburgers and some fries and a Coke. I didn't want the world's best burger, because I could get that at home, grilled on our farm. I wanted a burger instantly. Instant action. It was a symbol of what I'd missed so much.

We thought the cabby understood since he too was chanting a word that sounded something like "McDonald's." It started to pour down rain. I'd never heard such wonderful rain! He pulled into the center of the city. Some people scurried up wide sidewalks under colorful umbrellas. He stopped in the middle of a block and there it was. The little red sign with the golden arches inside of it. Ran Ying was very, very happy, too. She volunteered to go in. I told her I wanted six orders of fries, three Quarter-Pounders with cheese, and a few large Cokes. She came out with four white bags with little logos on them filled up. She even got a burger and fries. The driver communicated roughly, wanting to know where we wanted to go now. Ran Ying made him understand that we just wanted to cruise the wet, shiny streets of Hong Kong while we ate our food. I was almost tempted to go back and buy a few bags more just because I could, but I was too full.

Next came Chicago. American air space! The ground of the free. Our Northwest Orient flight flew from Hong Kong to Chicago first. Then we'd change planes, headed for Nashville. There were delays and the air over O'Hare was filled with planes, but who cared. They didn't have a gate for our plane, so we stopped in the middle of some runway. That was great. It was surprisingly hot today, the pilot said. What perfect English the pilot spoke! It was a hazy day; it even looked slightly polluted over Chicago and over the runways. It was beautiful pollution. We walked down a metal stairway, onto the runway. I could smell jet fuel. The plane next to us was also unloading, and coming off it were a lot of blond people speaking some Scandinavian language. I knelt down and kissed the runway. It tasted bad but I felt wildly happy. I was even happy to see the customs agent's dour face. Later, after we got through customs, we walked outside the airport, and just to really kiss the ground I knelt again on some grass and kissed it. I was HOME. Home like I'd never appreciated it before. In America.

We spent a few hours in Chicago, and then our flight to Nashville took off. I felt as if people could look at me and tell I had come from some oppressed country. A whole bunch of friends were at the airport waiting for us. Ran Ying's triplets and Ed stood waiting. I was shocked and strangely shy to see so many friends standing with their arms outstretched. But nothing hit me as much as when Rebekah could stand it no longer and burst toward me, leaping into my arms. Barbara had stayed home—she'd thought the baby was coming earlier that morning. I wanted to give all my friends a piece of me, but I wanted to get home and see Barbara and Jed and the farm, worse. Even Mary, one of my favorite waitresses from the Poplar House in Spring Hill, came to the airport.

# Back from the
# Death Zone_____

I wasn't home long when little Luke was born, on October 15. From the moment Dr. Kuykendall lifted Luke out of Barbara, he had a head of red hair. I held Luke after he'd been dried off by the nurses at Maury County Hospital and I wanted to tell this baby that he was born into a land of free people. If they would come with me when they got older, I would take my three children to places where they would know themselves better by learning of others.

Now that the anxiety of Luke's birth was over, I began to fully focus on the climbers. We had not heard anything from them for too long. No news this late in the expedition was a bad sign. By now they should have made the top. At first the news from base camp had been frequent and good. They were making their way up the mountain faster than anyone had dared hope. But then there were weeks of delays and bad weather. Now the momentum seemed to have reversed itself. At first their message from Tibet was "There's no doubt we'll make it. It's just a matter of time." Lately it had changed to "If we're lucky and the mountain lets us, we should get to the top."

One typically wonderful fall morning I walked into our trailer earlier than usual. I was hoping that on her way to work Terri Baker, my assistant, had picked up about fifty rolls of the color slides I had taken on the China trip. I couldn't wait to see how they'd come out. As I rushed down the narrow hall of our trailer I heard her saying something.

"Peter, I think there's a message on the answering machine you'll want to hear." I could detect neither sorrow nor delight in her voice. In one way I wanted to ask her what was up, but I went back to listen for myself. Terri had rewound the Code-A-Phone to the message she wanted me to hear.

"Hello, Peter. This is David McClain. Just wanted to know where you wanted the storm doors you ordered delivered to. They finally came in." Beep.

"Peter, this is Skip. Turn on both the _Today_ show and _CBS Morning News_ in the morning. Some of the climbers will be on."

I guessed that meant they were coming home. Or did it mean they were already home, or arriving home in the morning, or could they possibly be broadcasting live from Mount Everest? I'd heard ABC-TV was planning to broadcast live from the top of Everest, someday soon. I called Skip but he was out. The next morning, although they didn't mention names, both Jane Pauley and Phyllis George said early in their shows that some of the guys would be on. And they were. Lou and Wick were on the _Today_ show and Phil and John Roskelley were on CBS. For all of about three minutes each. They looked as if they'd just been let out of a prisoner of war death camp. But at least _they_ were alive. I switched back and forth to see what they had to say. Lou's face looked as thin as a narrow shoe. Most of his hair had fallen out. Wick looked like an actor in one of those movies where the characters begin at thirty and age to a hundred. Phil and Roskelley just looked pale and very thin. They all appeared to have lost huge amounts of weight—and TV makes you seem "fatter" than you really are. I guess Lou had been serious when he'd told me, "Living in the death zone slowly kills you." Their voices were very weak and they were not their normally quick-thinking selves. I couldn't wait to sit down with Lou, soon, and hear what had happened on Chomolungma. There was no way to tell anything in three minutes. But I understood that they had landed just a few hours before in Seattle, and that was where the interviews were coming from.

A few months later, Lou and I got together, and this is what he told me about the climb:

"After you left base camp, we started to work the next day, started up the mountain and got the camps going. Everybody was anxious to get started. We'd been there long enough to acclimatize so we wouldn't get sick. We started going up as fast as we could," Lou said. "After seven days in base, we were starting to get frustrated. You get high-strung climbers pumped up and then you turn them loose," he explained.

I asked him how the yakkers had done. Lou grumbled, then said, "The first thing that went wrong was that the yaks stopped below our Camp Three and dropped all the loads. Their leader got confused and tired and told them to unload too soon." I was at Lou's underground home hearing this. The Cascade Mountains rose up before us.

"When the yaks came back down for the second carry, I was really anxious to make sure they got the right place. So I went up that time and stayed with them. We'd already made it to 21,300 feet and got all of our equipment at the right place, fast." Ingrid was lying near us by their combination stone patio, trout pond, and hot tub soaking in some Cascade Mountain sunshine.

"The next day, while I was paying off the yak drivers, a team of four laid in our route to Camp Four, using a fixed rope to the top of the North Col. It took them eight hours and they did a beautiful job. That was Ershler, my son Peter, Geo, and John Smolich. Geo did a technical ice climb up the vertical wall for about forty feet, on which we later installed a ladder." That ladder would be the only one they'd use. At this point they were making surprisingly fast time.

Lou gave me a sheet of paper (see page 348) that had the dates and key events of the rest of the climb so that I could follow his story. The first entry after departing Seattle and arriving at base camp was:

*Sept. 4   Route to North Col (near Camp 4) established in one day by Ershler, Dunn, Smolich, and P. Whittaker.*

"Then the whole team started up to set up tents on Camp Four. We had tents and oxygen bottles and there were seven of us carrying—we had a real crew. No more yaks. It was deep snow and we were taking turns breaking our trail. At first it was knee deep, then it was thigh deep. Pretty soon I looked over and it was over Peter's waist. Peter had been leading and he stopped and we all collected at a place about two thirds of the way up to the north wall. We were still on a very steep place and avalanches were coming down on both sides of us.

"While we were stopped, John opened his pack to get out something to eat. I looked over at him and I said, 'John, what do you think of this slope?'

"He said, 'Frankly, it scares me.'

"I said, 'I think it's dangerous as hell up here.'

"And he said, 'I didn't want to be the first to say anything.'

"I said, 'I think this is really sticking our necks out, so let's get out of here before we go any higher; it's steeper up ahead.'

"Some of the younger guys said, 'We're almost there!'

"But I said, 'Yeah, I know, but I think we better wait because there is too much snow and we need to live.'"

Only Lou could say that they needed to live and say it so casually—as if he'd made the same kind of decision a hundred times. He had.

It was one of many times during the climb that Lou would have to analyze the dangers and risks after getting his team's opinions. He would have to decide whether to keep going, making great time, or turn back. On expeditions with lesser leaders, these decisions can tear apart the team, and kill people.

*Sept. 5–14   North Col slopes unstable, rest at base camp (Sept. 8–13).*

"Lou, didn't you tell me that just an inch or two of sliding snow can become a killing, crushing avalanche?" I asked.

"Yep. Just an inch of snow, falling six thousand feet, can build up to a six-foot-tall wall of snow. By the time it hits, an inch of snow can be a brutal snowpack. We were on this wall that was pretty steep." Lou was the kind of man who didn't like to say no, but he would if he knew it was for the health of his team, which included his son.

Right then, Lou told me, they backed off the mountain, but it was too bad because they had only about five hundred feet more to go before they got to the top of the North Col. It was about five hundred vertical feet and they could have made it but the risk was too high.

The snow was still unstable and deep for another day and so they were forced back down to lower camps to let it settle. They had to go all the way back to base camp after making such relatively easy progress to that point. Less wise team leaders might have gone on and maybe they would have made it. And maybe not. Lou's bottom-line goal was to bring everyone back alive. He would eventually be able to accept himself if they didn't get the summit, but it would be harder to know he'd made a risky decision and lost people's lives. This team did what Lou said because they trusted him.

"We waited at base camp for five days, then came back up and made Four. Camp Five was made just a couple of days later. We were making great progress again," Lou said, the speed of his storytelling increasing.

*Sept. 15   Route reopened to North Col, Camp 4 established.*
*Sept. 18   Roskelley and Wickwire put in route to Camp 5 (24,700'), turned back by storm.*
*Sept. 20   Camp 5 established by Roskelley, Wickwire, Ershler, Smolich, Dunn, and P. Whittaker.*
*Sept. 22–28   Rest at base camp.*

"While resting at base camp we'd talked and decided we'd try to use the old Camp Five that the Japanese had used. The British had used it, too, in the thirties."

The sheet then reported a normally exciting moment on any climb:

*Oct. 2   First summit attempt—Wickwire, Roskelley and P. Whittaker reoccupy Camp 5. L. Whittaker suffers frozen eyes, turns back with Mahre and Wilson.*

"Using that Camp Five would turn out to be a mistake," Lou mentioned, "because of the winds. Some of the most incredible winds turned us back more times than anything else, more than deep snow or sickness. It was just the winds that were our biggest deterrent to making the summit.

"I've experienced bad winds, but trying to get to Camp Five and above, I found winds that were more powerful and more constant than any I had ever seen. The wind came through the worst between 4 and 5 P.M. The winds are always incredible on Everest but never had I seen any like these. We'd take a couple of steps when they let up a few seconds, then have to lie down on the snow when they came rolling through. They sounded like a locomotive running over us." I could see Lou remembering the force of the winds again.

"The wind was so powerful that it picked up Greg Wilson and blew him thirty feet or so. It also blew three food sacks that weighed forty pounds each. There was no room in the tents so we left them out and they were blown off the mountain.

"Somehow the tents stood up to the winds but the guys went hungry one day because we had lost all our food. We should have had it anchored or tied but we weren't figuring one hundred or one hundred fifty mile per hour winds," Lou reflected. About the worst thing a climber can do in the death zone is go hungry.

"The higher you get, the thinner the air is, so the winds don't blow you as hard. They move as fast, but there's less density. That wind created three failures and I was one. Three times we tried to go beyond Camp Five and three times we were stopped. One time we didn't make it more than a few hundred feet. One time my eyeballs froze."

"Your what?" I said, shocked.

"Yeah. I turned back a hundred feet below Camp Five, about 24,800 maybe, because my eyes froze. I was on the middle of a rope with Mahre and Wilson. Wilson had cracked a rib from coughing, which happens a lot up high. It's less dense up there and you're built for gravity pressure and higher air density down here, so your muscles are stronger than they need to be up in thinner air like that. About a week after, he was carrying light, but he was starting to work again."

Lou continued. "The wind was not so bad at the start and when we left everybody was keeping together good. A few hours out the wind was picking up again.

"I had a face mask on the day I froze my eyeballs. The face mask kept creeping up, so my vision was really limited behind my goggles.

316 · *ACROSS CHINA*

I opened my goggles and pulled it away. I wore sunglasses because it was so bright. They had a side shield that wasn't riveted on, and the thing blew away in the wind. I looked up and my hood was not as tight as it could be, so I was getting a lot of air blowing by the side of my goggles. Pretty soon the goggles seemed to fog up, and I figured that it was the ice blowing in." Lou rubbed his eye as he remembered.

"I asked the guys to stop. Dave was in the lead and I lifted up my goggles to look and clear the ice away, but there was still no vision. Then I knew it wasn't the goggles, it must be my eyes. I got Dave up to me and said, 'Dave, look at my eyes,' and he said, 'My God, they're all white and they're frozen over—white!'" Lou explained that climbing that high you lose your ability to react quickly.

"The conjunctiva was frozen white, but out of one eye I could see a little bit. I said, 'Dave, I can't go on this way.' I called Roskelley over and said, 'John, I'm going to have to go down and take these two guys with me. I need someone to walk in front of me that I can hold on to or look at and follow his shadow.' He said, 'We're only fifteen or twenty minutes away from camp.'

"I said, 'Yeah, but it's going to be longer than that in this wind.' He said, 'If it had been this windy an hour earlier, we'd have turned around, don't you think?' I said, 'Yeah, you can't climb in this now, but you're beyond the point of no return.'" I wondered if I'd be able to have a conversation making climbing decisions with a frozen eyeball.

Lou went on, saying, "I thought I'd better go back because I couldn't see and I'd just be a handicap. John said, 'Okay, we'll go into Five.' John was turning out to be one strong team player, which was something I had worried about earlier, having never climbed with him before, based on his bad-boy reputation. So they went into Camp Five and I was led back down to Four. My eyes had frozen in maybe ten minutes' time by the wind blowing across the eyes. My vision was slowly getting hazier. I fell ten or fifteen times coming down. Dave and I were tied together. Greg was in front leading." (Greg was the one with the broken rib, who'd been blown thirty feet by the winds.)

"We got into camp and I said, 'I'm going to stay here tonight and go down tomorrow to Camp Three. I told Greg and Dave that I didn't want to use them to take me down to Three. I told them, 'I'm going to go down alone, using the fixed ropes, in the morning.'

There was no first-aid kit in Camp Four so I didn't have aspirin to help and didn't sleep that night. The next morning I bandaged my eyes. It was a real burning kind of pain. I still couldn't see out of my right eye, but the left eye was a little better.

"I started out and went down the fixed ropes by myself. I had to rappel on the way down, but I'm used to doing that. I used to teach rappels in the military. I fell a few times, but as long as you have that ascender on, you're okay, you hang from it." (An ascender is a device that locks onto the rope, which a climber releases to continue on down.)

"There was about seventy feet to rappel and twelve hundred feet of fixed rope to get down. At the bottom George Dunn and Smolich and Ershler met me. They had walked about a mile from Camp Three to the base of the rope. I had radioed and said I could get down the ropes all right, but I could use a little help getting across the glacier. You don't want to walk the glacier alone on a rope.

"With as little sight as I had, there was almost no perception of depth. I'd see a place where I thought I could step and it wouldn't be where I thought it was. So I'd step and miss it and do a somersault and hang from my rope. About seven days later, my vision was just about back to normal again.

"After my eyes froze and I went back down the mountain, they were still trying to get to Camp Five and still not making it. Or getting to Five and not being able to go any farther. So everyone came back down to base camp and rested for what we hoped would be the last big push to the top." So far the team was doing pretty well, as far as Lou was concerned. Everyone was alive and despite a cracked rib, frozen eyeballs, bad avalanches, winds faster than a race car, and other normal extreme climbing conditions, there was still much hope.

# 50
## Who's Stronger? _____

"Originally I'd planned to be on top the first week of October and we'd only made one attempt and been turned back, bad. We hadn't even set up Camp Six yet, so I was starting to get worried. I started to think, 'There is a chance that we're going to miss this climb. If we do I'm going to buy a disguise and come back. I'll step off the plane with a hat and a beard and forget about it.'" For Lou even to admit that he wanted Everest that bad was a surprise to me.

"Every letter that came over here said, 'We know you are going to make it this time,' and I thought, 'If they only knew how much this depends on the right weather and so many other variables.'

On October 8th, one of the team came very close to dying.

_Oct. 8  Second summit attempt—Ershler, Dunn, and Smolich traverse North Face to Great Couloir, bivouac at 26,600' and cache gear. Dunn becomes ill from dehydration._

In this, the team's second summit attempt, Geo, Smolich and Phil were to climb across the North Face, camp there that night, and go for the summit in the morning. They planned to stay in a tent left there by a previous Australian team, but they could not find it. They came within a breath of dying that frigid night of October 8.

"Roskelley probably saved their lives," said Lou. "Ershler said over the radio, 'We're going to drop the equipment here and come off the mountain.' Roskelley said, 'Wait a minute, you guys are the top climbers in the world but you'll never make it down in the dark. You'll get killed going down. It's almost dark. You've got your equipment, you'll have to bivouac.'

"Ershler was real nervous. He wanted to bail off that mountain and get down to try to get to Camp Four. Maybe there they could live. Why bivouac at 26,600? That's too high, they kept saying. Roskelley gave them the greatest speech over the radio I ever heard, trying to tell them how great they were and how they could live through the night.

"It would have taken hours for them to come off in the dark," Lou said. "They'd have died trying to get down. They had sleeping bags, so they dropped all their gear and crawled into a little hole. One of our biggest fears was waiting till morning to find out if they had lived," Lou reported, sounding casual.

"So their conversation came down to 'Are we going to die here or are we going to die on the way down?'

"Roskelley kept saying, 'You guys are good enough mountaineers, you won't die up there. Keep each other awake, warm each other's feet, talk to each other all night long, and as soon as it's light, start down.' That's what they did and they survived the night."

"When they returned," Lou continued, "I thought I had three healthy guys and they were going to be going great guns in a day or two. Make another summit attempt. They said, 'We're ready to climb,' and I said, 'Great, you can be another wave. After we went to bed, at about midnight Ershler came over to my tent. He said, 'Lou, Geo is still throwing up.' I said, 'Then he's lost his dinner? How about liquids?' Ershler said, 'He hasn't been able to take liquids either.' I should have done something that night and I didn't. We should have put him on oxygen right then." Lou knew now that the clarity of his thinking was impaired at that high altitude, miles above sea level.

"In the morning I asked Ershler, 'How is Geo?,'" and he said, 'He is worse.' I said, 'Get him in here and let's check him over.' He came in and he had blue lips and blue fingernails, which meant lack of oxygen. There was something wrong." Another understatement.

"Geo groaned, 'Lou, I feel awful. My stomach is killing me and I'm so nauseous but nothing's coming out.' I said, 'What was the last food you ate and kept down?' He said, 'It was three days ago.' He hadn't even been able to keep down liquids. The guy was dehydrated. I said to Carolyn, 'Carolyn, can you get liquids in him?' She had an IV there, so we punctured a vein and she rigged up the bottle and we warmed up the IV in a pan of boiling water. There was an oxygen bottle and so we put him on oxygen. We put a mask on him and turned it up as high as it would go. It was hissing out. He was lying there and you could see a little color coming back. He took the mask off and said, 'Boy, do I feel better.' He was getting the fluid and the oxygen. We said, 'Geo, we're going to take you down the mountain; you are sick and we are going to get you to the doctor.' The doctor was at base camp."

"We got him up early the next morning and started down the mountain. He was carrying his own pack; he wanted to do it. About ten or fifteen minutes down the trail the oxygen was wearing off because he could hardly move. Geo suddenly said 'Lou, I've got to throw up again,' and he gagged. I let Geo set the pace and I got Dave Mahre to help me.

"Fortunately, John started down with us because I don't think two of us could have done it. We got down a ways and Geo was still throwing up. He got weaker and weaker. Where the trail comes down by the river Geo couldn't walk and right there he said, 'I don't think I can make it.' By then it was almost dark." I remembered the exact spot as we had hiked up that high before I left the team. It was even fairly easy for me and Geo could normally run circles around me.

"I said, 'Geo, if you stay here, I don't think I can save you. I don't think I can keep you alive. We're going to try to carry you.' He said, 'Okay, if you can support me, I'll try walking.' So Mahre and I got on either side of him. He first put his arms around our necks; he was limping and not talking anymore; he was really hurting. He had lost his coordination so his feet were kind of stumbling and tripping, staggering. He couldn't support himself standing up anymore. We still had about four miles to go and we were practically carrying him and he was still throwing up. We would stop and rest him about every five hundred feet." Lou glanced down at his feet.

"It was dark, but I could see we were going to make it. We promised him a lemon-lime pop when we got to camp; we had about four left down there. He was not dead weight yet; he could still support himself some, which was great. Otherwise, it would have been really hard to get him down. I was figuring on piggybacking it at the last to get him in.

"I said, 'On three, everybody yell "Ed!"'' It was pitch-black and we'd just rounded the corner by the glacier and had a ways to go. We didn't have any flashlights either. So we kept yelling and finally Ed said he heard these weird noises and he came and helped us. He said Geo had almost no discernible blood pressure and if we hadn't brought him down, and if Carolyn had not given him the IV, he would have died. After that Geo was not in the picture for the summit," Lou said. Understatement number 20.

_Oct. 9   Third summit attempt—Wickwire, Roskelley, and P. Whittaker attempt to traverse North Face from Camp 5. Stopped by cold and severe wind few hundred feet beyond Camp 5._

This meant that they'd now made three summit attempts and had yet to establish Camp 6. Things were looking very bad. They were getting desperate when someone suggested that they put in a new Camp 5, straight across from the old Camp 5, locating it in the Great Couloir, directly below the summit, at 24,800 feet.

But who was going to do it? Geo was out of the picture now— originally considered along with Phil to be on the first summit team. Whoever led across the mountain to set up new Camp 5 would wear themselves out. They could not be a part of the final ascent team. Everyone knew Lou would have to decide.

"We talked a lot about this one. It got pretty tense. 'Instead of going up the way we'd thought, let's leave the North Col, traverse across and set up a new camp.' This was toward the end of the expedition and we were just kind of devastated. We said, 'You know we must make a new Camp Five. Staying on this exposed ridge is killing us.' And so Wickwire and John and everybody agreed."

Except Peter, his son. The decision that Lou faced next would be one of the hardest he'd ever have to make. Would he pull his son off the summit team and replace him with Phil (since Geo was out)? This was Phil's third trip to Everest. This was probably Wick's last chance.

"Making that new camp," Lou explained, "meant a big support team. It meant asking some guys to sacrifice. If the summit team went over alone, they would never have the strength to carry the gear to this camp, and then to a new Camp Six, and then go up. So we needed some people to donate their energies, and know that they weren't going to go up," Lou stalled a moment, seemingly wondering if he had made the right decision.

"I asked Peter to support with Dave, Wilson, and Smolich. 'Cause there's no way anybody is going to make it unless I get some support people to go over. It was a little touchy to pull Peter off the first team, because he was on the first team for quite a while. Then because both of Ershler's teammates had gotten sick, Geo and John, and they were unable to function as a team, I had to make just one team and I did that. The final team was Wick, Roskelley, and Phil. It was quite tense but Peter accepted it and led across to that new camp and did an incredible job." Lou was very proud of that mature reaction by his young son, his first time on Everest.

*Oct. 17 P. Whittaker, Mahre, Wilson, and Smolich pioneer traverse across North Face to put in new Camp 5 (24,800') at foot of Great Couloir. Wickwire, Roskelley, and Ershler occupy new Camp 5.*

"That was the first time that route had been taken across that wall to set up new Camp Five. Nobody had ever walked over there. It was just an incredible route. There were all kinds of avalanche conditions.

"That traverse Pete took was a technical trip. They carried the summit team's gear in, got them set up, put the tent up and everything, and then they bailed out. There was not enough room for everybody to sleep at the new Camp Five. So those three were our last hope.

Without Ran Ying as my translator, I would have never experienced all I did in China.

Lao Li, in shades, with his former commune friends on the Inner Mongolian Plateau

An old man on a melancholy stroll through the alleys of Beijing

Zheng Ziquan was very proud that I tried on and bought a pair of the peasant sandals he makes in Chengdu.

A distant view of Baiyinnar, the Mongolian village of seven families where I lived. Its name means "Have-a-Pond."

The home of my Mongolian family, with "Mongo Mama" in the doorway and "Mongo Papa" on his motorcycle

Mongolian wrestlers at a celebration of their rebuilt temple. One of these incredibly strong men would soon give me my own "personal demonstration." The wrestler on right was the eventual champion.

At a Mongolian celebration in the village of Wu Lan Tu Ge Su Mu, this drunken horseman rode wild through the crowds, whipping people with his reins till he was subdued here by his brother.

Mongo Mama's herd of horses runs free as do all Mongolian horses in this area of the grasslands.

Mongolian elders wait for a horse race to pass them during their summer festival.

On Mongo Mama's table, under glass, are family portraits representing four generations. She's the one in traditional Mongolian headdress, and her husband's grandfather is on the right. Others include her son, above, now serving in the People's Liberation Army.

Mongo Mama's youngest son on a Mongolian wooden saddle. His name means "Wide-Open Spaces."

Mongolian dancers act out the animals and spirits they represent, exhibiting grace and power.

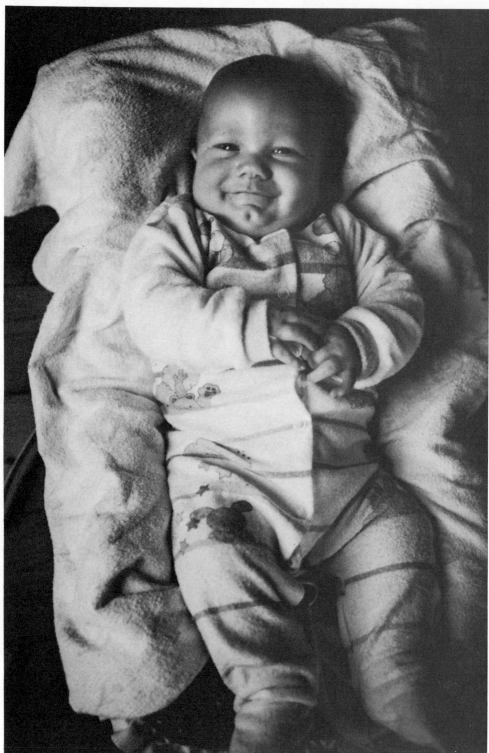

Luke Jenkins, born on October 15, 1984. He was given "most special gift of red hair."

The sheet registered some good news next:

_Oct. 18   Ershler, Wickwire, and Roskelley climb Great Couloir to 26,600'._
_Establish Camp 6 50' above cache._

There would be no more higher camps unless something horrible happened. Humans are not supposed to stay above Camp 5 for more than a couple of nights anyway. Something bad did happen when they got to Camp 6. Two bottles of oxygen had been carried up to Camp 6 by Ershler, John Smolich, and George Dunn on summit attempt number 2. When they had to bivouac, they stuck them in the snow. Phil dropped one of them at a lower elevation, one hundred feet or so from where they bivouacked. By the time Wick, Roskelley, and Phil got up there, the bottle Phil dropped had been avalanched away. They found only one bottle holding the sleeping bags down. So now there could only be one going with oxygen. That didn't matter to Roskelley, for he was planning to go to the top without. A near superhuman effort.

"Losing that bottle was tough luck. The next morning, two would try for the summit without oxygen, and Wick with oxygen." Lou's pace was fast now.

The team's fourth attempt was reported on the sheet like this:

_Oct. 19   Fourth attempt—all three turned back at 27,000' due to_
_Roskelley's dizziness._

But there was much more to it than those few words report. It's true that they turned back because Roskelley was dizzy. But the day that Wickwire, Ershler, and Roskelley left on attempt number 4, the weather was the best of the whole climb. It was an ideal day, clear and with no winds. They were walking up the mountain, going good. Wickwire had oxygen, and the other two did not. Wickwire wondered why he was not going as fast as he felt he should, because he had the oxygen. John was feeling funny. John had taken codeine because some past frostbite was hurting real bad and this made him dizzy. He was stumbling. John looked in trouble and so they started back down. They came back down to their tent and Wick went to shut off his oxygen tank and found it was not turned up all the way. That kind of spooked him.

I could see the emotion replaying in Lou's eyes as he told me the next part of this incredible expedition. "I called them on the radio at their Camp Six and said, 'It's over. You guys did one phenomenal job. John, don't feel bad about it, you did great. Wick, we tried.' I was ready to come home and have somebody say, 'Oh, you didn't make it again.' I was ready to say to them, 'Damn, we did the best anybody could do up there. I have no feelings of guilt. We didn't let anybody down, we came back alive. I don't care who thinks we didn't do a good job.' As far as I was concerned, we were successful just by staying alive." That was the most emotional I'd ever seen Lou.

"They said they wanted to try one more day. I said, 'Okay, we'll give them one more day.' A lot of times, spending the night that high will take the will to conquer out of you."

"Dave Mahre said, 'Lou, they're just going through the motions, they're not motivated anymore.' I said, 'I think you are right. They've been up there too long.' This was going to be the third night. But Wickwire was willing to give up his oxygen bottle, the only one. And probably his last chance to get to the top of the mountain. That was an incredible sacrifice. It was Ershler's bottle that went down, so it was up to Phil to climb without oxygen. Ershler wanted to come down the mountain that night. He said the climb was over. Wickwire and Roskelley sat there and talked Ershler into staying. They talked almost all night.

"I figured I had a team going but I didn't know who. It all depended on how they felt that morning because overnight that high up you could change your mind. You could be bummed out, you could be getting short breaths, you could have no feeling left in your toes. So you never make a decision till morning anyway.

"When they called me in the morning at six-fifteen, it was Wickwire. I asked, 'Are you on the mountain?' and he said, 'No, I'm in camp and they're heading up.' I said, 'Great. The weather isn't as good, but we'll let them try it. This is it, Wick.'

"Wick said, 'They left fifteen minutes ago.' And I said, 'You going to stay?' He said, 'Yeah, I don't think I could have done it; there's just one bottle. I didn't feel good about it, but I think Phil is stronger than I am, and I think that they've got a chance of making it.' I said, 'We'll see what happens today, but you guys come down tonight— this is it. I mean, we've got to get off, and you guys have been up there long enough; we don't want another one like George.' Wickwire said, 'Okay.'

"So that day, the two of them fought it out, went all the way up.

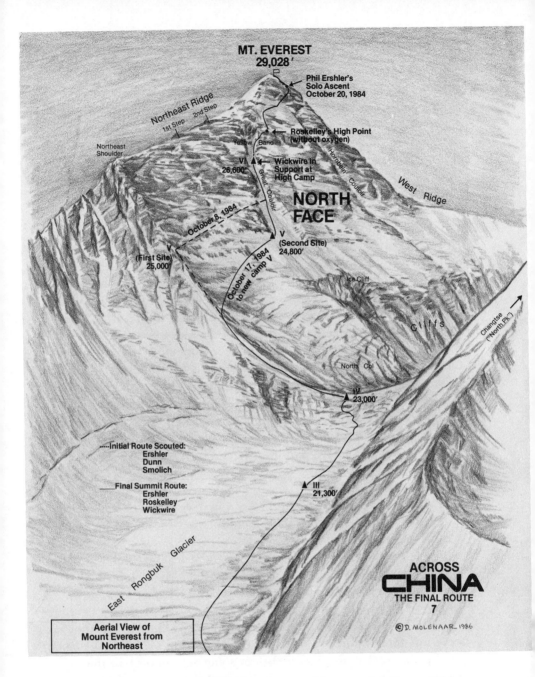

MT. EVEREST
29,028'

Phil Ershler's
Solo Ascent
October 20, 1984

Northeast Ridge
1st Step    2nd Step

Roskelley's High Point
(without oxygen)

Northeast
Shoulder

Yellow Band

VI    Wickwire in
26,600'    Support at
High Camp

Hornbein Couloir

NORTH
FACE

West Ridge

October 8, 1984

Great Couloir

V
(Second Site)
24,800'

(First Site)
25,000'

October 17, 1984
to new camp V

Ice Cliff

Cliffs

Changtse
("North Pk.")

North Col

IV
23,000'

-----Initial Route Scouted:
Ershler
Dunn
Smolich

____Final Summit Route:
Ershler
Roskelley
Wickwire

III
21,300'

ACROSS
CHINA
THE FINAL ROUTE
7

©D. MOLENAAR 1986

East Rongbuk Glacier

Aerial View of
Mount Everest from
Northeast

Our team's route was neither easy nor without great drama. This American team made history by pioneering a new route, making several attempts in high winds, and reaching the summit very late in the year. The dotted line shows the original route from which they were turned back by killer winds. At the last moment the team put in a new Camp 5 and continued from there to Camp 6. From Camp 6 there would be failed attempts and the expedition would be called off. But Ershler, Roskelley, and Wickwire would not give up and decided to make a daring last-ditch attempt for the top.

John led, doing a beautiful job, and Phil led too. Then John saw Phil, healthy and strong. John had no feeling left up to his knees or to his elbows. His core temperature was down to the point where he was in danger of hypothermia. Phil was warm because he had the oxygen. John thought he could make the top. But he told me later, 'I thought I might make the top, but I didn't think I could make it back. It wasn't worth it.' And I said, 'Great, John, it wasn't worth it; no amount is worth your life.'" A few years earlier, no doubt John would have pushed on, but now he's got a young son whom he wants to teach to hunt elk and see grow up.

"John's core temperature dropped to the point where his hands and feet felt like clubs, and he said, 'I can't make it, Phil. But I think I can get down okay.' So Phil said, 'I'm going down,' and John said, 'In a few weeks, you'll be mad at yourself, Phil. Do you feel like you could go on?' Phil said, 'Yeah, I probably could,' and John said, 'Why don't you go on? I can get back down.'

"Coming down, John was walking like a mummy. When he got to Camp Six, Wickwire immediately took his boots off and put John's feet under his, Wickwire's, armpits. He gave him hot tea. Wick said I was real worried about John, then. I was worried about everybody. Meanwhile, Phil was going on alone. Steve, our cameraman, was filming Phil with a telephoto lens from far below as Phil neared the top. Steve was also relaying Phil's progress with his radio. For us, it was like hearing the greatest Super Bowl game ever played. Carolyn even made popcorn.

"Then Phil just turned up the flow on his oxygen bottle and went faster than he had before because he didn't have John. So he took off by himself and went for the summit.

"Phil felt responsible for John. He felt he had to help John down the mountain. So he needed John to urge him on. If John hadn't said, 'Phil, go on, I can make it,' Phil would have gone back down with John. Phil was committed to John's living.

"So Phil cranked it up and made the summit by himself. He knew Steve was filming him, so when he got to the top of the world he started waving. He also had with him some very important things. He carried Chris's trumpet mouthpiece and some things of Marty's. He dug a hole, buried them at 29,028 feet and came back down."

*Oct. 20  Summit day—Ershler reaches summit using oxygen.*

# The Light from
# a Wood Stove

A calf-killing blizzard blew against the north side of our farmhouse.
It was piling up snow against the house, the barn, the old smokehouse, and any cow that might be lying down this night trying to
birth a calf. Probably by now Shocker had small icicles on his body. I
couldn't understand why he always stood up against the outside of
the red barn instead of going inside it. It was past two A.M. Both of
the wood stoves that heated our just-completed, restored farmhouse
had burned their wood, and the house was cooling down very fast.
When it was below zero and when the north winds blew loud, the

house always cooled off quickly. I'd been back from China for a little over three months.

I wanted to stay under our blankets but baby Luke, little Jed, and long-legged Rebekah kicked off their covers almost every night. I got up and went downstairs to fill both stoves with hickory and locust wood. Our new wood floors were made from local walnut and I had to be careful to keep from slipping on their slick finish. The big, black Buck wood stove that heated our kitchen took two armloads to fill up. The moonlight reflected off the new snow and lit our ten-foot-tall stained-glass window a soft blue.

Our other smaller stove was in the family room/library. The only time it could be used as a library was when the children were asleep. When they were awake, and in here, it had the energy of a boxing gym. We'd paneled this room with some cherry, grown wild on the Tennessee hills. This little blue stove kept the wood burning longer than our black one did, and there was still a flame inside when I threw on more locust. I left the door of the stove open and sat in my chair and watched it burn. Almost nothing calmed me more than seeing, feeling, and smelling the slow burn of aged hardwood. The branches of the hundred-year-old maple trees that surrounded the house hit the tin roof when the wind moved them. Bits of ice fell from the maple branches and made sliding sounds as they raced down the frigid tin.

The orange glow from the burning wood was the only light in the room. On the mantel stood a stone carving by an Old Master sculptor, Chen Jing Xiang. His subject for this classic sculpture was a beautiful Chinese maiden. He'd delicately carved her hair so that it was flowing down her back. She lay on a lily pad. While reclining she gazed back at a bird that had a very long tail and looked like a peacock. "The bird was surprised to find a woman more beautiful than itself." As a carver of stone, this man from the China coast was surpassed by no one in the world. Chen Jing Xiang told me it was one of the best things he'd ever sculpted, but "you have heart of artist, it will be good for carving to be loved across ocean, in your home." He agreed to sell it to me, even though his leaders did not want him to.

What made his work even more astounding was the stone he used. It was from the very famous Long Life Mountain. From the outside, the stone from Long Life Mountain looked like an ugly rock. But running through it were veins of white and red and a fleshy orange mixed in sometimes with a smoky black. To me, the impossible part of the carving of the stone was figuring out how to take the different veins of colored rock and know that where the lily pad would be was the exact place where the stone was ivory-white. How did the artist know there would be enough of the red to make the bird and delicate orange for the girl's face and hands? They said it took decades to master this kind of carving. Chen Jing said he could _feel_ where the colors in the stone would be. Chinese artists have been carving such stone for fifteen hundred years.

Since I'd come home from China, there were few days that I did not think of something or someone there. Since winter had come to our farm I'd been wondering about how Jin Mie, our head yakker, was doing. I recalled an invitation he'd offered me. "You come back my favorite time of year. It is winter because we will kill the goat, the sheep—we can have meat, not so much work to do. We sit together and drink, have food, sing, dance." I was ready for some good goat meat and Tibetan singing. Thinking of our yakker's goat made me think of the "six-star-rated" seafood meal at the fishing village, before we were forced to leave. I remembered the Delicious Garden and Shirley's aged eggs back in Chengdu.

Through the window I could see a small group of cows, their hunched backs to the winds, trying to live through a cold, blue-moon night. It was so hostile outside tonight, I couldn't even imagine Mount Everest this time of year. Who would be drawn to climb her after another winter passed for Jin Mie and his people? Would Wick ever go back? Or Lou or Papa Dave? I doubted it, unless Lou led one more expedition with the hopes of getting his son Peter to the top. This winter, Peter was helicoptor-skiing instructor at Snowbird. As for the others, I suspected Geo, John Smolich, and Greg would return. Everest to these men is a must if they plan to continue as professional, ultimate climbers.

For John Roskelley, it was the MOUNTAIN that had said, "No." He'd be back. He needed it more than any of them. For most people it took a few years, if ever, to get back the inspiration for another "extreme climbing" expedition. Roskelley was known to come home after being gone for four months and leave a few months later to bag another summit. Some climbers never stopped thinking of the waiting mountains. There were many peaks left, even for Phil. When a piece of the bark on a log flared up, I wondered, would I ever go back? I did not crave another mountain, but I hoped to go back to Tibet.

By now the fire was blazing, helped by the strong draft the wind created in the chimney. Sitting up late like this had become a habit since I'd been home. I would often wake up and not be able to stop thinking about an experience in Mongolia or the driving of Parnelli Yak. But recollections from my journey around China could hit any-time. I'd jump in my car to go on the most ordinary errand and I'd think, "This freedom of movement is not even conceivable for my Chinese friends, like Lao Li or Muran." When I'd drive by Smokey's, a local honky-tonk, I'd think about all those people in there dancing and watching cable TV. They never worried about what member of the opposite sex they were seen with, or whether they'd been given permission to be friends. They just listened to the song "She's Been Cheating On Us Again."

Our weather this time of the year, mid-January, was not very dif-ferent from Inner Mongolia's. I remembered that Mongo Mama told me, "Whole winter will be free." They spent most of their time in the small cooking room with the fire in the brick cooking box burning, creating smoke to keep their kang warm. If the snow be-came so deep their cattle and horses could not paw through, then Mongo Papa might have to go out and feed them some of the grass we'd cut by hand. I fed my hungry cattle hay every morning in the winter. The medal of Genghis Khan that Mongo Mama gave me sat on our stone mantel in our kitchen.

I closed the doors on the wood stove. My hands warmed as I lin-gered near it. I didn't want to go back to sleep because I loved the sounds of the storm outside wailing around our house. Regardless of what storms blew through Red China in its future, I knew now that her people could not be stopped. Oppressed and slowed down, yes. But the stone carver would still create his art, and Mongo Mama would not forget Genghis Khan, and Ran Ying's father would find ways to get more books. The Long Life Mountain stone would sit on that mantel for as long as I lived here, reminding me of a wider world, far from the USA. I would not forget Mongo Mama, or Ran Ying, or Jin Mie, or the "Little General," for they were China to me now. If some new horrible political movement was inflicted upon China, I would think of how it would hurt them. If China became a better place I would be glad for them. China was no longer a red flag to me, or Chairman Mao, or a billion swarming black-haired people. China was my friends.

I would remember Everest, too. Whenever I felt that I was getting too old or too tired for adventure, I'd think of Lou and Papa Dave, climbing Everest in their fifties. Prayer-stones and copper pots from exotic lands sat in their homes, calling them to far-off countries and further challenges. I would remember, too, something Phil told me that Marty always said: "Never settle for less."

I walked back upstairs, feeling that my firemaking had warmed the house. The shiny lacquer-ware screen I'd bought for Barbara stretched seven feet and rested beside our bed. It had taken a Chinese artist almost a year to paint its beautiful birds and landscapes. It took two months to reach Tennessee on a slow boat from China. Before getting back under my covers I checked the kids. They were under their blankets for a change. As I drifted back to sleep, I found myself wondering what Bhutan looked like, where exactly it was and how one got there. I was asleep when I heard the soft sounds of Luke crying. I warmed him a bottle in the microwave and settled back in the rocker to feed him.

I found myself wishing my family had a kang so that we could sleep warm and safe on cold nights like this, just the way they do in Mongo Mama's room. When Luke finished, I settled him down. The house was silent. I stumbled into bed and was asleep before I could think of Bhutan again.

# Epilogue

Since I returned home to the USA, many things have happened to the people who brought this book to life. Death has come, homelands have changed, babies have been born, life-styles altered, avalanches struck, family reunions attended, mountains climbed, hay cut, degrees granted, and cheeseburgers eaten.

John Smolich, a friend and member of the climbing team, said to me when we were together one beautiful Himalayan afternoon at the base of Mount Everest that after this expedition, he'd be going on one more long adventure, an expedition to climb K-2, the world's second highest mountain. Then he planned on getting married, setting up his own guide service, lessening his parents' worry, and climbing in the Pacific Northwest. On June 21, 1986, while climbing on K-2 on the China/Pakistan border, John lost his life in a killer avalanche. He was loved by many and that was in evidence at the memorial service friends and family had for John in Portland on August 16, 1986. The guys at RMI are having a bronze plaque made memorializing John, and it will be permanently placed at K-2.

Skip and Susan found each other in Greece, were married by the local Greek minister on Santorini Island, and on September 26, 1985, Quinn Van Yowell, their baby girl, was born.

Lou and Ingrid settled back into their stone home in Ashford, Washington, where it took a few months for Lou to recover from life in the Death Zone. In 1985, Lou went to Peru with Greg Wilson to participate in the Rio Abiseo Research Project, an archeological dig of a lost city hidden till now in tropical rain-forest wilderness. He and Greg scaled burial sites one thousand feet up on almost vertical cliffs. Lou continues running Rainier Mountaineering, climbing Rainier, and has a previously unclimbed mountain in the Himalayas he is working on getting permission to climb. The name and place are at this writing secret.

Peter Whittaker was working as a ski instructor at Snowbird in Utah, taking skiers up in helicopters, when an avalanche swept him away, doing serious damage internally and to his legs. He almost died, and some thought he'd never climb or ski again. But this past winter, Pete was back in Snowbird helicopter-guiding and this summer was again guiding people up Mount Rainier. He has begun his own guide service to take clients around the world.

The week after returning from Everest, Jim Wickwire was back practicing law at the firm where he's a founding partner. Two of his daughters are now in college and Jim is headed somewhere "BIG" in 1987 to again test his gifts on the highest mountains of the world.

Carolyn Gunn returned from Everest and moved to southwestern Colorado, high in the Rockies, to work as a vet, ski, live in the mountains, paint, write a book, and climb. She went to Peru with Lou and Greg and will surely feel the call to the least-known corners of the world again.

Phil Ershler came back to America a hometown hero, having climbed the world's highest mountain. Being a committed, professional mountaineer, Phil has in the past few years led climbers on expeditions to the highest peaks in South America and Alaska, as well as continuing to guide on Mount Rainier. He's been speaking about his Everest conquest, and plans more peak-adventures to China and the Himalayas.

Dave Mahre says he's "still the same ol' guy, working, sleeping, eating, and climbing." Dave still serves as mountain manager of the White Pass Ski Area in Washington State, as he's done since 1962. He's active in mountain rescue, as always, and most important to Dave, he's playing ball, going to local lakes, water-skiing and sailboarding with the ever-growing Mahre family. Dave's now got thirteen grandchildren.

Tibet, a country I hope to return to someday, has opened up more to foreign travel. However, this summer word has gotten back that because of infighting between the Chinese Mountaineering Institute and Chinese International Travel Service, Tibet has closed back down, leading some China-watchers to speculate that it could close down completely.

John Roskelley was "whacking weeds" the day we talked on his family's new mini-farm east of Spokane, Washington. Although John has been to Nepal and Bhutan since returning from Everest in '84, and is scheduled to be back on the China side of Everest for the fall of 1987, there is much evidence that the "mountain cowboy" is slowing down some, mostly to spend more time with his and Joyce's four-year-old son, Jeff, teaching him to hunt, fish, do gymnastics, read and write, and grow up to be a strong man like his father some day.

Greg Wilson's ribs have healed long ago, and he has made five trips to South America guiding climbers. He also guides on Rainier and wouldn't have it any other way.

George Dunn, known throughout the world as Geo, fully recovered from his near-death sickness on the '84 climb and has led climbs up Mount McKinley in Alaska. He just finished his two-hundredth summer climb of Rainier. Betting people say Geo will someday stand on top of Everest. I hear his old yellow Datsun 240Z is still running fast.

The wind still blows very cold out of the North against Mongo Mama's home, and she and her family are well.

Ran Ying set up an appointment to become an American citizen a few months after coming home from our journey across China. She canceled because she still wasn't sure if she wanted to give up her Chinese citizenship. Her triplet sons, Michael, Patrick, and Ron Adwell, are now five and live with Ed and Ran Ying in Nashville where Ed's getting a Ph.D. at Vanderbilt. Ran Ying graduated from Bethel College with a B.A. in 1985. On November 22, 1985, she made her decision, and became a U.S. citizen.

Back home, Luke is now walking, sort-of-talking, and we are looking forward to a cool and beautiful Tennessee fall.

# *If You're Ever in China . . .*_____

If after reading this book you find yourself traveling in China, you might like to visit some of the places you've read about, meet some of the people, taste some of their incredible food, and perhaps buy some of the things they make.

Lhasa Rug Weaving Factory
Lhasa, Tibet

The Delicious Garden Restaurant
Chengdu, Sichuan Province

Straw Peasant Shoes
Zheng Ziquan
265 Shaanxi Street
Chengdu City, Sichuan Province

An Yingjie & Ma Yongchi
Muslim Beef Noodle Restaurant
Lanzhou Panxiuan Road
Lanzhou City, Gansu Province

Baotou Carpet Factory
Baotou City, Inner Mongolia

E Nongfu "Muran" (the manager)
Wu Lan Tu Ge Su Mu Tourist Center
Damao Qi, Inner Mongolia

The Stone Carver
Fuzhou General Carving Technological Factory
Fuzhou, Fujian Province

General Department Store
Wu Si Road
Fuzhou, Fujian Province
Phone: 50016

Fujian Carving Art Gallery
General Factory
Liu Yi Road (Wang Zhuang)
Fuzhou, Fujian Province
Phone: 42773

Fujian Tourist Souvenirs Manufacture and Supply Corporation
Fuzhou Branch
Wu Si Road Central
Fuzhou, Fujian Province
Phone: 33491

# *So You Want to Climb*___

Perhaps some of you would like to begin a relationship with the mountains. Please look into Rainier Mountaineering, Inc., and their guided trips up Mount Rainier. Contact Lou Whittaker at R.M.I. for more information:

Rainier Mountaineering Inc. (R.M.I.)
201 St. Helens
Tacoma, WA 98402
Phone (206) 627-6242

If you are more advanced, you may want information about international programs and trips conducted by individual guides. These trips include the Himalayas, South America, China/Tibet, Africa. Contact:

Peter Whittaker's Guide Service
Summits, Inc.
201 St. Helens
Tacoma, WA 98402

Or:

International Alpine Guides led by Phil Ershler, Eric Simonson, or Joe Horiskey. Their addresses are:

| Phil Ershler | Eric Simonson | Joe Horiskey |
|---|---|---|
| 14309 SE 17th #F-7 | P.O. Box 155 | 201 St. Helens |
| Bellevue, WA 98007 | Ashford, WA 98304 | Tacoma, WA 98402 |

Or:

Roskelley School of Mountaineering
E. 16641 Foothills
Spokane, WA
99207

P.S.
If you would like to write Peter or get a copy of his newsletter, "Our America," address your letters to:

P.O. Box 20
Franklin, TN
37064

# Key Events in China/
# Everest '84_____

Aug. 6    Depart Seattle.

Aug. 20   Base camp reached.

Sept. 4   Route to North Col (near Camp Four) established in
          one day by Ershler, Dunn, Smolich, and P. Whittaker.

Sept. 5–14  North Col slopes unstable, rest at base camp (Sept.
            8–13).

Sept. 15  Route reopened to North Col, Camp 4 established.

Sept. 18    Roskelley and Wickwire put in route to Camp 5 (24,700′), turned back by storm.

Sept. 20    Camp 5 established by Roskelley, Wickwire, Ershler, Smolich, Dunn, and P. Whittaker.

Sept. 22–28    Rest at base camp.

Oct. 2    First summit attempt—Wickwire, Roskelley, and P. Whittaker reoccupy Camp 5. L. Whittaker suffers frozen eyes, turns back with Mahre and Wilson.

Oct. 3–4    High winds prevent movement above Camp 5.

Oct. 8    Second summit attempt—Ershler, Dunn, and Smolich traverse North Face to Great Couloir, bivouac at 26,600′ and cache gear. Dunn becomes ill from dehydration.

Oct. 9    Third summit attempt—Wickwire, Roskelley, and P. Whittaker attempt to traverse North Face from Camp 5. Stopped by cold and severe wind few hundred feet beyond Camp 5.

Oct. 17    P. Whittaker, Mahre, Wilson, and Smolich pioneer traverse across North Face to put in new Camp 5 (24,800′) at foot of Great Couloir. Wickwire, Roskelley, and Ershler occupy new Camp 5.

Oct. 18    Ershler, Wickwire, and Roskelley climb Great Couloir to 26,600′. Establish Camp 6 50′ above cache.

Oct. 19.    Fourth attempt—all three turned back at 27,000′ due to Roskelley's dizziness.

Oct. 20    Summit day—Ershler reaches summit using oxygen.

# Bibliography_____

*Everest*
Bonington, Chris, and Charles Clark. *Everest: The Unclimbed Ridge.* New York: W.W. Norton & Company, 1983.
Rowell, Galen. *In the Throne Room of the Mountain Gods.* San Francisco: Sierra Club Books, 1977.

*Tibet*
*Avedon, John F. *In Exile from the Land of Snows.* New York: Alfred A. Knopf, Inc., 1984.

Harrer, Heinrich. _Return to Tibet._ Translated by Ewald Osers. London: Weidenfeld and Nicolson, 1984.

Harrer, Heinrich. _Seven Years in Tibet._ Translated by Richard Graves. Los Angeles: J. P. Tarcher, Inc., 1981.

Hopkirk, Peter. _Trespassers on the Roof of the World._ Los Angeles: J. P. Tarcher, Inc., 1982.

*Rowell, Galen. _Mountains of the Middle Kingdom._ San Francisco: Sierra Club Books, 1983.

## China

*Butterfield, Fox. _China: Alive in the Bitter Sea._ New York: Bantam Books, 1983.

_China Reconstructs,_ North American Edition. San Francisco: China Books and Periodicals. (To order magazine, contact China Books & Periodicals, 2929 24th Street, San Francisco, Calif. 94110.)

DeLand, Antoinette. _Fielding's Far East._ New York: William Morrow and Company, 1986.

*Hinton, William. _Fanshen: A Documentary of Revolution in a Chinese Village._ New York: Vintage Books, 1966.

*_Journey into China._ Washington, D.C.: National Geographic Society, 1982.

Lord, Bette Bao. _Spring Moon._ New York: Harper & Row, 1981.

Mosher, Steven W. _Journey to the Forbidden China._ New York: The Free Press, 1985.

_National Geographic Atlas._ Washington, D.C.: National Geographic Society, 1981.

Prawdin, Michael. _The Mongol Empire—its Rise and Legacy._ Northampton: George Allen & Unwin Ltd., 1961.

Terrill, Ross. _The White-Boned Demon._ New York: William Morrow and Company, 1984.

*Tiger, Lionel and Reinhart Wolf. _China's Food: A Photographic Journey._ New York: Friendly Press, Inc., 1985.

*Highly recommended books.

China

cigarettes - buy best brand offer
never tip
lead bags for film
above 18,000 ft - deterioration
dust masks